Praise for

LET YOURSELF BE LOVED

"This story brims with hope, unflinching love, and the reminder that there is purpose and meaning in every moment of life. Elizabeth Leon shares her story with candor, joy, and a level of wisdom that's been hard won through suffering. I have had the privilege of watching Elizabeth navigate some of the very challenges she writes about, and stand amazed at the way she has risen with grace and dignity. *Let Yourself Be Loved* will remind you that God is faithful, that no suffering is without purpose, and that God is 'able to do immeasurably more than all we ask or imagine, according to his power that is at work within us' (Ephesians 3:20)."

— LISA BRENNINKMEYER
Founder of Walking with Purpose, Author of *Be Still*, *Rest*, *Walking with Purpose: 7 Priorities That Make Life Work*, and over a dozen women's bible studies

"Elizabeth's writing is passionate, lyrical, and deeply felt—raw and real, you can feel the pain in its pages but also get to witness a journey towards healing. Incredibly personal and moving, her style is such that reading her words is like listening to a close friend whose voice you trust and enjoy. To those who have suffered such loss or known someone who has, the book is a testament to the work it takes to assimilate loss into our lives, a valuable window into understanding grief, and a guiding light that can help lead others towards grace and peace."

— JOE WHITMORE
EVP Global Marketing, Sony Pictures Entertainment

"Intimate, tender, and at times even funny, Elizabeth Leon reminds us all what it means to be human. Reading *Let Yourself Be Loved* is like sitting with your dear friend as she holds your hand and recounts her story with heartfelt candor. And yes, the story is heart-wrenching, but it's also surprisingly joyful and hopeful. In generously sharing her personal grief, Elizabeth reassures us that our traumas are not ours alone. Indeed, she invites us to open ourselves up to the lessons that come from life and death. For anyone experiencing any kind of loss, I encourage you to read this beautiful book."

—DEANN HELINE
Executive Producer/Co-Creator of *The Middle*

"In this introspective, absorbing memoir, Elizabeth Leon chronicles a love she birthed long before her baby took his first breath and will endure long after he took his last. Choosing to continue her pregnancy after a life-limiting diagnosis is, for her, no choice at all. Channeling all her love, her strong Catholic faith, and a resolve backed by research, she sets out to do everything in her power to provide her son, John Paul Raphael, with as much life as she can pack into whatever minutes they would share outside the womb. 1,690 minutes, to be exact.

"How can a mother let her child go after fighting so hard to keep them alive? For Leon, this is not an intangible question but is rather a visceral decision to fight her own instincts when her precious baby forgets to breathe for the very last time. Faced now with the unmitigated grief of child loss, she tackles an equally daunting challenge: packing as much life and purpose as possible into every minute she has left in her own lifetime. And carrying his memory when she can no longer carry his 4 lb. 1 oz. little body.

"Bereaved mothers from all walks of life will see themselves reflected on these pages—the parts that are lovely to see and the parts that take some digging to uncover. But through it all, one beautiful image will emerge: that they, too, are a fierce and worthy mother. Even if mothering looks nothing like what they planned."

—RACHEL LEWIS
Author of *Unexpecting: Real Talk on Pregnancy Loss*, Founder of Brave Mamas, a community for bereaved mothers

"Elizabeth Leon and her husband, Ralph, are just settling into a second marriage for each—with nine children in their new blended family—when they discover that Elizabeth is pregnant at age forty-five with their first child together. They are over the moon with delight at this confirmation of their love, until they discover that their baby is likely to have Trisomy 18, said to be 'incompatible with life.' Anxiety and fear become constant companions, not knowing whether their beloved John Paul Raphael will even survive nine months in the womb; yet, throughout it all, John Paul Raphael is loved and cherished. Leon is honest, vulnerable, and courageous in this gripping memoir of grief and hope. Joy and pain intertwine as the family learns to trust in God's mercy and tender care even in the valley of the shadow of death. You will find yourself believing that miracles are indeed all around us, all the time . . . and that you can let yourself be loved."

—LARAINE BENNETT
Co-Author of *The Temperament God Gave You*, *The Temperament God Gave Your Spouse*, *A Year of Grace: 365 Reflections for Caregivers*, and others

"*Let Yourself Be Loved* is a book that opens your mind to the joys and sorrows of infant loss. I encourage you to pause and listen to this powerful story by Elizabeth Leon. You will learn about how to be brave during life's most difficult moments and to let yourself be loved, even when it hurts."

—EMILY JAMINET
Author of *Secrets of the Sacred Heart*

"I was privileged to get to read Elizabeth Leon's emotional and sincere toil as she tells the heart-breaking story of John Paul Raphael. The love and honesty Elizabeth shared by opening the details and reality of bearing her experience and pilgrimage of her son's life, death, and memories was so touching. I couldn't put it down and kept reading till the late hours to hear more of how JPR touched his family and is still being used by God. So much of Elizabeth's testimony reminded me of my own loss of three babies, especially Steven Thomas, who died in my womb at 20 weeks. I know the Leon Family will continue to touch people with their own little saint. I am happy to have a new saint to ask to intercede for my family. Dear little Saint John Paul Raphael pray for us."

—SAM FATZINGER
Author of *A Catholic Guide to Spending Less and Living More*

"As a neonatal clinical nurse scientist with over forty years' experience, I welcome Elizabeth Leon's book *Let Yourself be Loved: Big Lessons from a Little Life*. Elizabeth's poignant telling of her experience, reveling in the joy of a late pregnancy with her second husband only to then face a most likely devastating prenatal diagnosis, highlights many of the trials lived by others. Her at times brutally honest sharing of her deepest feelings and effects on her relationship with her husband, nine children, extended family, and community provides a valuable window into the complexity of childbearing not often discussed. It is with pride in my perinatal nursing profession that I read of Elizabeth and Ralph's compassionate, individualized, family-centered care surrounding John Paul Raphael's birth, life, and death. The exemplary care this woman and family were provided in such an acutely traumatic clinical situation should be a template for all women experiencing perinatal loss. . . . [In] Elizabeth's story . . . we not only hear her voice, but she has managed to enable her readers to listen to the strong and powerful voice of her son, John Paul Raphael."

—gRETCHEN LAWHON, PHD, RN, FAAN
Clinical Nurse Scientist

"Elizabeth's story is deeply moving and inspirational. She vulnerably and courageously reveals her encounters with the rawest human emotions, giving the reader permission to do the same as we navigate our own life's tragedies and traumas. But, as the title reveals, Elizabeth's story is a story of love, about letting ourselves be loved—exactly as we are. She brings to life the richness and meaning of journeying together with open hands and open hearts, touching our universal longing to be fully seen and received."

—DE YARRISON
Founder of You Are Made New, a healing ministry for women

"Powerfully, tenderly, bravely written; a book which belongs in every pregnancy resource center, every obstetrician's office, every pediatrician's office. A tremendous resource not only for grief counselors but for post-abortive women. *Let Yourself Be Loved* is the message of a woman who has experienced both the anguish of losing her son and a journey of faith. It is also the legacy of a little boy who left us all with a very powerful message."

—MARYANN LAWHON
President of Pennsylvanians for Human Life, Founder of the VOICE of JOHN

"Despite enduring the devastating loss of my own son after eighteen years, I could never comprehend the sorrow of preparing to say hello to a precious child one moment and goodbye only hours later. Betsy's account of how she summoned the strength and courage to do this work for her sweet baby boy is awe-inspiring. Her faith in God and his plan for John Paul Raphael amazes me. I have leaned on God in my own journey but never have I trusted his plan as completely. Betsy has inspired me to reexamine my own faith and my own understanding of God's plan and purpose for me and my son, Jay.

"I am so grateful to Elizabeth for writing this book. Her exquisitely explored journey of loving her stricken son and loving God for sending him has uncovered layers of buried burdens within my own grieving heart. She has opened my eyes and my heart to the infinite value and divine purpose of every human, no matter the length of their time here on earth or the circumstances surrounding their departure. What a gift this book is to me and will be to all who read it."

—ERIN GALLAGHER
Bereaved Mother, Program Director of This Is My Brave

"*Let Yourself Be Loved* is a treasured look into a mother's innermost feelings about the loss of her baby. In a dehumanized world, readers will be honored by the privilege of entering so personally into her private pain and sharing her journey from tragedy to light."

—FATHER STEFAN STARZYNSKI
Author of *Miracles: Healing for a Broken World*

"Elizabeth Leon's *Let Yourself Be Loved* shares the lessons learned from the fleeting, glorious life of her son John Paul Raphael. With honesty, courage, and the grace that comes from profound love and loss, Leon shares a memoir not only of her grief but also of her deep abiding faith. Leon reminds us that, though we all suffer loss, the measure of the loss is also the measure of our love. While we may grieve time and time again throughout our lives, we are never alone. 'I am with you always.' (Matthew 28:20)."

—CHRISTINE SHIELDS CORRIGAN
Author of *Again: Surviving Cancer Twice with Love and Lists*

"Elizabeth's honest and wide-open love of God shines brightly on every page. Her unwavering faith and her intense love for her family and her dear John Paul Raphael carries the reader through the storm, knowing that in the chaos and pain of deep grief, there is always deeper and even everlasting love."

—JULIANNE HAYCOX
Author of *Conversations with Grace*

LET YOURSELF BE
LOVED

BIG LESSONS FROM
A LITTLE LIFE

ELIZABETH LEON

*Carol,
Beloved ♡
In Christ,
Betsy*

VIRGINIA BEACH
CAPE CHARLES

Let Yourself Be Loved

By Elizabeth Leon

ISBN 978-1-64663-571-9

Library of Congress Control Number: 2021917841

Scripture quotations taken from the (NASB®) New American Standard Bible®, Copyright © 1960, 1971, 1977, 1995, 2020 by The Lockman Foundation. Used by permission. All rights reserved. www.lockman.org

Published by

◤ köehlerbooks™

3705 Shore Drive
Virginia Beach, VA 23455
800–435–4811
www.koehlerbooks.com

nidcap®
FEDERATION
INTERNATIONAL
voice of the newborn

Endorsed by the NIDCAP Federation International, Inc.

In loving memory of
John Paul Raphael Leon
January 4-5, 2018

All for the glory of God.

TABLE OF CONTENTS

A LETTER TO THE READER:

GRIEF WILL COME to all of us. It is universal but also deeply personal. Grief doesn't have to be shiny. It doesn't have to have a purpose, a meaning, or a reason, but I learned that, when I was ready, there were riches to be found in the wasteland of grief. I discovered treasures that transformed my heart and became a message of love and hope for the world. I came to see grief not as an enemy to be feared, but as a teacher.

If you are holding this book and have experienced your own devastating loss, I humbly offer my story as a way—one way—through the darkness of grief to peace, purpose, and even joy. My prayer is that in some way, this book brings you comfort, and that through my story, you draw closer to the One who is Himself love, consolation, and hope.

Your heart is tender, holy ground. I want to honor the sacred landscape of your loss while encouraging you to engage your story more deeply. I have provided questions for further reflection at the end of the book as a guide. While no words can lessen the agony of your grief, I desire to come alongside you and whisper that you are not alone. We can walk through this together. *Let yourself be loved.*

—Elizabeth Leon

1

NEW BEGINNINGS, SECOND CHANCES

You never know when you will be surprised by love.

"God is always good, and we are always loved."
—Ann Voskamp

THE STORY OF JOHN PAUL RAPHAEL is a grand love story, God's from the very beginning. It is the saddest story with the happiest ending. A tragedy with a plot twist of joy. A story that taught me the beautiful agony of surrender and the radiance of hope. Through our baby, light flooded the darkest caverns of my heart and seeds of grief sprouted into spectacular blossoms of peace, purpose, and joy. Not the miracle I wanted, but a miracle I would learn to love.

My husband, Ralph, and I were married on June 1, 2013. He was fifty and I was forty-one years old. Long, windy roads led us to the right place at the right time to meet and fall in love. We had each endured detours we never could have imagined. My first marriage of sixteen years ended in 2010 when my ex-husband chose another woman. After spending over a year trying to save my marriage, I finally accepted the inevitable. We were divorced and the marriage later annulled. Ralph and his first wife had been married twenty-one years when she lost her second battle with cancer, also in 2010. It was inevitable that we brought wounds and scars into our new marriage, along with nine broken-hearted children, five of mine and four of his.

Our families were both members of the same large, suburban Catholic parish and had known each other for years. Ralph's three daughters were occasional babysitters for my children. His youngest, a boy, and my oldest daughter were the same age and had attended Catholic school together for eight years. In addition, I often provided meals to Ralph and his family during his wife's long illness. The week before she died, Ralph stopped me in the narthex of our church after Sunday Mass. He explained that his wife was near death, and he asked if my husband and I would sing at her funeral.

My first husband and I are both musicians and spent many years singing together in the music ministry at our parish. In tears, I gave a short explanation of how my marriage was disintegrating, but, while I could not speak for my husband, it would be my privilege to sing for them. It is a poignant detail that the last time my ex-husband and I ever sang together was at the funeral of Ralph's first wife.

Over the next few years, Ralph and I saw each other occasionally at church or at the Catholic school our children attended. Two of our children were in the same musical production in the spring of 2011, and we saw each other several evenings in a row at the play. Neither of us knew any other Catholic adults who had been married and no longer were, and a text friendship developed as we shared struggles about single-parenting or life after marriage. In time, Ralph asked if he could come sit with me on my front porch swing, and we slowly fell in love.

At our wedding reception, we had a big sign that declared: *All the Roads Led to You.* Love was a miraculous and unexpected gift to find after tragedy, and even more surprising with such large families. When Ralph's mother found out we were dating, she exclaimed, "All those kids! You can't — it's too much!" For sure, the Lord had

His hand in bringing us together. A few years into our marriage, we discovered a Gaelic phrase that perfectly fit our feelings for one another: *anam cara*. In the Celtic tradition, *anam cara* means "soul friend," the person with whom you can share your innermost self and reveal the hidden intimacies of your life, mind, and heart. This special love cuts across all conventions to create an act of recognition and belonging that joins souls in an ancient and eternal way.

With each other, we were home.

Like most couples in love, we had many conversations about our future plans. Despite approaching middle-age, we stood in the front of the church at our wedding and promised God and the whole congregation we would willingly accept children as a gift from the Lord. I am confident I heard some good-natured chuckles at that point in the ceremony! Yet I still secretly longed to welcome another child, even though our lives were complicated. A baby seemed like too much to ask for after the unexpected blessing of our love and marriage. I didn't feel like I *deserved* to want more. Plus, we were already in over our heads with the reality of daily life. We still had seven children under our roof, ages five to eighteen, all mourning their first family and adjusting to our new one. I let my desire for a baby rest silently in my heart and trusted it to God's providence.

I consider motherhood a privileged vocation. Motherhood had given shape and purpose to the past twenty-two years of my life, and I never regretted giving up my professional goals to stay at home with my children. For two years after my ex-husband left, being a mother also meant being a single parent. My five babies and I were afraid and alone. I was flattened by grief and disappointment, but I fought to keep our family from sinking and did everything I could to preserve the life my children knew. Through God's grace, we survived and learned to breathe again in the rubble of their dad's departure. Our spirits triumphed, a testimony to the power of prayer and the support of those who held us up. That time blazes brightly in my memory despite how traumatic it was for us all. I feel nostalgic for the intensity of my bond with my children as we clung to each other in the maelstrom our lives had become. As years passed, I rejoiced in seeing the unique beauty of my children unfold day after day. I celebrated the miracle of their existence and the privilege of sharing my life with them. I wept at their sadness and the wounds I could barely even soothe.

My five children—Maggie, Leah, James, Nathan, and Clare—are the way I live my heart out in the world, their names etched on my soul more deeply than any tattoo. I adore my stepchildren too: Meaghan, Alicia, Carrie, and Andrew. They are children of my heart and I choose to love them along with their dad. I cheer them on in their successes and cry for their disappointments. I miss them when they are gone and pray for them and their needs. I wish there was not a difference. That isn't even the right word. I would give my life for any one of the nine of them. But the presence, the noise of the five children who grew beneath my heart is louder. It is more insistent and more of my responsibility.

I know that my stepchildren may appreciate the love I shower on them, but they don't long for it. It is not my life's work to make sure they know how precious and loved they are. I can never make a dent in the loss they carry from their mother's death. I know I am a mother-figure to them on some days, but often just a friend. And that's ok. I accept the limitation of my role in their lives. But the children from my heart, my blood, and my body? They are woven into the fabric of my life and I in theirs. We have a connection that goes far beyond vocation or responsibility. We are communion and legacy.

God used the first years of our marriage to help Ralph and me wade through some hard territory. We had healing to do to find freedom and surrender in how we loved each other and ourselves. I carried deep wounds of rejection, abandonment, and betrayal from my divorce and from my own parents' divorce when I was a child. We began to spend an hour together every week in front of the Blessed Sacrament in our small chapel at church. We often attended daily

Mass during the week and were both involved in Catholic small groups. My journey through shame and anxiety took me all the way to Mexico City to seek healing on a pilgrimage to the Shrine of Our Lady of Guadalupe. The Lord slowly softened our hearts and increased our commitment to each other and to Him, then blessed us with new life.

On Memorial Day weekend in 2017, we headed to the Chesapeake Bay for a getaway. Memorial Day was the anniversary of our first date in 2011 and we often tried to find a way to spend special time together on that weekend. A priest we loved was offering a one-night couples' retreat, so we paired the two, booking two nights at a historic inn not too far from the retreat. We spent the first two days kayaking in the bay and relaxing in Adirondack chairs at the shady waterfront. The oak trees outside the historic manor towered over us and I gazed out at the expanse of water.

Shyly, I shared with Ralph that my period was several days late. In fact, I had never been this late and not been pregnant. Ralph took my hand and we spoke with honesty, awe, and perhaps a little anxiety as we considered this possibility. We drove to the retreat the next morning and surrendered our marriage and family to the Lord during those twenty-four hours of prayer. As we packed to return home, we both wanted to know for sure. We stopped at the first place we could find, a CVS in La Plata, Maryland, and I took a pregnancy test in the bathroom. I sat in the dirty, dumpy stall after peeing on the stick and tightly closed my eyes, counting the minutes in my head. I wasn't sure anymore what I wanted the test to say. This would be my seventh pregnancy after five living children and one miscarriage.

"I am supposed to want it to be negative," I thought, "because I'm old and our lives are complicated and hard." But that wasn't true. I longed for God to break boldly into our lives and say, "Here I am in the middle of your marriage and the three of us are having a baby because I love you and I want to share this blessing with you and the whole world!" I could barely admit this dream to myself.

At the end of three minutes, there it was: a little plus sign. A baby. Our baby. Ralph was waiting outside the door and I slowly walked to him with the stick. What did he see on my face? Could he tell I was vulnerable and shy? Did he know I needed him to share my excitement? Slowly, I lifted the stick so he could see the little plus sign. His eyes met mine and we shared a long, meaningful look. Neither of us was naive to the impact of that little sign, but then he threw his arms around me and kissed me deeply. I felt awkward in my dazed excitement. Adrenaline surged through us as we each considered all the ways our lives were about to change.

We headed home after buying Slurpees to celebrate. My mind raced. I spent the drive reading from websites about being forty-five and pregnant. We knew there were many risks associated with "advanced maternal age." Miscarriage rates were high. There was a higher possibility for birth defects and chromosomal abnormalities. The statistics reminded us that when you are older, a healthy baby is not a sure thing. It didn't matter. I loved this little peanut already. I was sure she was a girl. I loved that she was a pin of light shining from the trinity of love between Ralph and the Lord and me.

But I was not yet at peace. The honest truth is that I hovered in the space between protecting my heart and falling in love. Our baby's presence felt so surprising, like a butterfly that landed on my nose. I was afraid to breathe lest it fly away. I finally admitted to Ralph how I had longed for a baby from the beginning of our marriage, but that it felt like an undeserved blessing. My spirit, long broken from the hardships of life, didn't feel worthy of a glorious coda at the end of my fertility, like the majestic organ improvisation after the opening hymn on our wedding day. I felt selfish to want more and wasn't convinced our family could handle it.

I remember thinking, "Well, this is a big complication." Was I really loving and generous enough to start over with a little one now at my age? How would we tell the children? How would we afford this? How ridiculous would I look walking into preschool again at fifty? Would a miscarriage just be better for all of us? The worries flew through my head and my heart at alarming speed.

I am so sorry, little one, that I had so little trust and faith in those first moments. My selfish weakness was loud. I was afraid. But it didn't take long for me to rest in the truth. A miscarriage wouldn't be better. *You are our child. You are loved and wanted. We are already celebrating you.*

The spring of 2017 was already a challenging season of uncertainty and suffering. One of our daughters had spent several weeks receiving inpatient treatment at a mental health hospital. We were entrenched in helping her find stability while navigating new medications and dramatic side effects. Ralph and I held the news of our baby as a secret treasure between us while we tried to help our daughter through her struggles with an eating disorder, self-harm, and a serious anxiety diagnosis. I remember thinking that this poor baby was conceived in tears and fear. My concerns for our teenage daughter mingled with my new love for this tiny speck in my womb and my worry that this little life might not be here to stay. My faith was my lifeline, and I took all these unknowns to the Lord and laid them at His feet.

The week after the marriage retreat, I called my obstetrician and made an appointment to see the doctor. I felt shy on the phone. The whole idea of our baby was so new, so tender and fragile. I was afraid to breathe. I felt old and a little ridiculous. But, we loved our baby. Ralph and I sat together in that deep mystery of total love, knowing there were no guarantees.

When we arrived at the first appointment, I walked into the obstetrician's office convinced everyone was staring at me and could see how old I felt. I laughed at myself because of course I didn't look pregnant yet at all. Anyone who cared to glance my way would probably assume I was there for a menopause visit. During the appointment, the doctor explained all the dangers we had already researched online. Since I was only eight weeks along, it was too early to detect a heartbeat in the office, so the first step was to get an ultrasound to confirm the pregnancy was progressing. We made an appointment at an imaging center near our house for later that week.

Arriving for the ultrasound, I remembered the excitement I felt during my younger pregnancies, but now I was scared and vulnerable. I took my time in the bathroom putting on the paper gown. I was afraid to admit how much I was already in love with this baby. I had the sense this was the first of many moments when that love could be crucified. In the chilly exam room, I lay on the table squeezing Ralph's hand. The tall, Russian technician didn't seem alarmed by my advanced maternal age. While she spread jelly over my stomach, she cheerfully told us about the healthy baby she had in her forties. She pressed the wand on my abdomen and there was our baby! Only a tiny circle in my womb but with a strong beating heart on the screen. Our child.

Smaller than a kidney bean, the technician told us. I felt a release inside me seeing the tiny life Ralph and I made. *O, Lord, guard and protect our child.* Having many children already did nothing to dim the joy and wonder of creating a new life with this man, the love of my life. Our baby was real and already a part of us both. With tears in his eyes, he cupped my face in his warm hands and kissed me deeply. He held his forehead against mine. Whatever lay ahead, we would face it together.

It was grueling to help our daughter fight for her life while knowing our baby's future was also not a sure thing. The possibility that we could lose one or both of these beloved children was very real. I vowed to do whatever it took to protect them both, while knowing it was almost entirely out of my hands. I tried to console myself: Even if I miscarried, I would always remember this beautiful child. I had lost a baby on March 4, 1999 at five weeks gestation, a small child my first husband and I chose to name Samuel Peter, despite not knowing the gender. Our new baby would always be with me, one way or another.

I headed to the mall later. My love needed an outlet, something tangible to see and touch. I felt shy and embarrassed as I wandered through baby aisles for the first time in ten years, looking for a treasure that was just right. Gently and gingerly I lifted and touched and smoothed blankets and small stuffed animals. I felt unworthy moving through the aisles of beautiful baby clothes and gifts. My heart was still bruised from the brutal end of my first marriage. The pure, innocence of these baby gifts reminded me of bringing my five children into a marriage and family I believed was faithful, solid, and loving. I was wrong then; what if I was wrong again, not about Ralph, but about thinking we could give our child what he or she needed?

I didn't feel pure and innocent anymore; I still carried shame and disgrace from being unloved and unwanted by my ex-husband. I couldn't protect my other children from pain. What if I couldn't protect this child either? Already, he or she would be born to a wounded mother in a messy family. I dug deep to find faith and courage and searched for a small, gender-neutral baby gift to see and touch. I went home empty-handed and feeling foolish. Some discouraging inner voice criticized me for daring to dream of welcoming our baby.

These struggles were part of a lengthy healing process I had been working through for several years. Despite the many blessings in my life and the consistent love of my husband, I was plagued by self-doubt and self-rejection. Childhood wounds from my parents' divorce and the trauma from my own divorce often convinced me that I was not worthy of love and belonging. It felt safer to hide my dreams and desires so I could not be hurt or rejected. For decades, I hid behind perfectionism and control, but after my divorce, that false fortress came crumbling down. Now, I struggled with anxiety, depression, and PTSD as years of hurt bubbled to the surface.

Through God's grace, I began the slow process of untangling the trauma and lies that bound my heart. I was only just learning to listen to my heart and trust what I heard when I found out I was pregnant and finally admitted my dream of having a baby with Ralph. It would be many months before I would see how the Lord used my journey with our baby to keep healing my heart.

Still disappointed from my shopping trip, I turned to the internet and found a sweet, soft yellow duck, half stuffed friend and half tiny blanket. I ordered it as a surprise for Ralph. When it arrived and he opened it, I tearfully shared that our baby deserved at least one special gift from his mommy and daddy, even if it ended up just being a remembrance of his or her brief life. We tucked Duckie away in a drawer for our eyes only, but I loved knowing it was there. For our baby.

Over the next two weeks, my pregnancy symptoms began with the same nausea and vomiting I experienced with my previous babies. Even though we weren't ready to share the news, it became clear we would need to tell our fourth daughter about the baby. Maggie was home from college and she could tell something was not right with Mom. We knew she was one of our children who would happily welcome the news of a new sibling.

We invited her into our room one night to ease her concerns about why I seemed so "off." As she sat on our bed, we told her to close her eyes; then we put Duckie in her lap. She looked down and we could see her begin to process what it meant. I nodded at her shyly and then we both cried. I explained I was secretly throwing up all the time, but I wasn't really sick. She was relieved and we felt so lucky to have her love and acceptance, along with her promise to keep the secret. Later, I shared the news with a friend over lunch. Each announcement made the surreal more and more real. I grew more hopeful as the days and weeks slowly passed, even while absorbed with caring for our other children and helping our daughter heal.

At twelve weeks, I had another ultrasound and was relieved to see the baby, now the size of a kumquat, developing on the screen. Ralph held my hand in the warm, dark room and we watched perfect little arms and legs dancing in black and white. *Sweet baby, we love you so much already.* The technician printed out dozens of pictures. Ralph picked one to carry in his breast pocket every day. Remembering many of our concerns, the doctor was quick to reassure us that at this stage, once you see a heartbeat and other signs of normal development, the miscarriage rate drops significantly.

Encouraged by healthy wiggles and a strong heartbeat, we gathered our ultrasound photos and invited our older daughters over for dinner. Leah, a high school senior, and Maggie and Andrew, both sophomores in college, were living at home that summer. James, a high school sophomore, was away at music camp for six weeks, and Clare and Nathan, ages nine and twelve respectively, were at their dad's house for the week. We hated not telling them all together, but this was the only time we could get the three oldest girls—Meaghan, Alicia, and Carrie—together, so six out of nine would have to do.

I felt nauseated, both physically and emotionally. It had been a running joke for the last four years that we surely wouldn't go and have a baby. Ralph used to tease the kids every time we called them together that we were pregnant. Now that we actually were, I was wary and uncomfortable. I felt so protective of our baby, remembering the little kidney bean on the screen. Our baby was loved and not a mistake. I desperately wanted each of our children to feel the same way, and yet the reality would likely be far from it. Despite all of our efforts to put together a happy, blended home, we understood that each of our kids still missed and grieved their first family. An unexpected pregnancy would make a messy situation even messier.

At the end of a fun dinner, Ralph said he had one more thing to talk to them about. He pulled out the accordion of ultrasound pictures from our recent visit and held them up. Shock and silence followed. Someone asked, "Are those baby pictures? Are you pregnant?" The words sounded like an accusation. I could barely make eye contact with anyone. I let Ralph do the talking, and he filled them in on the story thus far. No one said much. The older girls left fairly quickly, and we knew the real conversation would happen between them all via text, out of our earshot.

One daughter did come and give me a hug, though.

"Congratulations," she said, and I knew she meant it even if she was shocked. I appreciated her kindness and bravery. I had written our son James a letter at his music camp out of state to give him the news. He was hard to reach in person and had no phone, email, or social media during his time there. When Clare and Nathan returned from their dad's house later that week, they were next. Nathan was surprised, but mostly upset that others knew before him. Clare, our youngest, finally had the reaction we wanted from all the kids. She jumped up and down and cried, "I'm so happy! I'm so happy!" She even let me take a video of her laughing-crying excitement. I was so thankful for the innocence and joy of our little girl.

Ralph and I understood how hard our family was for all our kids. It's difficult when your parents remarry and you have step-siblings. Having a new half-sibling is worse. The reality of the physical love required to create a baby is embarrassing for any child to think about. We knew our children might consider a new baby a betrayal of their other parent. I also knew teens and young adults in their early twenties were developmentally self-centered and couldn't help focusing on how this would affect them. It was difficult to face their disappointment and lack of enthusiasm, though. Our baby had beaten odds already just by being here. We loved him or her so much and hoped our other children would share that love eventually. Handling their complex emotions about our growing family was hard, even as we understood and empathized with their many feelings. We were so grateful for Maggie and Clare and their enthusiasm. We would have to trust that God would move in the hearts of our other children and that this little one would work some baby magic of his or her own.

2

OUR LITTLE BOY

It takes courage to surrender with no certain outcome.

*"Trust in the Lord with all your heart and do not lean on
your own understanding. In all your ways acknowledge Him,
and He will make straight your paths."*
—Proverbs 3:5-6

GIVEN MY ADVANCED maternal age, Ralph and I planned to
have genetic testing done. We knew no diagnosis or condition would
cause us to compromise or terminate our baby's life, but we felt it
was important to be as informed as possible in order to face any
challenge. We desperately hoped our little one would be healthy, but
we knew it was all in God's hands.

At fourteen weeks, I had an appointment at a maternal fetal
specialist's office near our house. Noninvasive prenatal testing (NIPT)
analyzes small fragments of placental DNA circulating in a pregnant
woman's blood. It determines the level of risk that a baby will be born
with certain genetic abnormalities, commonly the Trisomy conditions.
The packet in the waiting room talked mostly about Trisomy 21 or

Down's Syndrome. I thought a lot about Trisomy 21 and how full of joy children with Down's Syndrome were. I was sure there would be hardships, but we would embrace and celebrate a little boy or girl with that special condition. The information also mentioned Trisomy 18 and 13, but only briefly, as most of those children did not survive.

Ralph had to work the day of the screening, so our son Nathan, twelve at the time, came with me to the appointment. Nathan was excited for his first ultrasound experience. As we waited in the dim room, I was grateful his presence kept me in strong "mommy" mode and didn't allow my mind to wander to my fears. The technician arrived, and soon our tiny baby was on the screen. I held my breath and prayed silently until I could see that little heart beat again. Our baby had grown so much in four weeks. While the tech focused on measuring the neck folds that can indicate a complication, Nathan used my camera to take videos of the screen. My love for my baby overflowed and a few tears slipped out of my eyes as I remembered the somber reason for the ultrasound: searching our baby's body for anything that could be wrong.

After the tech was finished, the doctor came in and was very encouraging. Nothing on the ultrasound indicated a problem. This did not mean there weren't any, but the measurements for the nuchal folds, which were related to Down's Syndrome, all looked good and the rest of the baby's anatomy was developing normally. I let a little more hope creep into my heart.

After I wiped up my belly, Nathan and I walked down to the lab where they drew my blood for the first trimester screening and the NIPT. The first trimester screening measured different hormone levels in my body that could affect the pregnancy. It also gave a statistic about the likelihood of certain genetic anomalies. As a general screening test, it is considered less accurate than the NIPT. NIPT is relatively reliable at indicating the presence of chromosomal abnormalities and perfectly accurate at telling the gender of the baby. We would have all these results within the week. After the bloodwork, Nathan and I headed home, happy to have seen our little baby and encouraged by the ultrasound. The blood test results would give us the most complete information yet, however. I shared the details with Ralph later at home and tried to put it all out of my head for a few days as we waited.

The following Friday I got a phone call from Kate, one of the genetic counselors at the maternal fetal medicine practice. She asked if I was free to talk, and I quickly made my way to the front porch so I could have some privacy. Mentally, I prepared myself for whatever she might say. I longed for Ralph to be there with me, but I sat down and let her know I was ready. Kate said they didn't have the full results of the NIPT testing, but the lab had come back with the results of the first trimester screening: She was very sorry, but our baby had a one in five chance of having either Trisomy 18 or 13.

She was compassionate and knew how hard this was to hear, especially since it was an incomplete result without the NIPT data. The tests showed a very, very low likelihood for Down's Syndrome so she did not consider that a risk, but the chance of our baby having either Trisomy 18 or 13 was as high as the test could predict. "What does that mean?" I asked quietly. She said one in five were the worst odds you can get on this test.

White noise slowly filled my head as her words swirled in my brain, but I remember being very composed on the phone. I asked a lot of clinical questions about statistics and the likelihood of false positives. Kate said they would get back to us as soon as possible with the other test results. "No problem, I totally understand," I heard my own upbeat voice answer and we hung up.

I sat in my favorite chair on the front porch. It was a beautiful, warm, sunny August morning. The flowers were blooming, and I looked across the street at the mountains in the distance. My children were quiet inside the house, and this nice lady Kate had just told me that our baby had the worst possible odds for having the two worst chromosomal abnormalities, the ones I wouldn't even read about. The silence stretched on as I sifted this information around in my head and heart. My emotions began to churn as the immediate shock wore off. I called Ralph at work and tried to give him the information I could barely process. I was crying by this point and felt fear and sadness begin to overwhelm me. A train roared through my head. Ralph was calm and supportive, reminding me this was just a preliminary test and we would have to wait for the other results.

"We are in this together," he soothed. "No test result can change how much we love our baby and how much God is with us."

I tried to let his words console me.

I don't remember going back in the house and getting through the rest of the day. These new and terrifying possibilities swirled in my mind as dozens of different scenarios played out in my imagination. The younger kids left that evening for a weekend with their dad, which meant Ralph and I had a lot of free time to sit with this information. We snuggled side-by-side in bed that night with our laptops. While Ralph finished charts from the office, I forced myself to begin looking at these words that had a one in five chance of becoming our reality. Trisomy 18. Trisomy 13. Incompatible with life. Stillborn. Babies not born alive. Babies that live only minutes or hours. Cleft palates. Club feet. Clenched fists. Heart defects.

These felt like nightmares.

I forced myself to read stories of families with babies who lived and died with Trisomy 18 or 13. I looked at pictures of babies with these conditions. I had seen our baby on the ultrasound already—could he or she still have a physical condition that would be hard to look at? Would we be able to tell yet? I read about babies who died in the womb. Babies who died during delivery. Babies who lived only minutes. Babies who needed immediate surgery then died. Babies who couldn't suck or feed or breathe. And the worst part of it was the data no longer applied to a hypothetical baby. It could be my baby. There was a one in five chance that these horrible, life-threatening conditions would be our baby's reality.

I knew it didn't matter one bit to us what was wrong with him or her; we would love our baby fiercely every moment going forward. But I was scared, even as we clung to hope. One in five was just a statistic. My research was just hypothetical, right? Just numbers. Not a diagnosis. Love filled my heart for the fragile, innocent life within me. We prayed and Ralph held me while I cried, knowing we just had to wait. We prayed again the scripture that would become our lifeline:

Trust in the Lord with all your heart and do not lean on your own understanding. In all your ways acknowledge Him, and He will make straight your paths. (Proverbs 3:5-6)

Coming out of the gym the following Tuesday, my phone rang and I saw the number of the genetic counselor on my screen. Rain poured down as I rushed to my car to take the call. Kate let me know right away that the results of the NIPT were in and that the testing ruled out the possibility of our baby having Trisomy 13 or 21. I didn't have time to feel relieved before she continued. The test showed our baby had an 87.5 percent positive predictive value of having Trisomy 18.

Her words hung thickly in the air of my car. The silence stretched on. Even the raindrops outside my car stopped pinging on the roof. I was suspended in time; it was if a knife slipped and sliced my skin, leaving blood bright on the cutting board, but I had yet to feel the pain. The whole world paused with me while these terrible words made their slow, certain descent through my ears into my brain and down to my heart.

When they arrived, I knew instantly that everything had changed. Kate's words reverberated within me like a loudspeaker: *87.5 87.5 87.5.* On the other end of the call, she was gentle but oblivious to the shift in my universe as she forged on, presumably answering questions I no longer remember asking. She taught me about the positive predictive value and what that meant. She said there could be false positives based on the difference between placental DNA and fetal DNA, but that really, we had to assume the test was accurate. Did we want to schedule an amniocentesis? Were we interested in termination, because she had to offer that, and did we want to know the gender? Her words ran together in my head. I could barely think. *87.5. Was that high? Trisomy 18—which one was that again?*

She was so nice and kind as she delivered these horrible words to me in my car in the rain. My tears poured freely and my throat clenched as I tried to process everything she said. This was not the answer we were hoping for. I couldn't say much to her other than, no, we did not want an amnio. And no—we would never terminate so please don't discuss it again. And yes, please, the gender.

A boy, she said. Our little baby was a boy. We were having a probably (*87.5 percent but that didn't mean for sure, right?*) very sick baby boy.

After I hung up with Kate, I called Ralph distraught. I could barely speak. It seemed heartless to burden him with this information when he would have to go back to work, but I couldn't hold it without his strength. I could barely get the words out about Trisomy 18. I knew that we would pour over all this when we were together later, but I also had to tell him—it seemed so important, really the only thing that mattered—that he was having a son. I was having his little boy. I tried to smile because it really made me so dizzyingly happy to be having his little boy, but the echo of my weekend research screamed in my head. *A little boy who will probably die. Statistically, he may not make it until birth. He could be dead already.* This child that we longed for, this child who was already a miracle, would probably die at some secret moment inside me and I wouldn't even know. I couldn't process it. The shock and fear overwhelmed me.

After Ralph and I hung up, I drove straight to the adoration chapel at our church to give it all to Jesus. The Lord gave me a beautiful gift because as soon as I walked into the chapel, the only person there walked out. I went straight to the altar and fell at the Lord's feet on the marble floor and sobbed, pouring out my heart. I had few words, only a lament of sorrow. Disappointment, fear, confusion, and anger churned together in one throbbing storm of emotion. "Please heal our baby," I cried over and over. I knew this child was God's from the very beginning. I knew I would be called to surrender the numbering of his days to God. But I didn't have to like it. I didn't have to accept it in the first thirty minutes of receiving the news. Right now, I could wail and moan and fight and say, "No, NO! This is not what I want!"

I felt every dream and hope I had for our baby collapse. I was terrified about what the future would hold for him (*Our boy! We were having a boy!*) and for us.

Ralph and I clung to each other at home that night. We began the painful, sad process of sharing this news with our family and diving deep into the online world of Trisomy 18. We learned that it is caused when there is a third copy of the eighteenth chromosome in every cell of the baby's body. This extra chromosome causes many issues with how the child's body develops and is able to communicate with itself. We read, again, that very few Trisomy 18 babies are born alive. Those that are rarely live more than a few hours or days. Fewer than twelve percent make it to their first birthday. Sadly, boys had worse outcomes than girls. We became experts at explaining the impact of 87.5 percent positive predictive value. Eventually, we clung to the only place we could find hope: 87.5 percent was like one in eight. They aren't great odds, but there was still a chance our son could be healthy. We did not know for sure. The only way to know definitively was to do an amniocentesis, which posed a slight risk to our baby by occasionally causing the pregnancy to miscarry. We would not take that risk.

I think now there was relief in not knowing definitively. One chance in eight was important for me to cling to hope. I feel sheepish because of course my faith in God demands that I believe there is always hope, despite the odds. But humanly, the numbers mattered. I see now that I had not yet learned to completely surrender. I still needed science to give me the slightest of odds so my rational brain could feel a sense of safety, however false it might be.

In faith, we clung to the hope that our Lord was very close with us and certainly with our baby. He had a plan for his life that would unfold in the way it was planned from all eternity, as hard as that might be for us to accept. Please know this was no Pollyanna faith. This was faith that I fought for moment by moment and came to only after bleeding at the cross with Jesus, sobbing and wailing before the Lord and begging Him to help us. It came after crying out that we were desperate and nothing without Him.

Realizing our little one's life could be very short, Ralph and I needed to be able to love him and pray for him by name right away. I wanted Ralph to decide our son's name. His beautiful father's heart chose John, the beloved son of the elderly Zechariah and Elizabeth from the bible, and Paul, the saint whose powerful conversion and deep love for the Lord have been very meaningful to Ralph and me. John Paul. Since John Paul was already a very special baby, I wanted him to have a very special name. I added Raphael, his daddy's name in Spanish and the victorious angel whose name means "God Heals." *John Paul Raphael Leon.*

We sat in the wake of the devastating news of his potential diagnosis. We keenly felt, in painful technicolor focus, the universal truth that most of our lives are out of our control. All we can do is trust and surrender to the Lord, confident of His presence and love, but with no certainty of outcome. Our plan was to fall in love with our baby and embrace whatever time we were given. This felt like a terrible plan. I wanted a plan that included changing the test results and making him healthy.

We spoke with our obstetrician by phone after he got the report from the specialist, and he confirmed everything we had heard from the genetic counselor and researched ourselves. We shared our decision not to have an amniocentesis in order to keep John

Paul Raphael as safe as possible, even though it was the only way to definitively diagnose Trisomy 18 before birth. We knew our baby was happy and secure for the time being in my womb and blissfully unaware of his possible condition. We would do nothing but pray and wait until my twenty-week sonogram on September 20, five weeks away. Five weeks felt like an eternity when I now feared my baby could die at any moment and I wouldn't know it. My OB said I could come to the office any time just to check for a heartbeat until I was able to feel movement to reassure me that he was still alive.

As we looked ahead, my OB, the geneticist, and our own medical research confirmed that most Trisomy 18 babies show some kind of distinct abnormalities on the twenty-week ultrasound. This would be our chance to see his body more closely and weigh the odds again. If the ultrasound showed normal development (a one-in-eight chance!) as it had at the fourteen-week sonogram, we would have every reason to be hopeful.

This was delicate and holy ground. Under normal circumstances, I could safely anticipate twenty-five more weeks of pregnancy, but even if we made it that far, twenty-five weeks was still a long time to watch and wait and pray. To sit in uncertainty. To "hope for the best." I tried to surrender to how powerless we were, but my human frailty compelled me to wake up every day convinced there had to be something I could do. This was an intense supernatural challenge. How did I stay hopeful and committed to praying for a miracle while acknowledging the very possible reality of needing to let him go long before we ever imagined? I had to do both. I needed to prepare mentally and emotionally for all possible outcomes.

We were fortunate to have an incredibly supportive OB practice that embraced the dignity of John Paul Raphael's life and the beauty that still exists even with a devastating prenatal diagnosis. We also learned that, should we need it, there was a perinatal hospice program in their office that would support us through a negative outcome. Having the word "hospice" enter my life at this stage was agony. It all was. This wouldn't be a true story of John Paul Raphael if I didn't share the constant fear that was present every moment of this journey. Yes, we had a deep faith and deep trust. We prayed constantly for our baby and surrendered it all to the Lord. But humanly, fear was ever-present. Surrender and trust don't always take that away. The more we loved John Paul Raphael, the more I could not breathe as I contemplated the realities that could be our future.

We were blessed to be surrounded by a strong network of family and friends. We knew we could count on the prayers of our community to help and hold us during that time. We mustered up our courage and sent out a huge email to our people to introduce them to John Paul Raphael and share with them our need for intercession for his health and healing. This support was invaluable and the love we got back touched us deeply. We had dozens of emails from friends and family in response, promising their support and their prayers. This was a raw and vulnerable time. Our beautiful child's life was at stake. Asking for help was at least something I could do, but I was so tender and fragile that it took me weeks to receive the kindness and love of our loved ones' replies. Their compassion brought the risks too close. A huge part of me wanted to grab Ralph's hand and go into hiding until the whole pregnancy was over. It was hard to let people see how scared I was and how much I was hurting, especially when there was nothing anyone could do. It took courage I didn't always have to open up and share our love and fear for our beautiful child.

I decided to buy John Paul Raphael one more gift, a soft, snuggly blue baby blanket to go with his Duckie. One of the many hard things about this pregnancy was not responding to my body's instinctive need to nest. My hormones urged me to prepare and plan for everything a healthy baby would need. I longed to create a lovely and nurturing room to welcome and celebrate John Paul Raphael, but we weren't going to have a baby shower or decorate a nursery with 87.5 percent, so I just bought a blanket. Blue Blankie gave me something concrete to hold on to when there wasn't much else.

3

HOLDING ON TO HOPE

Our greatest sufferings are an invitation to joy.

"We have this hope as an anchor for the soul, firm and secure."
—Hebrews 6:19

RALPH AND I had been saving money for several years to take a five-year anniversary trip to Italy. When we found out I was pregnant, we quickly decided to move up the trip, anticipating that we would be bouncing a happy nursing baby instead of going overseas on our fifth anniversary. With the news of John Paul Raphael's possible diagnosis, our trip was no longer a vacation but a pilgrimage. The timing was ideal. We would spend nine days alone with each other and our beautiful son as we waited for the date of my twenty-week sonogram on September 20. We might never be able to take John Paul Raphael on another family vacation, but we could take this one, just the three of us. Praying for his healing also gave focus to our trip. Every church, every altar, every Mass, every saint—they were all opportunities to lay our hearts and our need before God all over the country of Italy. We prayed at the tomb of St. Paul the Apostle, St.

John Paul the Great, St. Francis of Assisi, St. Clare—so many warriors to intercede for one sweet small baby and his scared mommy and daddy. We prayed for a miracle of total health and healing but given the statistics, we mostly asked for the gift of him being born alive.

I had a very moving experience in Rome at Michelangelo's Pieta in the Basilica of St. Peter. I had visited once as a fresh, young twenty-one-year-old, straight out of college. Here I returned, wounded and scarred from my first marriage with nine heart-broken children and one (maybe) very sick baby who I longed for with all my heart.

Oh, my mother. I see your face and your sorrow. You know my heart. You know what I carry. You know completely what it is to carry your son in your womb and in your arms and through his life, knowing you will surrender him to death. I know that the swords that pierce my heart are nothing in the light of His and your suffering, but I know you see me, my sweetest mother, and you know.

So much of our journey with John Paul Raphael was about faith—about being a beacon of hope and clinging to trust in God and surrender. But sometimes, like here at the feet of Mother Mary cradling her dead Son, it was about a terrified little girl who could not possibly walk the path laid out before her, who felt crushed beneath the load of her sad, lost, hurting daughter and the eight other children she must love and support. Living in the land of uncertainty and maybes and positive predictive values was exhausting. I didn't feel strong enough to carry the burden of responsibility for our son, even with Ralph. Contemplating Mary and Jesus, I finally felt as powerless as I really was.

You know and you hear, my mother Mary. I trust you with my baby and my own heart. Please let him live.

We took pictures of John Paul Raphael in my belly wherever we went in Italy. My belly at the Coliseum, my belly at St. Mark's in Venice, my belly on the ancient stairs of Assisi. When you aren't sure how long your baby will live, it is important to build whatever memories you can. Ralph found a special sandalwood cologne in

Rome at the Basilica of St. Paul's Outside the Walls that he wanted to get as a signature scent for John Paul Raphael. We began to spray it on his Blue Blankie and his Duckie, both of which had traveled with us to Italy. I spent every morning lying in the hotel bed trying to feel John Paul Raphael move. Willing him to move. *Are you alive in there?* We were in Italy for the nineteenth and twentieth weeks of my pregnancy. It was certainly the right time for me to notice his movements. Panic and fear grew day after day when I felt nothing. Could he be gone already? We certainly knew a medical crisis overseas was a possibility. I was so desperate for him to be alive, but all we could do was hope, pray, and wait. Finally, during our last days in the beautiful light of Venice, it came. The fluttering. That feeling inside that I knew for sure was our little boy stretching his limbs. Love and relief flooded my heart. I cried, knowing that, at least for now, he was still here and the three of us were together.

Returning home, Ralph and I faced many challenges. Ralph was back at work full-time and I managed the daily demands of four children at home and all the various activities and work that brings. We still struggled to find the best care plan for our daughter and her mental illness. We found her a service dog named Gage. We hoped he would be the key to increasing her personal safety and facilitate her return to school.

As my twenty-week ultrasound loomed closer, I remembered with longing the naïve hopefulness of my previous pregnancies. My biggest worry from those sonograms was finding out the gender and whether that fit with my plan. I laughed unkindly at the innocent, young mother I was. It never occurred to me then to worry about my baby being "incompatible with life." And now I clung to the security of not-knowing. Yes, there were statistics and numbers and research, but there was safety in a place where the answer was neither yes nor no. Possibilities lived there. Hope lived there. Healthy babies that learn to ride a bike and go to college one day still lived there. The end of that not-knowing was an ultrasound appointment behind a locked door marked "September 20."

When the day came, Ralph and I arrived back at the office of the maternal fetal specialists, nervous and subdued. I tried to focus on the hope that I could still feel John Paul Raphael moving and that soon we would be able to see his sweet face again. But the larger reason for this visit weighed heavily upon us. We told ourselves and we told others that most babies with Trisomy 18 will show unique characteristics in some way on the ultrasound. I expected to see something really obvious, like a misshapen heart that would never work outside the womb or his brain not fully formed. A loud and clear sign. But as the ultrasound progressed, we saw a lot of perfect baby parts in all the right places. Tears rolled silently down my cheeks the whole hour seeing our boy. We fell more in love with him and soaked in each fuzzy gray shape, imagining him as chubby flesh in our arms. I also held my breath at the sword that could pierce any moment if the tech paused or made too many notes. But John Paul looked good to our naive and uneducated eyes. Ralph was hopeful. "He looks healthy to me," he whispered in my ear.

After a thorough exam, the tech excused herself and we waited. Fifteen minutes later a new doctor entered briskly without making eye contact and without introducing himself. This was not a good start for two emotionally fragile parents. I felt Ralph bristle next to me at the doctor's rudeness and lack of bedside manner. The doctor began his own ultrasound and made several anatomical observations in a casual way. Each point seemed small, and he shared them without gravity and seemingly without a lot of concern: a small septal defect in his heart, slightly short femurs, hands that looked clenched. The doctor showed us the brain and an area where normally you would see the beginning of the corpus callosum, the brain tissue connecting the left and right brain hemispheres. He didn't see it, but he also suggested it could still develop later and sometimes wasn't visible until twenty-two to twenty-four weeks. We told him that Ralph had a perfectly healthy nephew who also does not have a corpus callosum. Maybe this could be a hereditary issue? And finally, the doctor showed us the choroid plexus cyst. One-third to one-half of Trisomy 18 babies have one of these. And so did John Paul Raphael. But again, the doctor addressed this in an uneventful way. He said the cyst itself wasn't harmful and sometimes perfectly healthy babies have them too. Overall, the doctor was noncommittal about his findings, although he did say they could suggest Trisomy 18. Maybe it was just my hopeful heart that heard the second part: "Or they could be nothing."

After the doctor left, I lay on the table in the dark room trying to take it all in. It was so much. The words spun in my mind and my heart was tender and fragile. I didn't even know how to be with Ralph. This was our son the doctor was talking so casually about. The little guy wiggling all over the monitor, that I could feel dancing about in my belly? How could he be "incompatible with life" when he was so obviously alive? He wasn't just measurements and body parts and statistics. He was a gift we desperately wanted, but were not convinced we would ever receive in our arms.

Hidden in my heart was my secret hope that John Paul Raphael would be the one person to really care and be grateful that Ralph and I were married and in love. Because that love created him. Our son would somehow validate the love Ralph and I shared. I believed if all nine of our other children were honest, they would rather us not be married. They'd prefer we were still with their other parent, or at least alone and not imposing a stepparent upon them. Even though I understood that, I longed for John Paul Raphael to love us both the same and need us both and affirm the value and purpose of our union. Maybe that would finally make us a real family. I was in my forties and scarred from divorce and rejection. I had yet to really believe in my own beauty and worthiness. A second marriage can feel like it isn't as real as the first marriage, especially if the second one does not bear fruit. But here he was, our fruit! The pregnancy apps gave babies a new fruit size every week as they grew: poppy seed, lime, lemon, avocado, banana. John Paul Raphael was growing and saying, "I am here! I see the love of my mommy and daddy and I am so happy they are together."

I knew it shouldn't matter whether anyone else believed in or understood our love. I shouldn't expect our children to understand that the love Ralph and I have for each other is greater than the love we shared for their mom or their dad. That is not meant to be disrespectful to either of our first spouses, but one thing Ralph and I have learned is that suffering expands you. I am not the same person inside that I was when I was married to my first husband. It isn't just time and maturity that changed me. The experience of living through my divorce and grappling with my ex-husband's adultery and rejection dramatically changed me. Through healing and rebirth, I have a much greater capacity to love. The same is true for Ralph. He lived through his first wife's slow and painful death from cancer. That was no easy task. His heart expanded through grief and loss. I know we both loved our first spouses with all our hearts, but in sorrow, our hearts stretched to hold pain. Ralph and I also love each other with all our hearts, but it is a deeper and richer love because of loss. Through God's grace, that love blossomed into a child that has nothing to do with a first wife or a first husband or our old stories. He was our future together.

When we were first married, I struggled with feeling second, like I was second best or was just holding another woman's place until Ralph could return to his "real wife" in heaven. I feared that somehow, without children, our marriage didn't count. But here we were with a baby coming. It didn't matter one bit that this was my seventh pregnancy or my second husband. I wanted every little thing that every mother in love wanted from her baby. To see her husband's eyes in his tiny little face. To see her own hair or hands on a new tiny body. To see this beautiful blending of two souls and bodies into a new creation and marvel at the mystery and the gift.

Ralph and I walked away from the ultrasound a little stunned. There had been so much anticipation of finally knowing, and yet, somehow, we still didn't know. We tried to process what it meant and how we felt. The doctor recommended a fetal echocardiogram to take a closer look at the heart and then follow up with another ultrasound in a month. We talked to my mom in the car and tried to make sense of it all. Was the diagnosis clear? Did we know now? There were several questionable findings, but John Paul Raphael also looked really healthy. My mom shared her concern about the stress of being held in limbo as we waited for more tests in the coming months. But outside of an amnio, what else could we do? We sent a text to the kids and some close friends telling them what we could. All this new information settled over me slowly like syrup. Mentally, I re-visited every image and every word. As the day went on, my heart began to unravel. There was relief that September 20 was passing but stress that we still didn't know his condition for sure.

I heard a small whisper though, a gentle, tender, almost imperceptible voice inside me. We knew that 95 percent of Trisomy 18 babies show themselves in some way by twenty weeks on ultrasound. John Paul Raphael showed us five different signs that were all consistent with Trisomy 18. Yes, they were each small. Independently, none were life-threatening. They could each resolve and not be present on a later ultrasound. But they were here now, and together painted a picture of our perfectly imperfect little boy, our John Paul Raphael, who I had to begin to accept—(*I don't even want to write it . . . can I please say maybe or could?*)

I needed to accept that John Paul Raphael had Trisomy 18, but how could I do that and not give up hope?

How did I look at the realities of the ultrasound and still believe a miracle was possible? Was it a rejection of faith to only see the science in front of me or a rejection of reality to cling to faith and hope? How could I try to prepare for one path while still desperately hoping for another? Did they automatically cancel each other out?

My tears fell heavily that night. A cloak of sadness settled on my shoulders like a weighted blanket. In a shallow attempt to manage the situation, I began to sift through stories on the internet and did more research. I tried to find the one website or testimony or journal that would contradict our previous findings and say instead, "Whoops! No! Those markers don't *really* mean he has Trisomy 18. Just read my story and see!" But the opposite happened. The more I read and researched, the more likely it seemed that he did. Ralph says that in medicine, if you hear galloping, think horses, not zebras. And here we were clinging to the possibility that we were carrying a zebra, not a horse. Was it possible there were five independent markers that each meant nothing and we could have a perfectly healthy baby? Yes. I believe in miracles . . . but that was different than pretending John Paul didn't have Trisomy 18.

September 21 was a long, sad, lonely day. Numbness seeped through me. I felt disconnected as I read stories and blogs about others' experiences with Trisomy 18. It was surreal to accept that some aspects of those stories were going to be our story as well. We may have a stillborn son. We may bury a tiny boy. We might have to learn what to do or not to do if he turned blue and couldn't breathe. He may have a feeding tube. And we may have to find the strength to share this whole valley of tears with our nine other children and our families. I didn't feel brave anymore. I didn't want to share my grief with anyone except Ralph. I wanted to go away with him and suffer privately and come back when it was over and we were neat, tidy, and healed. That was not one of my options. Instead, I looked at this landscape that Ralph and I needed to learn to navigate and my knees buckled. *"Hello, grief. Come on in. You can have the room at the foot of the stairs to my heart where you are going to live . . . forever."*

An unavoidable tidal wave of grief was probably coming our way. Other painful feelings were already present. Failure. Shame. An expectation of myself that I should have made a perfectly healthy baby and I didn't. I should have given this to my husband, but I couldn't. My body betrayed me somehow. I felt embarrassed about my hopes and dreams about our baby and what John Paul Raphael meant to me about being married again and bringing our love to life in the world, blah blah blah. An ugly inner voice said, "*What foolishness. You never deserved that. Why would you even hope?*" Somehow John Paul Raphael being "incompatible with life" took away from our marriage too. My inner critic hissed, "*See? You can't even have a baby together.* You aren't as real as you thought. Maybe it's because of how old and fat and ugly you are. What were you even thinking?"

Many times, Ralph and I struggled to understand each other. He was much better at trusting and staying in the moment. I have deep faith and hope, but I also needed to try to understand the experience of what might lie ahead. I wanted to feel and touch the different possible endings to our story. I coped by trying to make the impossible unknown less scary by learning about it. For instance, I called a funeral home the same week as the ultrasound. As a mother, it was horrifying and agonizing to think about having to bury a son I hadn't even met yet, but I felt the tiniest bit better after calling the funeral home. I survived it and that one thing felt a little less terrifying. Ralph was sad and frustrated, though. He felt like I was burying John Paul before he was even born. He wasn't wrong. Maybe I needed to bury the version of our son that science predicted we weren't going to get. I needed to bury the eight-month-old nursing to sleep in my arms. The two-year-old running around his train table. The three-year-old learning to use the potty. The five-year-old going to kindergarten.

I wanted that little boy so much. I imagined him with floppy brown hair and chocolate brown eyes like his daddy. I loved every version of him. I already had so many dreams and hopes for him. Maybe he would be a priest and preside over our fiftieth wedding anniversary. Maybe he would unite our blended family even more. I knew that he was God's perfect child, fearfully and wonderfully made, but I needed to grieve my own dreams for him and let them go. I had to make the shift from plan A to plan B and that was a dreadful process. We would bury something of each of us, my heart and Ralph's heart, along the dreams we had for our baby boy. I also embraced and loved the baby he was right then with whatever unique abilities or disabilities he might have. But it was all fresh and new. I knew John Paul Raphael was alive, but he still felt close to death. I wanted to cherish every moment I had with him safely in my belly while accepting the truth that it might be the only life I got with him. Or there could be more. Only God knew. His plan, His child, His perfect timing.

We had another specialist appointment the following week and met a third doctor in the practice for the first time, Dr. Hassan. We immediately felt comforted by his grandfatherly and gentle manner. He started the appointment by asking us to tell him about our baby. My heart and body relaxed at the gift of this invitation. The medical assessments and concerns related to our baby weighed us down and it was easy to feel like all these professionals forgot the patient was also our *son*.

Dr. Hassan listened intently as we talked about John Paul Raphael, and he seemed to understand our hearts and our goals. We accepted the likely possibility that our son had Trisomy 18. We understood the implications of this for his life and probable death. Dr. Hassan accepted that our number one goal was for John Paul Raphael to be born alive and that this desire would direct all our care decisions. We were still unclear about the level of medical intervention we wanted to pursue at birth, however, as it was not evident exactly what John Paul Raphael might need. Dr. Hassan looked at our chart and felt it was likely John Paul Raphael would need immediate heart surgery at birth in order to survive. Half of his heart appeared much smaller than the other half and he recommended that we see a world-renowned fetal cardiologist at Children's Medical Center in Washington, DC as soon as possible. His office would set up the appointment.

As overwhelming as this new information was, I felt comfort in Dr. Hassan's care. I knew from my research that with these tiny babies, working with a hospital or neonatology ahead of time was sometimes very helpful, but I had no idea how to go about it. Now at least our baby would get some very thorough testing and we could begin to formulate a plan.

Ralph and I got up at five a.m. the following Tuesday to drive downtown to the Children's National Medical Center. I was scheduled for a fetal MRI at six a.m. Heading all the way into the city for such intensive testing made the dangers we faced all the more real. Our baby's condition and his care decisions could be a matter of life and death. I wanted to get it right. Ralph stayed with me as I was prepped for the MRI. Although the procedure was non-invasive, I had to curl up on my side in the tiny imaging tube for over an hour. I managed well for a long time in the ear-splitting noise, praying for our baby and trying to say the rosary in my head while not moving. Eventually my swollen, pregnant body began to ache and the tube seemed to shrink. It was comforting to see Ralph out of the corner of my eye, but it was hard to stay calm as the technician and radiologist took their time scrutinizing John Paul's brain. After another ultrasound and an echocardiogram, we met with the heart specialist and received encouraging news. In her professional experience, our baby's heart should function just fine at birth and need no surgery. This was a huge relief. Decisions related to invasive, painful, and risky surgery are hard for any parent, but when your baby may be very small with a life-limiting condition, they are even harder. The birth weight of Trisomy 18 babies tends to be lower than normal. Most surgeries can only be performed when babies have reached a certain weight. If your baby's life is expected to be short, there is the added complication that he may not survive the surgery or, if he does, may spend all of his brief life connected to machines or in pain. To have heart surgery taken off the table was a monumental victory.

The last half of the day was spent with the fetal care team: a genetic counselor, the pediatric radiologist, a neonatologist, a geneticist, and a nurse practitioner and attending physician from the palliative care team who work to assist families with potentially life-threatening diagnoses. We were humbled to receive such thorough support from nationally acclaimed professionals. We knew all these results could not change Trisomy 18, but they provided extensive information to give our beautiful baby every possible chance to live. One by one, each team member reviewed John Paul's records and tests and shared their observations and recommendations for his condition and anatomy. One additional concern mentioned was the amniotic fluid. The volume measured on the high side of normal, and if it stayed high or got higher, it increased my chances of pre-term labor. Polyhydramnios, an elevated level of amniotic fluid, is often caused by swallowing difficulties present in the baby. A healthy baby will routinely swallow amniotic fluid allowing the fluid level in the womb to stay constant. If the baby cannot swallow well, an abnormality often seen in Trisomy 18 babies, then he or she is not digesting enough amniotic fluid and not absorbing it well. This has the double effect of not reducing the amount of amniotic fluid and also causing the baby to be smaller or under-nourished from fewer nutrients. Polyhydramnios can also be caused by a tracheoesophageal fistula, an abnormal connection between the trachea and the esophagus. These are common in Trisomy 18 babies and require surgery to repair. After delivery, a baby with a tracheoesophageal fistula is unable to be fed orally and must have a feeding tube. The radiologist noticed that John Paul Raphael's stomach was small. He was concerned that John Paul might have a fistula or a defect in swallowing, both of which would require a surgical repair. This raised the question again of whether we would want to perform surgery on a baby that could be very small with a potentially very short life.

These were all difficult questions based entirely on possibilities. It was incredibly reassuring, however, to have so much professional and emotional support to finish out my pregnancy. The team said over and over that they were available for more questions, consultations, or to facilitate transferring information to the delivery hospital or even to tele-conference with my OB if needed. Until we were flooded with information and support, we didn't realize how much we needed it. We were so afraid and wanted to protect and save our baby. We knew these professionals might not be able to fix the unfixable, but I was comforted to feel cared for during this incredibly painful time.

Overall, we were encouraged by the visit. It re-kindled my hope that John Paul Raphael might not have Trisomy 18, but I also felt reassured that if he did, there could be hope for a more positive outcome. One thing the specialists made very clear, though, was that structure did not indicate function. Just because his anatomy looked good, with Trisomy 18, we had no way of knowing what the brain was capable of telling the body to do.

That was the most challenging aspect of his potential diagnosis. We could not plan or predict how John Paul Raphael would fare once he was born and his body was asked to take over. The very nature of Trisomy 18 exists in the presence of a third eighteenth chromosome. In some unknown way, the extra chromosome inhibits the ability of the brain to tell the rest of the body what to do. We had to plan for all scenarios, from delivering a healthy baby to delivering a Trisomy 18 baby who had a very brief life to having a Trisomy 18 baby who was able to come home from the hospital and live for weeks or months, or possibly years. Our deepest desire was for John Paul to be born alive and to open his eyes so we could at least see and love each other outside the womb for a little while. We allowed this longing to shape all our decisions around the rest of my pregnancy and his birth.

We also needed to reconsider the hospital at which we would deliver. Our plan had been to deliver at Fair Oaks Hospital with one of the doctors from the practice that delivered my five other babies.

But if John Paul Raphael was going to need any kind of surgery or specialized care, he would need to be at the very best hospital, necessitating an emergency transfer for him and possibly not me. This was not an option for us. We needed to be sure to give him the best possible care and still keep us together at every point. That meant delivering at Inova Fairfax Hospital where there was a Level 1 Neonatal Intensive Care Unit (NICU) along with a pediatric surgeon, should we need one.

This was the first of many hard decisions in the coming weeks that felt so important to get right. This was our very tiny, sick baby and we, as his parents, were given the grace and the strength to make the best possible decisions for him and to advocate for him in every way. The weight of that pressed on me. I realized that to "get through life," I had compartmentalized my fears and concerns about John Paul Raphael's care. In order to focus on helping the other four kids in the house, I unhealthily numbed or shoved aside my anxiety, fear, and stress about John Paul. As the next appointment drew near, the anxiety would stir back up again and I would fall apart. By twenty-six weeks, we were so grateful John Paul was still alive, but I started to panic. Time was moving quickly and the unknowns would reveal themselves one way or another in the next fourteen weeks, possibly sooner. I desperately wanted our little boy to be healthy and continued to pray for that miracle. Mostly, I just wanted him to stay.

4

THE SHADOW OF DEATH

*When you come to the end of yourself,
you can be found.*

*"Even though I walk through the valley of the
shadow of death, I fear no evil, for You are with me;
Your rod and Your staff, they comfort me."*
—Psalm 23:4

AT MY NEXT OB VISIT, we went over all the information from
the specialists. We were pleased to learn that one of the doctors
still had privileges to deliver at Inova Fairfax Hospital and agreed to
deliver John Paul Raphael there for us. We also met for the first time
with the perinatal hospice coordinator who shared resources around
having to say goodbye to our baby. We had many hard decisions to
make. I felt the pressure of having to think through every possible
outcome and what we wanted for John Paul Raphael and for us in
each scenario. It was critical to create a clear birth plan, but the
strength to do that still eluded me.

At twenty-eight weeks, I also felt every bit the old, tired, giant pregnant mother. The emotional strain of my pregnancy was a huge weight, but in a very real way my actual weight had increased substantially. Not just with pregnancy weight gain, but also from polyhydramnios. My belly measured thirty-four weeks due to the excess fluid in my womb and I started to feel the pressure against my lungs. Walking, breathing, and sleeping became more challenging day by day.

At my next specialist appointment with Dr. Hassan, John Paul Raphael was very active on the ultrasound. We had had so many scans that Ralph and I were both becoming skilled at reading the screen and following the measurements. I held my breath as the tech measured each of John Paul's bones and the circumference of his belly and head. Each of these measurements had a gestational age associated with the size. The goal was for the size to match the gestational age. John Paul was wiggling all over the place. His head consistently measured big. His belly and legs were always small. We scrutinized the size of his bladder and his stomach. Was he drinking any fluid? Could we see fingers on his hands? Did his fists look clenched or his feet still perfectly curved?

We knew that most Trisomy 18 babies, if they survived into these later weeks of pregnancy, usually fell off their growth curve eventually. They gained weight slowly and steadily like any healthy baby, but then just stopped growing. Each visit took several hours as they did Doppler scans of heart rates and blood flow through his brain and umbilical cord. Eventually, Dr. Hassan would come in and share some bit of encouragement, however small. He knew we were clinging to hope and loving our baby at every moment. He was very supportive and we were so grateful for his kindness and the generosity of his time with us.

There was intense relief in visiting with John Paul Raphael during these appointments and watching his ever-beating heart. Looking back now, I can still feel the anxiety pressing on me like a thick, painful blanket. My heart beat heavily, the sound pounding in my ears. My skin was hot and prickly, and my eyes scrutinized the monitor, staring intently at our son. We carried hope and fear, tossing them back and forth between our two hands. It was achingly beautiful to be held in the web of unknowing with our sweet baby. And even when Trisomy 18 seemed sure, what that meant for our baby was a great unknown. He was with us today, but could be stillborn. He was alive now, but that didn't guarantee he would survive delivery. He was practicing breathing in the womb, but that didn't mean he would be able to breathe on his own after birth. It was exhausting to tip-toe across thin ice day after day after day.

The week before Thanksgiving, my polyhydramnios increased significantly, measuring thirty centimeters of fluid. A normal range was between eight and twenty centimeters. This significantly increased the risk of premature delivery and the pressure on my lungs. It was no longer just my anxiety causing me pain in my chest cavity. Dr. Hassan and my OB conferred and decided I should receive steroid shots in order to improve John Paul Raphael's lung development and increase his potential for being able to breathe should I deliver early. Dr. Hassan insisted this was just prophylactic, but I felt on edge about what the coming weeks would hold. The doctors recommended not leaving town for Thanksgiving since we wanted to stay close to our health care team. Each of these decisions felt like life or death for our beautiful boy.

Ralph and I had committed to this journey with John Paul Raphael before he was even conceived. We were nearing the final battle, though, and I was already physically and emotionally drained. While there was no turning back, I doubted my ability to forge ahead. The light of my faith flickered. I forgot to rely on God and felt dwarfed by the mountains towering in front of us. Time pushed us on, though, whether we were ready or not. Ralph and I really needed to work through the rest of our birth plan. I had spent time online reading examples from other parents in similar circumstances, but

I felt frozen when it came to finalizing our own plan. I was stalling. This plan would itemize our greatest fears. How could we be sure exactly what procedures we wanted or didn't want before John Paul was here? What if I wasn't ready to make those decisions? What if I couldn't yet face my fears? It took a lot of strength, grace, and prayer to work through the whole process with Ralph. It was so tender to acknowledge the dreams we had for our baby and let them touch the reality of his condition and what it would mean for his life.

For instance, we knew we did not want to put our baby on a ventilator if his body couldn't breathe. We accepted that not breathing was one of the most common reasons Trisomy 18 babies die. A ventilator was not a solution, only a delay of the inevitable. But if I went into labor early and he was born at twenty-eight weeks, then maybe we would want extraordinary measures. If he couldn't breathe due to Trisomy 18, that was different than being unable to breathe because his lungs were immature. But how would we know the difference? And if we put him on a ventilator and he lived for days or weeks, how would we know if he could ever breathe on his own without removing the ventilator? And even if that gave us more time, was more time with a baby on a ventilator what we really wanted for John Paul Raphael or for us? It felt like any decision needed to have contingency A, B, and C. Even being a seasoned parent, making these decisions for our little one felt like way too much responsibility. I desperately wanted someone to just tell us the "right" thing to do, but only Ralph and I were given the grace by God to love and advocate for our child. We had to find the strength to do what must be done.

In an effort to feel more prepared, I read more birth stories from other little Trisomy 18 babies. As I read, I found myself crying out to God, *"No! I don't want this!"* Not because I didn't trust Him, but because I was so weak and these scenarios were impossible for my mother's heart to absorb. For instance, I knew now that most Trisomy 18 babies who are born alive die from apnea. They "forget" to breathe. These episodes may be rare or frequent, brief or extended. But for most Trisomy 18 babies, at some point, they just stop breathing and they don't start again. There is no way to predict when an apneic episode might occur or which of these might be the last. I was horrified, but I had to find a way to normalize it. I read several heart-breaking accounts from mothers whose babies died this way. They described their color changing. The agonal breathing. The discussion on when or if to give morphine. The question of whether or not the baby is in pain or distress as they die. I read about oxygen and feeding tubes and tracheostomies and how long you can keep your deceased baby with you before their body begins to change dramatically. I read about cuddle cots that keep a dead baby chilled so you can have more time with them and comfort bears that are made to weigh the same as your lost child. I read about tiny plastic caskets that look like take-out food containers and making baby footprints and handprints and recording his heartbeat. I learned about photographers that donate time to take photos in the hospital for families who have lost or will shortly lose a baby. I cannot remember right now how I managed to absorb all of this information, accept that it was my future, and still get out of bed and take care of my family.

We decided to go away for Thanksgiving against medical advice, hoping that I wouldn't go into labor. Ralph and I traveled to Scranton, Pennsylvania with our children, Andrew and Maggie, to celebrate with my mother and grandmother and extended family. John Paul Raphael continued to be active and stayed safely tucked inside my belly while we were away. When we got back, Ralph and I had appointments with the Fetal Care team at Inova Fairfax Hospital to introduce ourselves and to prepare for all the possible scenarios at John Paul's delivery. Ralph and I worked carefully over the holiday to finalize our birth plan and deliver it to the team. We took a tour of the NICU and talked about the rules and regulations that would apply to John Paul Raphael if he was admitted. For instance, any baby under four pounds or thirty-six weeks would automatically be admitted to the NICU. If John Paul Raphael clearly showed himself to have Trisomy 18, though, they would let him stay with me. If he needed oxygen or other non-routine care, however, he would have to go to the NICU. There were challenges with the limitations of visitors and family in the NICU, though, and it was hard to figure out how this was all going to work for our family. We felt very supported by the fetal care team, however. They understood our top priorities: that John Paul Raphael be born alive and that we not be separated. We believed they would do everything possible to make those things happen and give John Paul Raphael the very best care.

We were so grateful to be surrounded by a team of doctors who respected John Paul Raphael's life and believed it was worth saving. Never once did a doctor question our plans. In my research, I read many stories of families who felt their baby did not receive every opportunity because of a Trisomy 18 diagnosis or who felt unsupported by staff for choosing to embrace this little life. We felt the total opposite. With the exception of the doctor at the twenty-week ultrasound, we only met professionals who showed compassion for us and our little boy and who were committed to giving all of us the very best care. My aunt who works with premature babies was surprised to find out that I was given steroid shots in light of John Paul Raphael's likely diagnosis. She said that usually wasn't done for Trisomy babies because the doctors didn't think it would make a difference. We were so thankful that Dr. Hassan respected our desire to treat my pregnancy and our little boy as if he did not have Trisomy 18 since we didn't know for sure.

While we were at the Fairfax hospital, we took time to meet with Fr. Stefan Starzynski, the hospital chaplain who also had a healing ministry and a history of miracles with babies. It was beautiful and hopeful as he prayed with us. I knew we were held in God's hands, but it broke my heart to consider that the miracle could be how God used John Paul Raphael's very short life for His glory. We clung to hope and made acts of surrender minute by minute.

As the calendar turned to December, we returned to my OB for yet another appointment. After the routine checks, the doctor asked us to come into her office. We were shocked to hear her say that there had been some kind of misunderstanding. She was very, very sorry, but there was no way she could deliver our baby at Inova Fairfax Hospital. *What?* I was sure I had not heard her correctly. This same doctor had looked us in the eye four weeks prior and agreed she would deliver at Fairfax. Now I was thirty-one weeks pregnant, we had an entire plan in place at one hospital, and she had changed her mind. We were devastated. We would either have to deliver the baby at Fair Oaks Hospital without the higher level NICU, without a pediatric surgeon, and without the Fetal Care team—or we could choose Inova Fairfax and the additional medical support, but find a new obstetrician. How would we find a new doctor at thirty-one weeks? With an extremely high-risk, complicated pregnancy and a mother of well-advanced maternal age and a baby who had Trisomy 18? We were both too shocked to process how angry we were. The doctor was apologetic and offered explanations for how the mix-up occurred. She took full responsibility for not sharing this information weeks earlier, but it didn't change the outcome.

I cried deep, guttural sobs of grief and exhaustion. I was empty and had no reserves left to handle this news. I stared out the windshield of our minivan and held my giant belly as tears rolled down my cheeks. I just wanted everything to be okay and nothing was okay. Ralph was my anchor and simply drove us home, his silent strength coupled with his own worry for me as much as for John Paul Raphael. Though I endured physical hardships for John Paul Raphael during my pregnancy, the weight my dear husband carried was immense: his own equal love and concern for our baby plus his desire to protect and carry me through this valley of tears.

This was an unbelievably stressful and upsetting development, but at this low point, God moved quickly. Ralph and I decided that night that providing the best care for John Paul Raphael was more important than who delivered him. We decided to stay at Inova Fairfax Hospital and called my OB to let her know. She said she would place a call to the Fetal Care team at Fairfax to give them the news and see if they had any suggestions for a new doctor. By the next day, we heard from the coordinator that Dr. Kathy Wolfe and her practice were willing to take on our case; we would meet her the next day. Ralph and I arrived at her office a little late after fighting rush hour traffic. We were clearly the last appointment of the day and it was obvious they were stretching their hours to accommodate us. I was comforted to see scripture passages painted on the walls. When I left my urine sample in the bathroom, there were colorful mirror markers out for patients to write an inspirational message. *You are beautiful! God loves you!* The nurse doing my vitals was welcoming and friendly. When we finally met Dr. Wolfe, she gave me a big hug and asked us to tell her about our baby. The tears began as we told her about our family and our deep love and concern for John Paul Raphael, our fear and sorrow, but also the confusing information we had received: the NIPT test and other factors indicated he had Trisomy 18 while several aspects of his health and anatomy were not consistent with that condition. She understood our decision to forgo the amniocentesis to confirm the diagnosis and listened intently to our fears and questions. When we were through, she told us about two sweet Trisomy 18 babies she had delivered in the past. She shared her own faith as well as her recent pilgrimage to visit the Blessed Mother at Medjugorje in Bosnia-Herzegovina. She told us that she believed completely that God had our little baby in His hands, no matter the outcome.

I cried and cried as she spoke. At the eleventh hour, God had provided a loving, Catholic doctor with relevant experience to take care of us. I felt so reassured. Dr. Wolfe led us to an ultrasound room in her office and agreed with prior observations that John Paul just looked too healthy and too active to definitively have Trisomy 18. She was cautiously hopeful for us.

Over the next three weeks, I had multiple appointments with both Dr. Hassan and Dr. Wolfe. John Paul Raphael continued to grow, but so did the amniotic fluid. The baby had also shifted sideways. The combination of a lateral presentation and high fluid levels had us on red-alert that my water could break, and I was told to limit my activity as much as possible. The concern for John Paul Raphael was two-fold: in a sideways position, if my membranes ruptured, there was a high risk for a cord prolapse, a condition where the umbilical cord drops into the birth canal prior to the baby. This is a potentially life-threatening emergency due to the possibility of the cord pinching and depriving him of oxygen. Equally worrisome was that a large amount of fluid rupturing in a gush could also cause a placental abruption in which the placenta is ripped away from the uterine wall. This would also be fatal for John Paul Raphael in a very short period of time. Adding to our other anxieties was the high risk of an emergency delivery, certainly by C-section. We needed to modify our birth plan to account for this. If I had to receive general anesthesia in order to deliver our baby alive in an emergency situation, there was no guarantee he would still be alive when I was awake and alert in a few hours. Because we wanted John Paul Raphael's life to unfold in a natural way, our birth plan stated that John Paul Raphael was not to be put on a ventilator. If he had Trisomy 18, we would accept the limitations of his condition and allow his body to breathe or not breathe, however agonizing that would be for us as his parents. As much as I was desperate to keep him alive, we had to consider the long-term quality of his life. A ventilator was not an option for us.

But if I was going to be unconscious from anesthesia, I still wanted to be able to meet him alive. We made the challenging decision to amend our birth plan to request he go on a ventilator *only* in this situation to maximize the chance for John Paul Raphael and me to have time together. The process of having to remove the ventilator and potentially losing him quickly would be heartbreaking, but we both agreed this was what we wanted. I kept a copy of our birth plan in my purse because the doctors were very clear if I had a gush of fluid, I was to call an ambulance and go to the closest hospital. I would have to position myself on my hands and knees, my behind up in the air, and if I felt the cord drop, someone would need to hold it back in place. *Oh no no.*

Christmas was closing in and we hoped to make it through the holidays still safely pregnant. John Paul was very active and frequently shoved some body part or another into the top of my belly where Ralph and the kids could feel it and laugh and wonder about what position he was in. We had several 3D ultrasound photos that we loved, and we laughed about his "peanut butter" face, a result of the muddy graphics. I was fairly miserable physically with my enormous, fluid-filled belly. At my last measurement, the fluid was close to thirty-four centimeters. I was unable to walk or stand for more than a few minutes, and stairs were horrible. Despite the anxiety of what the coming weeks could bring, we were so thankful to have come this far with John Paul Raphael. We were cautiously hopeful that we would get to meet John Paul Raphael alive and love him face-to-face for as long as possible.

It was very difficult not to prepare materially for a baby. My desire to nest was very strong. My instincts did not accept that everything was not as it should be. It was sad not to have a baby shower or to externalize my deep love for our baby by preparing him a beautiful, soft, welcoming place in our home. We knew that if all our predictions proved wrong or God worked a miracle of healing, we had plenty of troops prepared to buy everything we would need in short order. I did make one, sad shopping trip to Babies-R-Us, full of tender grief. I browsed the tiny baby boy clothes as if in a dream, my love and longing so powerful and so fragile. I wanted desperately to buy everything a baby could ever want or need but understood that was foolish. Instead, I picked out three of the tiniest preemie outfits. We would need something to dress him in one way or another. Something to hold him in or bury him in. My throat squeezed and hot tears fell from my eyes as my fingers gently touched and held piece after piece of clothing. It was an impossible choice. One outfit to live in and one to die in? What clothing is best for a casket? I ended up with a two-pack of tiny, long newborn open nightgowns, a gray and white striped romper, and tiny fleece dinosaur pajamas, warm for under the ground. I cried and cried but was proud of myself for being brave enough to wade into a baby store on my own with my heart prepared to be pierced.

Earlier in my pregnancy, I had connected with a birth and bereavement doula, Laura Ricketts. She was an amazing resource and support for the volume of questions I had. She encouraged me to have supplies on hand to make all the memories we could in the hospital. She shared wisdom that we would never regret doing too much to remember John Paul. She sent me links to buy everything on Amazon: a photo frame with an opening for clay imprints of hands and feet and a small ornament you could press hands and feet into as well. I made phone calls to Now I Lay Me Down to Sleep, the organization that connects volunteer photographers with families whose babies are expected to die, but decided instead to reach out to a friend and share our story and see if she would be willing to take photos for us in the hospital. Johanna Waisley had taken photographs of my other children growing up and it meant the world to me that she agreed. As a mother of four young children, Johanna made a huge sacrifice to agree to drop everything and come to the hospital when we needed her. Ralph and I had been inspired to build a playlist for John Paul Raphael that included lullabies and songs about loving your child as well as many songs that focused on loss and missing someone precious. I had the playlist ready to go on my phone. I had done some preliminary packing for the hospital and had a list on my dresser of everything that we would need to throw in the bag at the last minute. In an effort to be prepared, we had the contact information for a funeral home, just in case.

We managed to have a lovely Christmas with our crazy family. The six youngest were home with us and our oldest daughter Meaghan and her boyfriend joined us for a slow morning of present-opening and brunch. John Paul Raphael wiggled away. I was touched that a few family members had included him in their gift-giving. I cried opening a soft, white lamb from my brother and sister-in-law. *Oh, Jesus, please let this baby live to love and hold this little lamb.* Our daughter Carrie gave Ralph and me each a necklace charm in the shape of a tiny foot with the initials "JPR" engraved on it and a tiny stone in the memorial color of Trisomy 18. Ralph's parents gave us an envelope with a cash gift in it for John Paul just the same as for all the other grandchildren. It meant so much to have his beautiful and important life remembered and acknowledged. I had encountered many friends and family members in the past months who had no idea how to handle my pregnancy. We spent a weekend with relatives who did not mention my pregnancy or our baby for the entire forty-eight hours. I am sure they were trying to avoid being hurtful, but it still stung.

Despite enjoying the holidays, I was caught in the middle of panic, fear, and depression. This journey was long and stressful and the hardest part was still in front of us. I numbed myself by spending time on my phone or watching movies and isolated myself from most of my friends. Even praying was hard, despite knowing we were walking God's path and there was no way to do it without Him.

We had back-to-back appointments with Dr. Hassan and Dr. Wolfe on December 27. John Paul Raphael had wiggled himself back into a head-down presentation, removing at least one of our many worries. The baby was active. My fluid was holding steady. We knew John Paul Raphael was small—his predicted weight at the previous week's visit was only four pounds, but he was still gaining weight from week to week. We were at the stage where we had to carefully balance giving John Paul Raphael as long as possible to grow and develop in my womb with the reality that many Trisomy 18 placentas stop functioning early, putting the baby at risk for dying in utero. John Paul Raphael wasn't due until February 2, but as we put all these pieces together and added the family factor of two college kids who would need to get back to school, we made the decision to schedule an induction on January 13. I would be thirty-seven weeks along. If John Paul Raphael did have Trisomy 18 as expected, delivering a bit early would not affect the outcome. And if he didn't, I had already received the steroid shots to help his lungs with any extra development.

I felt scattered and overwhelmed, giddy and scared. I was suddenly hyper-aware of John Paul Raphael's movements knowing that, despite all our tests and plans, we could still lose him spontaneously. We hoped and prayed that our little guy would stick to the plan and stay with us until January 13. I was so physically worn out and emotionally drained that it was hard to be hopeful. I had tried to be strong for so long, but I was running out of steam as we neared the end. I was so full of love for our baby and afraid to feel that at the same time. I explained to one friend that I felt like I had been living in the valley of the shadow of death for months, holding my heart in the slot of a guillotine. That's a stressful place to be, but it isn't really dangerous until it is time for the blade to fall.

I needed to prepare for the actual labor and delivery as well. We kept forgetting this part: Our baby needed to come out of me. Although I originally did not want an epidural so that I could be mobile more quickly after the baby was born, we decided to have one placed immediately when labor was induced so that if John Paul Raphael showed any signs of distress during delivery, I could transition more quickly to a caesarean section. We read that many families choose not to have fetal monitoring during labor. It is common for the stress of delivery to be challenging for smaller or weaker babies and if they were to die during the course of a natural delivery, the families did not want to know. But we were committed to doing anything possible to meet our precious boy alive, even if I had to have surgery to do it. We made sure our birth plan included fetal monitoring.

We spent the next few days quietly at home, letting our plan settle into my heart. January 13. God willing, I would be meeting my baby in two weeks! Ralph spent a few days at work, Maggie and Andrew hung out with friends, and the younger kids were at their dad's house for a few days. We celebrated a quiet New Year's Eve with good friends but were in bed before midnight. I remember the quiet, stillness of those days. We extended Advent as we waited in silence and hoped against hope.

On January 3, we met with Dr. Hassan to check on our baby. I smiled at John Paul on the ultrasound screen and watched his little heart beating strongly. The tech did all his measurements as we studied the screen; it seemed like his small percentages were getting even smaller. When Dr. Hassan came in to review the numbers, he delivered the news we had been expecting but still didn't want to hear: Our baby wasn't growing anymore. It had been two weeks since the last scans, and John Paul Raphael had only gained sixty grams, a negligible amount.

Everything came to a halt around me. Here we were. I sat up on the table and tears filled my eyes as we listened to our caring doctor and his recommendations. In his professional opinion, the fact that John Paul Raphael had not gained weight was an indicator that something was not going right anymore. Whether it was the placenta or John Paul's own body we couldn't know, but Dr. Hassan didn't think we could wait until January 13 and still have a good chance of meeting our baby alive. In the lilting Middle Eastern accent I had come to love, he said, "I'm not saying you have to go *right* to the hospital . . . " It took our minds a little time to grasp his meaning. I had been barely ready to deliver at thirty-seven weeks and now our trusted doctor believed that our baby's safety in my womb was at risk. My womb had been his secure haven for the past thirty-five weeks and five days, but now it might not be. Dr. Hassan couldn't predict how quickly things could change for John Paul Raphael, but he gently and firmly recommended we move our plan up quickly.

We were already planning to head directly from his office to Dr. Wolfe's for an appointment. He would call and consult with her on our way. As we drove to Fairfax, my head spun and I held my belly in my hands. *Are you ok in there, sweet baby? Do we still have time? What do you need?*

Dr. Wolfe agreed with moving up the induction. Did I want to deliver tomorrow or this weekend? Did we want to wait until January 9 when she was on call again? I froze as she presented so many options. The impact of having to make this decision—to make the RIGHT one—weighed heavily on us. I looked at Ralph with big, scared eyes. *I don't know what to do. How do we pick the date? How do we decide what date our baby will be born, knowing it could very well be the day he dies? Can't we just let him stay in there? But what if he is dying already and we don't know it?*

We listened to John Paul Raphael's heartbeat again and Dr. Wolfe gave me another booster shot of the steroids to assist with John Paul's lung development. Hesitant to make any definitive predictions, Dr. Wolfe thought we could safely wait until early the next week to induce delivery. We prayed that was the right decision. We had an appointment to return to Dr. Hassan in two days, on Friday, January 5 to repeat the Doppler scans of the umbilical vessels, and do another biophysical profile. If everything looked okay, we would wait until Tuesday, January 9 to deliver. If not, we would go to the hospital to induce labor. Dr. Wolfe reassured us that if we changed our minds or felt something wasn't right, we could call her back at any time. Before we left the office, she gave me a wooden rosary from her last pilgrimage to Medjugorje held by the priests and blessed by Our Lady during one of her appearances. She must have known how desperately I needed something to hold on to and I was so grateful for the tangible reminder that this was all God's plan. I felt peace and comfort from Dr. Wolfe, and her faithful prayers felt like a hug from the Lord Himself.

We headed home emotional and worried about our baby. It was

a lot to process, but we trusted our doctors to assess the situation. We were blessed to have skilled providers helping us make a hard decision. They both felt it was safe to wait and see for a few days but reassured us we could also induce if we were scared. Scared wasn't a strong enough word. If we lost this gamble, John Paul Raphael would die before he was ever born, but I was also terrified to take him out of my womb before he was ready. I see now that I was the one who wasn't ready. Despite spending thirty-five weeks preparing for this event, I was unprepared to face the possibility of our son's death. I convinced myself that our doctors were right to think John Paul Raphael would be safe in my womb for another six days. We would trust their experience and knowledge. I prayed we would not regret it.

We also carefully processed the information that John Paul Raphael had stopped growing. We knew this was an undeniable sign of Trisomy 18. With so many scans and measurements, we'd focused on the science of fetal medicine, but we were still a mother and a father who adored and longed for their baby. Truth sank heavily into our bones: Our baby was made so imperfectly perfect that he would not be able to live a long life with us. There were so many unknowns. Would he survive delivery? Would we have minutes, days, hours, weeks, or months? Would we be able to bring him home? I couldn't wait to see his face, to touch his skin, to feel him in my arms. I couldn't imagine having a baby that might barely weigh four pounds. My fifth child, Clare, had been over nine pounds at birth! Would there be anything about his body that was hard to look at? How would we walk this road of suffering? We continued to hope for a miracle of complete health, but at this stage, an uneventful delivery and a few days to love on him would also feel like a miracle.

5

MIRACLES

Miracles are all around us, but the miracle you get isn't always the miracle you prayed for.

"'For My thoughts are not your thoughts,
nor are your ways My ways,' declares the LORD."
—Isaiah 55:8

ON JANUARY 4, 2018, we woke up early to the phone ringing. Bitter cold temperatures had canceled school. Ralph snuck into silent bedrooms turning off alarms so the kids could sleep in. He climbed back into bed with me and we held each other close, clinging to the quiet security of the three of us together, my giant belly wedged between us. "I don't want to go to work," he whispered. I didn't blame him. It was freezing outside and seven of us were staying home, warm in our beds. I told him how grateful I was for all the sacrifices he made for us. This was an understatement. Outside of the Lord, my husband was my safest and strongest place during my pregnancy. He was consistently selfless in protecting me and serving me and our family, putting everyone's needs before his own. We had cried together many times and shared deep gratitude for the gift of John Paul Raphael's life. Ralph was much better than me at accepting God's will and living in the moment, but I knew we were united in longing for our baby with every breath.

After he left around 7:30 a.m. I fell back asleep in the quiet house. I was curled up on my side deeply dreaming when I felt a pop and was awakened by a flood of warm water in my bed. My eyes shot open. *What was that?* I felt the warm wetness in the bed and knew my water had broken. Terror filled me. I lumbered out of bed, standing there in shock as the water continued to pour out of me. Panicked, I screamed for the children as thoughts raced through my head: *A gush of fluid is an emergency. Call an ambulance. But no, wait, we have a plan. We're going to induce. My water is breaking. My baby my baby my baby. He needs me to pull myself together.*

"Andrew, call Dad and tell him my water broke! Maggie, call Grandma and ask her to come over as soon as she can. Leah, call the doctor—I don't know the number—Google Dr. Wolfe in Fairfax." I managed to get a grip. The water still poured out of me. I shouted for towels and told Andrew to tell Dad to come home immediately. Clare stood nearby, terrified. I tried to reassure her that I was okay. This was going to be okay, but I didn't know if I believed my words. I knew I had to get dressed but couldn't even figure out what clothes to put on or where they were. Maggie called the doula and Leah was on hold with the OB. I called for Andrew to find the packing list on my dresser and to start trying to find the rest of the things and to call James to help. I found a dress to throw on and grabbed a beach towel to keep between my legs. While I was brushing my teeth, Leah handed me the phone with a nurse from Dr. Wolfe's office on the line. She told us to head right to Inova Fairfax Hospital. The kids were amazing and calm and did everything right to help me. They finished packing the hospital bags and put everything in the car. We decided it would be faster if we drove toward Ralph instead of waiting for him to get all the way home. Maggie hopped in the driver's seat of the van as I quickly hugged and kissed the other four goodbye. Grandma pulled up as we were leaving.

Despite my fear and worry for John Paul Raphael, I felt the power of adrenaline and I could finally breathe. While the fluid poured out of me, I filled my lungs for the first time in months. I paid close attention to my body in the car. No contractions. No blood. No pain. I felt more pressure on my pelvis, but that made sense because John Paul Raphael wasn't floating in all the fluid anymore. Ralph called and we found a meeting spot. We joined up shortly and I hugged Maggie tight. I could see fear etched in her face. Ralph hopped in the driver's seat and we were off. It was 9:05 a.m. when my water broke and now it was 9:30 a.m. I could see worry on my husband's face and hear the fear in his voice, but he was also a physician, trained to act in a crisis. He spoke quickly, asking questions about what happened and why weren't we going to Loudoun Hospital, which was much closer. He told me to recline my seat all the way back to take the pressure off my uterus and the placenta. I felt no contractions and no pain, but also no movement. Ralph called the emergency room and told them we were coming, that my water had broken and we needed a wheelchair ready to take me up to labor and delivery. I was a high-risk delivery. Amazingly, the deep freeze meant there was no traffic and the Capital Beltway was wide-open. We made it to Fairfax in twenty minutes.

Ralph pulled up in front of the ER and rushed inside. I hadn't felt John Paul Raphael move during the whole drive. I tried to tell myself this was normal. His giant pool just drained from around him— he must be stunned. I whispered prayers over and over. When the wheelchair finally came, I carefully lowered myself in. One attendant wheeled me to another and then we sat and waited. My heart beat wildly as Ralph left to park the car. The attendant put an ID bracelet on me and then an ER nurse came to take me to labor and delivery. She chattered about how she had never been upstairs before. I tried to keep the fear out of my voice as I told her we really needed to hurry and get upstairs quickly. She probably thought I was a nervous first-time mother. At the nurses' station in labor and delivery, they didn't seem to know what to do with me. I sat there for a few more minutes as someone made a phone call to the head nurse. I spoke up again with greater urgency, "I really need to get my baby checked." They finally wheeled me into a room on the other side of the nurses' station and a cheerful nurse came in and gave me a gown. She told me I could go ahead and get changed in the bathroom and then they would need to ask me some questions to check me in. I left the door of the bathroom open while I stripped off my wet dress and, almost in tears, stated firmly, "I really need to get my baby on a monitor *right now*. He has Trisomy 18." I don't know if she heard the desperation in my voice, but she responded quickly and said, "Okay, let's do that then." Another nurse showed up and they got out the fetal monitor as I lay down on the bed. They placed it on my belly and tried to find his heartbeat before the straps were even in place. When she couldn't find it, she offered encouragement with a note of forced optimism. "It can take a little while to find the heartbeat sometimes." A third nurse came in and together they found a faint rhythm but then lost it. The questions began and I tried to tell them about John Paul Raphael, but the fear paralyzed my thoughts and words.

The room quickly filled with people. One of the other obstetricians from Dr. Wolfe's practice introduced herself and said that Dr. Wolfe was on her way. For a brief moment, I heard a heartbeat on the monitor but something wasn't right. "That's too slow," I said, looking at the nurse with wide eyes. "That must be my heartbeat."

Ralph appeared by my side and looked at me with tears in his eyes and sadness in his voice, "No, honey, that's his heartbeat." Panic flooded me. *It's too slow.* The monitor showed his heartbeat at only forty-six beats per minute.

Everything seemed to happen at once. They needed me to take off my jewelry and my rings. Could they cut off my bra? What about anesthesia? They needed me to decide instantly: Did I want general anesthesia, which would be faster but would knock me out for several hours after delivery, or a spinal that would take longer to put in place but would allow me to stay awake? Maybe we didn't have that much time to get him out alive? *John Paul John Paul John Paul.*

I cried and choked out the words, "I don't know!" Where was Ralph? He was just right there. The bed was already being wheeled out to the Operating Room and I couldn't find Ralph. I was going to have a caesarean section because our baby was dying in my womb.

I was shaking and disoriented. Where was my husband? We had prepared so thoroughly, but I still didn't know what to do. What if I made the wrong decision? It was too much. On the way to the hospital, I had pulled the rosary from Dr. Wolfe from my purse and still held it wrapped around my hand. What a blessed detail. Because the rosary was made from wood and string, and not metal, I could keep it with me in the operating room. I clung to the Lord and the Blessed Mother and prayed for guidance.

"The spinal," I cried. "Do the spinal. I'm sure." I prayed with my whole heart that it was the right decision. *Please let him be alive.* I clung to the rosary beads and prayed aloud, "Jesus, I trust in you. Jesus, I trust in you." It all happened so fast. I recognized no one in the operating room. Many people spoke to me at once. Where was Ralph? I had never been in a situation that was this traumatic, this dramatic, and an urgent matter of life and death. Our child's life was at stake. Did all these people understand how much they needed to save our baby? Was he even still alive?

I startled as they quickly shifted me to the operating table. They asked to hang my legs over the side and curve my spine deeply. Another masked face was in front of me holding my hands and my head, trying to calm and reassure me. Someone else slid a needle into my back. I can't remember if there was pain. I clung to my rosary and my faith and whispered my prayers aloud over and over. *Jesus, I trust in you. I trust in you.* This was a runaway train, flying down the tracks with no guarantee of safety. *Where is Ralph?* The masked face in front of me said they were putting in the spinal anesthesia and that I would feel touch and pressure but no pain. I was rolled quickly to my back and a drape went across my chest. I could see more masked doctors or nurses by my belly, but recognized no one. Mercifully, Ralph appeared by my side in his own surgical cap, mask, and gown. He said he was shocked at how many people were in the room, but he sat by my head, stroking my hair and reassuring me with his presence. Without warning, I screamed as I felt punched in the stomach. Panic coursed through me, and Ralph was afraid the anesthesia hadn't worked as they cut into me. The anesthesiologist came close and held my face in his hands for reassurance. "It's just pressure. You're okay. No pain, just pulling and pressure." And then, at 10:33 a.m., time stopped and there he was.

John Paul Raphael. His flesh. His body. He was so long and so blue. He wasn't crying or moving. His eyes were closed as the surgeon laid his sweet, floppy body right on my chest. The flood of emotion was powerful and instinctive. *I love you I love you I love you he's not breathing he's not moving Jesus Jesus Jesus.* Someone asked if they should take him, work on him, but Ralph said no, please wait. Just wait.

Here was our baby. His face inches from mine. His closed eyes and adorable nose. I cupped his head and kissed his face. I drank him in. The tears poured from my eyes. He wasn't moving. Wasn't breathing. Wasn't crying. I was sure he was dead. But he was *here.* We had waited so long and fought so hard for this child and this moment. We knew the risks and understood how our hearts could be pierced. We chose our son beyond all expectation of outcome. Ralph thought fast and grabbed the bottle of holy water we'd brought from the spring of Our Lady of Lourdes in France, given to us by a faithful friend. We poured it over our hands and over John Paul Raphael's head and made the sign of the cross on his forehead, baptizing him in the name of the Father, the Son, and the Holy Spirit. *And he breathed.*

He was alive. John Paul Raphael was alive! Every effort of the last thirty-five weeks and six days was about this moment. Our son was here and he was alive. Joy surged through us and erased the panic, anxiety, and fear that we had lived with for the last nine months. The NICU team respectfully asked if they could take him briefly, reassuring me that he would stay close in the room. If I turned my head all the way to the left, I could still see him there on the warming scale. They weighed and measured him and someone exclaimed, "He peed!" He weighed four pounds, one ounce and measured eighteen inches—long and skinny. They diapered and swaddled him and fitted a cap snugly on his head before they brought him back to my chest. *Oh, my sweetest baby.* He was breathing and his little eyes opened to look at me. *You're here. You made it.* Ralph kissed me again. We were both crying.

Dr. Wolfe came around the drape after sewing me up to say congratulations. I hadn't even recognized her behind the mask. My tears flowed and I showed her my rosary, still clutched in my hand. I could see the relief in her eyes that, at least for now, our story was happy. I had no thought in my head at all of how long the happiness would last. I was completely and totally absorbed in my son because he was finally here and for this moment, he was alive. I was awake and Ralph and I were together with our son. He was alive. Joy.

The neonatologist on call that day asked if we wanted John Paul Raphael to go to the NICU for testing. Doctors could not thoroughly evaluate John Paul outside of the NICU, but taking him there meant I could not follow due to my own need for surgical recovery. The doctor said that if we kept John Paul Raphael with us, we needed to understand the limits of what they could do for him outside of the NICU. I was so grateful we had put so much time and effort into our birth plan, as hard as it was. We were clear that we wanted no extraordinary measures for John Paul so it was appropriate to keep him with us for now. He was wrapped up like a glow worm on my chest. He continued to breathe on his own, although slightly labored, and his skin had a blue tinge. It appeared that the only thing he needed was a little oxygen. Tubing and a portable oxygen tank promptly arrived. The nurses placed a nasal cannula and hooked him up to oxygen right there on my chest. He immediately changed to a little pink baby! A lay hospital minister arrived and asked if we wanted John Paul Raphael baptized. She was so sweet and kind and gave him a blessing.

Dr. Wolfe explained that I would be sent to a recovery room for two hours. She was somber as she explained that after the rupture of my membranes, my placenta had started to abrupt. It was pulling away from the wall of my uterus and suffocating John Paul Raphael in my womb. My instincts had been correct. He was dying and every second counted that morning. I feel breathless when I think about all the other possible outcomes—even a small traffic jam might have meant never meeting our baby alive. As it was, he was born without any signs of life. We have no way of knowing if he had a heartbeat upon birth, if in fact he was born still but the power and grace of baptism in Christ breathed new life into him. Either way, he was here and he was alive. That was miracle enough. Gratitude surged through me. *Thank you, Lord.*

I was wheeled to recovery and Ralph followed, accompanied by John Paul in a bassinet that could carry his oxygen tank. One of the nurses returned my phone and camera to us; I have no idea how or when she got them, but she gave us an amazing gift by taking dozens of photos during the delivery and even went back to my bag in the other room to get my phone for videos. These are a treasure to us. I have no idea who she was, but her kindness is beyond price.

We knew the kids and my mom were already in the waiting room, but Ralph and I needed a little more time just to be together, the three of us. The delivery was a whirlwind. When we were settled in the recovery room, Ralph placed John Paul Raphael in my arms.

Our son was perfect. He was swaddled so tight and had the softest pink skin and a perfect little nose. I was amazed to feel the complete absence of fear and anxiety. After a brutal and highly complicated pregnancy with so many unknowns, our baby was here and, for right now at least, he was safe and breathing. I was so completely in this present moment, full of love and peace.

In terms of John Paul Raphael's treatment, every sign and symptom indicated he had Trisomy 18. We had asked the genetics team to take cord blood at birth for a definitive diagnosis and expected these results to take twenty-four to thirty-six hours. It was evident to both Ralph and me that John Paul had characteristics that were unique to Trisomy 18—a larger head, lower birth weight, and low set ears. His little hands, while not clenched continually, relaxed themselves into a fist with overlapping fingers. He had a small bit of fusing between a few fingers and a few toes, but overall, nothing about him looked unusual to me. I loved looking at him. He was perfectly imperfect. His heart rate was steady and his color was good on the oxygen. We were prepared to let his life unfold in God's time.

After Dr. Wolfe came in to check on me, Ralph went out to get the kids. I tried to prepare John Paul Raphael for what was about to happen. "The crazy people are coming, sweet baby, and they are so excited to meet you and love you!" And there they were, our other loves. We filled the tiny recovery room that was only supposed to have a few people in it. The hospital, knowing that we expected his precious life to be brief, worked very hard to be accommodating. Squeals and hugs and awe and love and wonder filled the room as eight of John Paul's nine siblings came in with Grandma to meet him. What a glorious moment for us as we proudly introduced our beautiful baby boy to his family. Our children were full of tender love, shyness, and eagerness to hold and see him. One by one we passed him around. I could see them each falling in love with their baby brother. Clare and Maggie hugged me tightly, so relieved that I was okay; I hadn't even thought about their worry as their mom was rushed off for emergency surgery.

We have so many beautiful pictures of John Paul Raphael in arms after arms after arms. Hilariously, in the middle of the chaos, the recovery nurse still needed to check my belly every fifteen minutes. We would shoo the kids to one side of the bed and hold up a sheet for privacy and go right on with our gathering. Our nurse did a good job being tolerant of many broken protocols. We didn't care. It was an appropriate time to break the rules.

After an hour in the recovery room, Father Stefan Starzynski, the Catholic chaplain, came in to visit us with another priest friend. He was out of town on a sick visit when I arrived at the hospital and it took him several hours to drive back in the bad weather. He came to see us right away. Since John Paul Raphael had already been baptized twice, Father Stefan confirmed him into the Catholic church under the name of St. Paul with his godparents, Maggie and Andrew, present.

When Fr. Stefan left, the children drifted in and out. Evan and Travis, Meaghan and Carrie's boyfriends, each took a turn coming in to meet John Paul. Maggie sent out a big email blast to let friends and family know our beautiful boy had arrived safely. We were also able to get in touch with my friend Johanna who was going to take pictures for us of this priceless time.

As I neared the end of my time in the recovery room, we needed to figure out what would happen next. Protocol dictated that since John Paul Raphael was on oxygen, he should go to the NICU, but since I was still recovering and not walking yet, I couldn't join him there. There was also a strict limit on visitors in the NICU which was prohibitive for a large family and the likelihood of our baby's life being brief. I also couldn't easily take John Paul Raphael to the post-partum unit because there was not an oxygen supply in place for him in those rooms.

Recognizing the critical and unpredictable nature of his condition, the neonatologist was able to arrange for the two of us to be transferred to the newly-opened high-risk perinatal unit. This floor was designed for pregnant women in high-risk situations and had an oxygen supply available by the bed that could be used for John Paul Raphael instead of me. The room was big enough to handle our clan and the floor was quiet, giving us some distance from other new mothers and their healthy babies. The doctors and nurses were willing to go to a different floor to care for us both. Sweet John Paul was happily resting in Ralph's arms as we moved to our new room— he even spent some time sucking on his daddy's finger.

Babies are such an incredible gift from our Creator and newborns inspire deep awe. Our room was heaven on earth. The sacred holiness of these hours was tangible. None of us could get enough of holding John Paul, smelling him, or feeling his skin. He loved to hold our fingers. We kept him wrapped in his blue blanket and his Duckie was always close by. As soon as we arrived in the new room, Ralph took out John Paul Raphael's cologne spray from Rome and gave everything a good dousing. We all smelled like sandalwood. The scent still powerfully transports me back to the holiness and beauty of that day.

The doctor came in to check on John Paul Raphael and we were able to get a longer oxygen cord so that we had more "leash" to pass him around. We met Tia, his baby nurse, when she came to do vitals on John Paul and to talk about feeding him. John Paul Raphael did not appear to be struggling with any secretions in his chest or throat and there was no outward indication that he had a tracheal-esophageal fistula, an abnormal connection between the esophagus and the trachea that prevents the baby from being able to feed orally. The doctor said they could check his anatomy with a nasal-gastric tube, but they would have to do that in the NICU. We decided to see if he could latch on to my breast, and if not, I would go ahead and express colostrum so we could try to feed him with a small syringe. We knew that many Trisomy 18 babies were not able to suck and swallow well, but we hoped feeding him small amounts with the syringe would be successful. I spent some time holding John Paul Raphael to the breast, but he would not latch on. Tia helped me to express colostrum and brought a breast pump into the room. She encouraged us to hold John Paul skin to skin as one of the best ways to comfort and care for any new baby. This was so lovely. We unwrapped our little baby and lay him naked on my bare skin, then wrapped blankets around us both. I loved feeling him breathing against my chest. I longed for this. *You're here. We are together. I have you. You are safe. You are my child, my beloved son. There isn't anything I wouldn't do for you. Please be well.*

Johanna arrived later in the afternoon with her camera. I felt reassured that we would have beautiful memories of these sacred moments. John Paul Raphael was still doing well so we decided to take him off the oxygen long enough for Ralph and Tia to give him his first bath—with a paparazzi of sisters documenting every moment! I watched from my position on the bed and grinned at their squeals. "He's smiling!" Leah cried. My heart was so full. Everyone loved him now. They brought him over to me after he was cleaned up, and Ralph and I dressed him in his white puppy-dog gown and his new soft gray hat. He was so small, even in the preemie outfit. These precious moments were gifts we weren't sure we would ever have. I held each one tenderly. Due to the bad weather, our daughter Alicia wasn't able to get to the hospital from Virginia Beach, but Johanna took one family photo of nine out of ten children, Mommy, Daddy, and Grandma.

As Johanna was leaving, my father and step-mother and my brother, my sister-in-law, and my niece arrived at the same time, all of them driving from Philadelphia in a blizzard. What an act of love for my whole immediate family. We didn't know how long this beautiful child would be here, so they took that to heart and got right in the car. At the same time, we got permission from the charge nurse on the floor for our daughter's service dog, Gage, to be in the room as well. It was definitely a crazy love party.

What I remember most about these hours is calm and joy. There was no fear. Our room was a holy sanctuary and we rested completely, held in that sacred space. We took John Paul Raphael's footprints and handprints and laughed at needing to re-do them to get them just right. We recorded his heartbeat. We cut a tiny lock of his hair. We pressed his big toe into a small bit of clay that the hospital provided to send off to turn into a silver charm. Doctors and nurses and children and family drifted in and out of the room. By 10 p.m., Ralph and I were left alone with John Paul Raphael again. He cried a sweet little bird cry and slept and drank from the syringe as we held him close against our chests. There was a brief moment that caught my attention when John Paul seemed to grow suddenly still. His breathing was consistently slightly labored and his head bobbed with each breath. But for a few strange seconds, he was motionless. I watched and waited, trying to decide if this was Trisomy 18 revealing its unpredictable power. "Ralph—," I began, but then John Paul Raphael shifted and sighed and the moment passed. Ten seconds from start to finish at most. Maybe it was nothing. We all hold our breath sometimes, don't we?

Ralph and I were exhausted and managed to squeeze side by side in the hospital bed with John Paul Raphael tucked between us, his little head rising and falling as he worked to breathe, even with the oxygen. He looked at us deeply with his wise, newborn eyes. We spoke to him over and over and stroked his cheek and his back and the softest skin under his neck. Ralph was soon fast asleep, but I was determined not to miss a minute of the miracle and willed myself to stay awake, whispering to John Paul and soaking him in.

We had one perfect night, cocooned together in that bed, the three of us as close as we could be. Our own holy family. We hold on to that memory. One perfect night followed by half of a perfect day before our son's hourglass, crafted and held by our Loving Lord, dropped its last grains of sand.

6

SACRED SURRENDER

The Lord specializes in using the ordinary to do extraordinary work.

"The pieces of our lives are scattered everywhere,
we can never pick them up again; there is some peace in
immediately understanding that."
—Jayson Greene, *Once More We Saw Stars: A Memoir*

ON THE MORNING OF JANUARY 5, 2018, one hospital room was full of life. A grateful mother and father held their small son. Three grandparents, many siblings, two boyfriends, and a dog drifted in and out of the room along with a rotation of nurses, a neonatologist, geneticists, and a child-life specialist. The morning was spent caring for a newborn, feeding him with a syringe, changing his diaper, and passing him around. In addition, there was a lot of care for one mother in her recovery from a C-section—wound care, pain management, and trying to get her up and out of bed for the first time.

I woke early that day to the bright sun pouring into the room even though the temperature outside was frigid and schools were still closed. Ralph was asleep next to me in the hospital bed, and John Paul Raphael slept peacefully tucked between us. I shifted him to my chest and tried to capture a few of these peaceful, shining moments with my cellphone. I cherished the simplicity and beauty of just being mother and child. For the moment, there was still no fear. As with any new baby, Ralph and I had been up several times during the night. John Paul cried his little bird cry to have more milk and then again when he needed his diaper changed. We did not take these normal moments with our son for granted. I even thought to video Ralph changing a poopy diaper. I desperately wanted to stay awake all night long, but at some point, the rhythm of both of my boys asleep around me lulled me to sleep as well.

By 9 a.m., the hospital was busy and we had several carloads of family on their way to Fairfax to visit with us. As I shuffled back to bed from my first trip into the bathroom, I noticed John Paul Raphael was very still in Ralph's arms. His chest wasn't moving, his head wasn't bobbing. We stared and watched and there was no doubt this time. He wasn't breathing. Panic coursed instantly through me. All my research said that these episodes of apnea are "par for the course" with Trisomy 18. Yet as normal as they were for a baby with his condition, they were not normal to me. It was also how he was probably going to die. My mind flashed back to the moments the night before when John Paul had seemed frozen, but how it passed quickly and I hoped I'd imagined it.

This time was clear. I can't say for sure how long it was that he didn't breathe, but enough time passed that the apnea captured all of our attention. We painfully waited it out, frozen and still with him. Frantic thoughts and prayers coursed through my mind. *Come on come on come on, breathe, baby. You can do it. Breathe, John Paul.* Was it thirty seconds? Forty-five seconds? Longer?

I am so grateful for the work we did researching and preparing for this possibility. At many points, I wanted to run away, be numb in denial. But knowledge and planning were critical to fully enter into the experience of John Paul's life, whatever it would be. When you are holding your baby and he is not breathing, the instinct to do something, to do anything, is fiercely powerful. Nothing could have truly prepared us for this, but I had read stories of many other families who had been right where we were. We knew there was nothing we could do. Yes, medically, there were interventions. He could have been rushed to the NICU and intubated and put on a ventilator. Then he would breathe. And live. And, in my grief, I have wished over and over again that we had done that, done anything, to have more time with him. But in my heart, deep in the place of surrender and faith Ralph and I had carefully nurtured, we knew we could not intervene. It is no life to stay on a ventilator in a hospital forever. It was not a solution, only a Band-Aid. Since it appeared John Paul Raphael did in fact have Trisomy 18, we would be back at this very same spot when the ventilator was removed. We accepted the limitations of his life and felt equipped to face them. It is truly only with God and the prayers of our community that we found this courage.

Eventually John Paul Raphael opened his eyes a little wider and began to breathe again. The relief coursed through me and tears filled my eyes. We held him even closer, covering him with love and telling him not to scare us like that. We called for the neonatologist and Tia to check his heart rate. They reassured us that for this moment, all was well. The doctor spoke gently about the reality we already knew. This was the course laid out in front of us. There was no way to predict when the next episode would be or which episode would be the last, his final breath. We held on to the hope that many Trisomy 18 babies were in much worse condition. Needed far more than just oxygen. Couldn't drink milk or poop. We also knew some babies went home and lived for days or weeks or months. We longed for this outcome.

By noon, our hospital room was bustling. Everyone had arrived and my stepmother Joann was graciously dishing out homemade chicken soup, cheese, crackers, and veggies. We ate and chatted and passed our baby around the room. After lunch, Fr. Stefan popped in to check on us. He chatted and prayed with us briefly. As he was leaving, he turned and asked, "Would anyone like to receive communion?" What an abundant blessing from the Lord that Fr. Stefan was carrying the Blessed Sacrament and that Jesus came in His very Body, Blood, Soul, and Divinity to strengthen us for what was to come. Jesus knew what we did not and provided the gift of the Eucharist to fill us with grace and strength to endure His holy will. Eventually, several groups of people headed home. Our children Meaghan, Andrew, and Clare, and my father and stepmother remained behind with Ralph and me to spend more time visiting and enjoying John Paul Raphael.

You were there too, Jesus. I believe you filled that hospital room with your love and grace, your spirit and life, and came even closer as the time arrived for you to slip the soul of our most beloved son out of his body and into your embrace.

It happened while we watched, and yet I could not see it. What did you see, John Paul Raphael? Sweet baby, I pray you had no suffering at all, no grief, only love and trust as you left us and went ahead. One moment you rested in Meaghan's arms, looking up at her loving gaze. The next, some invisible thread snapped in your body and it was time. Your hour had come. Too soon. Minutes, years, and decades too soon.

I hope that in the same moment that your brain forgot to tell your body to breathe that Jesus was already there, holding your hand. That at just after one o'clock, when Meaghan said, "Something is not right," and passed you to Daddy who quickly passed you to me, you could already see your Shepherd's face as He came to gather you, His little lamb. I pray His gaze of love was already shining on you.

I watched you, John Paul Raphael, as you lay in my arms, your own gaze already looking away, past my face and past your Daddy's.

You locked on to something beyond us and never wavered as you began to die. We cupped your head and kissed your face, pulled you up close to our faces and necks and rubbed your chest and your back and tried to convince you to stay.

"Come on, baby, breathe. Come on, John Paul, you can do it, you can breathe." We begged you as we whispered into your ear. We prayed over and over. *Not yet, Jesus. It is too soon. I'm not ready. Not now. Not yet. I'm not ready for him to die.*

I held my own breath as we watched and waited and whispered and prayed. John Paul Raphael lay in my arms, enfolded in love as we all pulled in close, praying and begging him to stay. *Lord, have mercy on me. Please don't take him yet.* As the minutes ticked away and John Paul Raphael still did not breathe, my panic turned to understanding, and I knew.

"It's been too long," I whispered to Ralph, his body wrapped around mine and John Paul's, the three of us trying to be as close as we could be. Clare sat curled up at the foot of the bed. Andrew and Meaghan leaned in on one side and my dad and Joann on the other.

I wish I could see a holy, heartbreaking movie of that time as the veil thinned and we all hung together in that sacred space, life no longer separate from death. Joy and pain, love and grief—we hung weightless in this place with the mysteries of a lifetime, of eternity, unfolding before us. We had no choice but to surrender to it, this force profoundly bigger than our humanity, and we wept in wonder and sorrow as our beloved, beautiful, dear John Paul Raphael began to go.

The movie would show us huddled on and around the bed. Did we imagine that by surrounding our child, we could keep death away? Could we turn out the lights and bar the door and somehow be spared? As John Paul Raphael stopped breathing, his body became still. He was frozen, like any small child playing a game to see how long they could hold their breath. Only this time, the seconds turned to minutes. His color began to change from pink to gray to green. He forgot to blink and his eyes began to glaze over as he looked beyond. Eventually, I could see striations on his sclera and iris, and clinically at some point, I am sure his pupils were fixed and dilated.

The plot of this terrible scene includes John Paul gasping for breath at lengthy intervals, every five or eight minutes or longer, as if for a micro-second his brain said, "BREATHE!" and his body took a huge gulp of air. But just one. Each gasp ignited in me a weak hope that maybe he would start to breathe again. I couldn't help hoping, even though everything I had read about this process told me to expect otherwise. That occasional breaths as the body is dying are "normal." What a horrible, unthinkable normal. These gasps were followed by more whispers of love into his ears and our continued prayers that the Lord be close and somehow let us feel His presence in these unimaginable moments.

As one o'clock became two o'clock, I began to whisper my goodbyes. His heart continued to beat, although his heart rate gradually slowed. I don't know if his soul was still present enough to receive my love, but my mother's heart poured into him as I whispered my love over and over. A lifetime of I love yous. I told him how beautiful he was. How grateful I was to be his mommy. How he had already changed our lives forever. That I understood. That I knew he needed to go. That it was okay. That I saw it was so, so terribly hard for him to breathe. That we wanted him to be at peace and at rest and to fly ahead where I already longed to be going with him.

How I did this, how I gave my beautiful son permission to die, I will never know. Even while I accepted that I had no power and no choice, my human heart wanted to fight this with every option available. *Get the ventilator. We were wrong! We do want to intervene! Make him breathe! Someone please fix this!*

There was no rescue. Tia and the child-life specialist both arrived. We passed Tia's stethoscope around to listen to and monitor John Paul Raphael's heart rate, essentially to know how quickly we were losing him. Fr. Stefan, the hospital chaplain, returned to the room as well. I have a clear memory of looking up from John Paul and seeing Fr. Stefan praying and weeping as he sat on the couch next to the bed. His priestly presence bearing witness with us during this painful vigil was such a comfort.

Other than the imminent finality that my baby would soon be dead, the worst part of this time was the agonal breathing. Agonal breathing, or agonal gasps, are the last reflexes of the dying brain. The body uses the accessory muscles of the respiratory system to try and gather breath. The result can be a look of pain or a grimace, but it is just the body's reflex to do everything it can to breathe. Sometime after 2 p.m. John Paul Raphael began agonal breathing. The intervals of random breathing continued, but each breath was now a desperate gasp. His face was greenish at this point, his eyes glazed over but still open and so dark. The name is appropriate because with each agonal breath, his eyes and mouth opened wider and he appeared to be in shock and pain. I couldn't help but think that he wanted us to fix all this, to stop it, to make it better. And of course, I was frantic to do just that. Ralph assured me over and over that this was just a reflex. It was only the body's way of shutting down, of letting go. Nevertheless, it was traumatic to witness. We held him even tighter. We kissed him even more. We whispered words of love with all our hearts. We comforted him in every way we could. We covered him in our tears. I pray that at my own death someday, I am also surrounded and held by my family. And if in those moments I feel fear, I will remember how bravely our son surrendered to his death. And how, with God's grace, we will soon be reunited.

Eventually, we removed the oxygen tube from John Paul's nose so his tiny, perfect face was free. Ralph and I had previously discussed the possibility of giving John Paul Raphael morphine to ease any distress or potential pain in his last moments. Knowing that morphine also slows respiration, we were hesitant to request it, but the agonal breathing was devastating to watch. No matter how much Ralph tried to convince me that our baby was not in pain, my heart couldn't accept it. We asked Tia for the morphine and at 2:20 p.m., she administered a tiny dose. As we watched and waited, John Paul appeared to relax a bit. In our own agony, I turned to Ralph and whispered, "Will you sing him a song?"

My dearest husband has the most beautiful heart. He was suspended in his own suffering, longing to fix this, to save John Paul, to protect me and our whole family from this loss. I am sure the last thing he felt he had the strength to do was sing. But he would never refuse me this gift in these precious moments. I love Ralph's voice. Singing together has been part of our relationship from the beginning. When I have trouble falling asleep, he will often hold me close and sing Billy Joel or James Taylor. In this holy moment, he began to sing the comforting lyrics of James Taylor's "You've Got a Friend."

We all sang. With all our hearts—the seven of us and Tia. All of us crying and loving one little boy with one unexpected lullaby. As we finished the final chorus, John Paul Raphael took one last and final breath. Within a few moments his heart stopped completely. Time of death: 2:43 p.m.

7

STUNNED AND SHATTERED

Joy and pain are both God's love story.

"Fathers, mothers, whose soul has suffered my suffering,
everything I felt, did you feel it too?"
—Victor Hugo

EVERY TIME I RELIVE that day, there is a hush at this point in the story. Magically, I have inserted a long, reverent silence for as long as it would take me to process what just happened. From the moment Ralph and I held a positive pregnancy test in our hands on May 29, 2017, until 2:43 p.m. on January 5, 2018, we were on a runaway train. We lived in the land of uncertainty, hope, stress, fear, love, anxiety, and joy. All of it together. And here we were.

After. The thing we dreaded most and prayed earnestly to avoid still happened. It was done. Our baby was dead.

I knew deep in my being that my life and my heart had just been altered in ways I could not yet understand. This was trauma. But frankly, at 2:44 p.m.? And 2:45 p.m.? The rest of the afternoon and evening? There was a deep calm and profound peace. I think now of Christ's words on the Cross: *It is finished.*[1]

We didn't need to watch and wait and worry anymore. Every muscle in my body and every part of my soul and mind sighed a slow, deep, full release of all the fear held tightly coiled within me for the last thirty-six weeks and five days. I was relieved. What a strange word for that moment. I was not relieved that John Paul Raphael was dead, but I had worked hard every day to surrender to God's plan for our son's life. There was relief in knowing what that plan was. It had a number: 1,690 minutes.

We prepared so thoroughly for John Paul Raphael's birth and life. What happened now? I don't mean the lifetime of loss we would carry, but the reality of holding a dead child in my arms. Now what?

I am thankful I had also extensively researched this part of the journey. If it was possible my son was going to die, I did not want to be blindsided by this. I read blogs and scoured the internet for information from other families. I needed to know what my options were, to hear how other brave mothers and fathers made this terrible time the tiniest bit less terrible.

I knew that I wanted to spend as much time as possible still holding John Paul. He was my son. He was and is so deeply loved. And even though his soul was gone and his body lifeless, I grew that body in my womb, and I loved it deeply. We had so little time to get to know him. For families in our situation, the time we spend with our baby after his or her death is precious.

We spent just shy of twenty-two hours with John Paul Raphael in our hospital room after he passed. These were deeply spiritual, quiet minutes full of love. I confess, I was nervous about being with him after he died. Intimately encountering death was completely new to me. I had seen very few dead bodies in my life and all from a reasonable distance. There was no way to predict what this experience would be like. How would it feel? How quickly would his

---

1   John 19:30

body change? Would there be some disturbing alteration in his skin or his smell or how he felt to touch?

The hospital was perfect in accepting and honoring our wishes to stay with John Paul as long as possible. We were prepared to advocate aggressively for this but grateful there was no need. I don't even remember having a conversation with anyone about taking his body away. The staff seemed to treat our desire to keep him with us, to hold him until I was discharged, as perfectly normal. His nurse Tia reassured us that his body would be just fine. We would likely see no unusual changes as we continued holding and loving him.

I changed his diaper for the first time after he died. I laughed because he had pooped and it was actually a big mess to clean up! We lingered with his body to memorize every part of him. We touched every finger, toe, and fold on his smooth newborn skin, still warm. We kissed him and loved him no differently than if he were still with us. We made sure he was perfectly clean and then slowly dressed him in his new dinosaur pajamas. We put his soft gray cap back on his head and wrapped him in Blue Blankie. We took dozens of pictures.

We had called our family during the long vigil of his dying. Sometime after 3 p.m., my mom, Maggie, Leah, and Nathan returned to say their goodbyes. My stepdaughter, Alicia, and her boyfriend arrived that evening from out of town to meet and say goodbye to her new brother, all at the same time.

It was heartbreaking to watch our children come into the hospital room carrying their stunned and shattered love. I am sure each of them had their own fears about confronting death this closely; for my stepchildren, tragically, it was not the first time losing a close family member. But together our nine children loved their brother deeply and bravely, each in their own way, and even when perhaps they did not think they would. Our daughter Leah, who had been through so much that year, seemed to have a special connection to John Paul Raphael. We have many pictures of Leah grinning and holding John Paul during his life, but it is the photo of her holding him lifeless in her arms, tracks of tears visible on her cheeks, that is my favorite. We never know when we will be surprised by love. Leah was so brave to open her heart to him with the expectation of loss. My heart filled with love for each of our children as I considered the impact of this journey on them individually.

Nurses and other staff members stopped in throughout the afternoon to offer their condolences. We experienced so much love and respect for this one brief life. The impact John Paul seemed to have had on so many people consoled us. By 9 p.m., all the final words had been said and the hospital room was dark and quiet. We were alone. Ralph and I were tired and numb, but the nurses still needed me to get up and walk to continue my own healing.

One day post-surgery, I was finally free from all tubes and needles. Shortly after midnight, Ralph held John Paul Raphael for me as I slowly made my way out of bed, testing the feeling of my stitches and measuring my pain. When I was ready, he gently laid him back in my arms. We began our slow shuffle out of the room through the deserted hallways of the high-risk perinatal unit. Being separated from the other mothers and babies in order to provide oxygen for John Paul Raphael had the merciful secondary effect of eliminating my exposure to healthy, crying newborns and happy, celebrating families. Inova Fairfax Hospital had recently opened this unit and it bore the glossy, freshly decorated look of a nice hotel. The dim, silent corridors were lined with door after door, all but one open to show an empty hospital bed.

As grateful as I was to be out of bed and doing this completely normal thing with my baby, I couldn't help feeling like I was in some alternate version of *The Shining* as I shuffled along with Ralph, holding the lifeless body of our son in my arms. We saw no one, even as we rounded the corner at the nurses' station; the chairs sat empty. The buzz and beeps of the monitors were the only sound. In hindsight, I am so grateful for the darkness of the night outside the windows, the reverent hush in the hallways, the respectful absence of all ordinary and normal activity. Our world had stopped along with John Paul Raphael's heart. This was our funeral procession, this one walk the only one we would ever take with our baby. I want to pretend the whole hospital held its breath in shared awe and grief as one perfect, lost child passed by.

When we got back to our room, weary through and through, we curled up in the hospital bed, our little family of three, and slept deeply, John Paul Raphael tucked between us all night long. There was a ridiculous freedom in being able to sleep with him during that second night with no worry about his condition or his health. We just held him close with no further concern or fear.

The morning of January 6 dawned heavy and sad. Sometime during the night, grief covered me thickly and I woke in a dense, dark fog. My anxiety grew as I remembered that sometime today I would have to hand over my baby. We were communicating with the Office of Decedent Affairs and the funeral home to coordinate having John Paul's body picked up. This was the next agony to endure. I knew we had to let him go, that some stranger would take him, put him in a car, and drive him to a funeral home. I did not allow myself to dwell on the details of these arrangements, but I couldn't help the fleeting thoughts flashing through my mind. Would they put him in a box? Would they put him in a freezer? How could I allow this? Why couldn't I just take him home and hold him until we buried him? I knew some people did this; that it was possible and there was a device called a cuddle cot that would keep the baby's body chilled enough to prevent decomposition while still appearing "cozy." There had been so much else to worry about that we just never got that far.

A beautiful new nurse came in that morning and introduced herself. I was sitting on the couch holding John Paul Raphael when Monique walked into the room. She came and sat in a chair at the end of the bed and looked me deeply in the eyes.

"I am so, so sorry about the loss of your son. Could I please hold your baby?"

She came over and I offered her the lifeless body of my child.

She took him back to her chair. She held him. She oohed and aahed over him and commented on his perfect nose and silky hair and how handsome he was. She rocked him and talked to him like he was a living baby. She respected and honored his life. I have no idea how she knew to do this or if she understood the tremendous blessing of her presence and the attention she gave us that day. The value she placed on our son and the wonder she shared over his very creation affirmed what every new parent longs to hear: *Your baby is beautiful. Look what you made. This child is a miracle. A job well done, Mom and Dad.* I look back at her gift to us with marvel and gratitude. I wonder what in her own life taught her the profound importance of honoring our loss in this way.

After Monique left, Ralph and I passed several hours grieving. We cried and listened to John Paul Raphael's playlist of music. We sprayed the room with sandalwood again and tried to bond the experience of holding him with the music and the smell—something to help us re-connect to these profound moments well into the future. The genetics team came in and said the results of the cord blood testing were back and they confirmed the diagnosis we already knew. John Paul Raphael had complete Trisomy 18. It didn't matter. It was beginning to feel like nothing else would matter again.

Just after noon, Tia arrived with the shocking news that the funeral home would arrive at 12:30 p.m. Panic flew through me. Thirty minutes? We only had thirty minutes left? I had to finish needing my son sometime in the next thirty minutes? This news broke the dam holding back my maternal grief and it flooded out. The wails of deep, guttural sorrow I had been holding back gushed forth from my shattered heart. I clung to John Paul. Crazy thoughts raced through my head that included hiding him or racing out to the car with him or simply refusing to release my grasp. Ralph was so calm and so gentle and held me as I held our baby.

"I am so sorry I couldn't fix it," he whispered, "This is so hard. I am right here." Repeat. Repeat. Repeat.

As the minutes ticked on I couldn't help myself from picturing some orderly, wheeling in a sterile bassinet, depositing my baby's body in it, and leaving to rattle him down the hallway. A metal elevator. An old, foul smelling, green hallway in the basement with vaults of dead bodies on either side. A loading dock with a dark sedan and an open trunk.

"There is no way I am letting a stranger leave with our son," I told Ralph suddenly with a steady and firm voice, the voice of a mama bear prepared to draw blood to protect her cub.

Ralph looked at me, unsure how to safely respond. He heard the grief and agony and longing in my words—the sorrow that this story did not have the ending we wanted and that John Paul Raphael would not be coming home with us. He was leaving instead to go to some unthinkable location in a funeral home in Leesburg until we could make plans to bury him.

I could see him thinking. "What about Tia?" he asked me gently. "Would it be okay for Tia to carry him away?" Tia, the loving and kind nurse who had been with us each of these three days. Who helped Ralph bathe John Paul, helped me express colostrum, listened to his heart, answered our questions, and sat vigil with us and sang as he died. Tia, a mother with her own toddler at home. Tia, with big, gentle brown eyes who I knew was grieving with us.

"Yes," I whispered in a tiny voice, betraying my own heart. It took me months to realize that I was angry at Ralph for making me let go of John Paul Raphael, for finding a reasonable way for me to consent to the unreasonable. He let me blame him for as long as I needed to, wisely accepting that grief can, at times, be both irrational and childish.

Tia came in only a few minutes later, and I could tell it was time to say goodbye. We could not stop the tears. We carefully took John Paul Raphael out of his soft, Blue Blankie. I held him against my heart and wept as I drew strength from a well-spring far beyond myself and forced my hands to release him to Ralph. He wrapped him in a blue and white crocheted baby blanket the hospital had given us on Thursday as a gift. He held him out to me to kiss and say one more goodbye. He walked to Tia and together they stood and stared into that small, sweet face before Ralph kissed his son one last time and Tia slipped out of the room.

At this point in the movie in my mind, the scene should cut to a sunset and the score of Samuel Barber's "Adagio for Strings," or there should at least be some kind of weepy montage of grieving parent moments with a poignant soundtrack. Anything but the reality of those agonizingly slow empty minutes that ticked past as we sat in the silent stillness of the hospital room after Tia left with our son, minutes that stretched in front of me for the rest of my life.

There was no script for what to do now. I embodied all the clichés that became cliché for a reason: shock, disbelief, numbness, emptiness. I was dazed, torn apart, incredulous, frozen, aching. I longed for my own heart to stop so that I could be wheeled away alongside my son. You hear this from bereaved mothers—this surprise and astonishment that despite the death of a child, we go on. *Why am I still alive? I feel dead, but I am not.*

Over the next few days, the dead feeling came and went. It was actually preferable to the not-dead feeling, which was total agony. A raw cavern ripped into the very center of me. A fire of despair that burned brightly for months and months. An emptiness I am sure only other bereaved parents can understand. I recently found a quote from Victor Hugo who also suffered the loss of a child: *"Fathers, mothers, whose soul has suffered my suffering, everything I felt, did you feel it too?"*[2]

There is no scarcity in grief and suffering and I know comparisons are usually fruitless, but it was comforting during this time to convince myself that perhaps this was, in fact, the worst grief. That I have endured the worst life could throw my way. That something even more cruel wasn't lurking out there, waiting still.

2   Victor Hugo, Les Contemplations, IV, 1856

I am shocked at myself for writing that. Of course, I know there are worse things. A child's suicide. A child's long, drawn-out death by a painful terminal illness. An abduction that remains unresolved. A child who is murdered. A child whose death is somehow my fault. But I think it is human to want to think this is the worst of it, that life is not holding back its final knock-out punch.

I was discharged a few hours after John Paul Raphael was taken away. Monique brought in a wheelchair for me and I sat and looked around the hospital room, taking it in. I tried to burn every moment into my memory. As I was wheeled out, I looked back and saw a large purple butterfly[3] taped to the door, a sign to all who were about to enter that room: Please be delicate and gentle; all is not well.

Ralph went ahead to get the car and Monique was quiet as she wheeled me down the hallway and into the elevator. She seemed to know instinctively that these were moments that called for silence and dignity—to honor and respect our loss with her presence only. I felt intensely fragile leaving the hospital with an empty womb and empty arms. I worked to avoid eye contact. I had zero confidence in my ability to interact with anyone in a reasonable way. In fact, part of me really wanted to cause some kind of hysterical, raging scene. That would have been a lot more honest than rolling along quietly, as if I agreed with all of this.

The whole world looked and felt different. I barely recognized it or myself. The void where John Paul Raphael should be was enormous and tangible; it engulfed me in its presence, hovering over, around, and through me. I was powerless against its force. How could I be leaving the hospital without my baby? I knew I was in shock—so much had happened in the last fifty-two hours, really too much to process. Monique was gentle and sweet as she said goodbye after Ralph helped me into the car. She managed to wordlessly convey

---

3   The purple butterfly initiative was founded in the UK in 2016 by Millie Smith after she lost one of her twins shortly after birth. Purple butterflies are now placed worldwide on incubators of babies who are part of a multiple pregnancy when not all the babies have survived, or on the hospital door of a mother whose infant has died.

respect and empathy at the suffering we carried and that stretched before us into the future.

We played John Paul's music in the car and cried most of the way home. We needed to do anything we could to touch and feel our baby, even if it was bound to deliver brutally sharp pain. As we entered our neighborhood some thirty minutes later, I noticed blue ribbons attached to all the mailboxes on our street. One of our neighbors had heard the news and rallied those around us to show solidarity, love, and support for us and to recognize the value and beauty of our baby's life. It was a profoundly meaningful moment for us to feel that love and to see those blue ribbons standing at attention as we drove by. They gave honor, dignity, and meaning to an otherwise agonizing and empty homecoming.

When we came into the house, I carefully made my way upstairs to our room. Someone had cleaned up the mess of water and changed the sheets on the bed. There were flowers and a new soft, white blanket was spread on the bed with signs from the children on our pillows. *"You are so strong." "I love you!" "The pain you feel now can't compare to the joy that is coming."* I filled with love for these children who longed to do anything to help us feel better. My dad and stepmother had remained in Virginia to take care of them, assisting them in this act of love and making sure the house was peaceful and running smoothly for us.

I was physically in a great deal of pain. A caesarean section is major abdominal surgery. This was my first experience with this type of recovery. While I was emotionally drained, my body demanded attention. My milk was beginning to come in, an indignity I was prepared for but which was, nevertheless, terrible to endure. Nursing my other five babies was one of the greatest joys of motherhood. And while I am so grateful I was able to feed John Paul Raphael the colostrum I expressed in the hospital, as with all my previous babies, I had been blessed with an abundant milk supply. My breasts were already beginning to be painfully full with milk that had nowhere to go. My body knew it was supposed to have a baby to feed. It hadn't yet caught up with the news; frankly, I hadn't yet either. *I want my baby. I want to feed my baby. I need to nurse my baby.*

Ralph helped me into bed and I tried to find a comfortable position. Between my abdominal incision and my painful breasts, it wasn't easy. I immediately took pain medication and very possibly something stronger to help me escape from reality for a few hours. If there was ever a time I needed to give myself permission to medicate, this was it.

We went to Mass together the next day. I was desperate to stay home and hide, but I needed the Lord. I needed to be in the church and pour out my heart through prayer in His presence, but I just wanted to be alone or invisible to do it. It was physically and emotionally challenging, but with Ralph's help and six children by our sides, we did it. I felt exposed, sure everyone could see deep inside me and see the failure and shame I harbored that we had lost our son. We didn't protect him. He died. It felt strangely biblical, like we should be pitied and shunned lest the same misfortune pass their way. I knew in some portion of my rational brain these were lies, but I was not processing well in any way.

I remember vividly, however, what happened before communion. Without warning, the cries of a newborn baby filled the church. My heart froze. My body tensed. My milk let down and a raw, visceral grief burned like excruciating fire through my whole being. *No no no—make that baby stop! That should be my son!* I screamed in my head. *Oh, Jesus, my Jesus, why is that not my son?* We sat in the back of the church and Ralph just held me while I wept before the Lord.

We spent the next few days trying to make plans for John Paul Raphael's funeral and burial. I was grateful I had taken the time during my pregnancy to consider this possible outcome and make some arrangements. We had already selected a funeral home and I had the information to reach the man in charge of selling the cemetery plots. The funeral Mass would be held at our home church of St. Theresa and John Paul would be buried in the Catholic cemetery at St. John the Apostle in Leesburg.

Sunday afternoon, we drove to the funeral home to finalize the details. I was filled with dread and anxiety but also an irrational excitement. John Paul Raphael was at the funeral home. I could not wrap my head around the details of where he was or how he was being kept. I wanted to trust in the dignity of this timeless profession to care for the dead, but I couldn't bring myself to think too much about it. Interiorly, I was fragile and brittle, with hysteria lurking just under the surface. Having never done any of this before, I could not predict whether I would keep it together.

When we arrived, Ralph and I entered the formal parlor of the colonial home and greeted a tall undertaker named Arnold. I wondered if he was the one who took John Paul Raphael from the hospital. I wanted to insist immediately that he return my baby, but instead we made ridiculous pleasantries and were escorted to a small salon in the back. Thoughts of John Paul consumed me. How could we be expected to pick out holy cards when I was not holding my baby? *Just bring him to me!* I kept looking at Ralph with wide eyes, certain he could hear the screaming in my head. The agenda of the meeting continued on without my consent. The details were horrifying. A photo album of baby caskets was item number one. My research into infant loss had also prepared me for this part.

"These all look like Styrofoam to-go containers. I am not burying my son in a to-go box," I announced firmly, and likely with a tinge of hysteria. Although I didn't catch it, I am sure Ralph and Arnold exchanged a silent glance. Arnold tried a small sales pitch to highlight the nice features of these outrageous, small white boxes trimmed with shiny pink or blue ribbons.

"Yes, but they are still plastic, correct? You want us to bury him in plastic?" I posed this question steely-eyed, daring him to respond.

Ralph squeezed my hand tightly and gently spoke the most perfect solution, but one that might not even be possible. "Maybe Chris St. George could make him a small wooden casket. I'll call him right now."

Chris and Jodi St. George are a beautiful, holy couple, friends from our church with seven children of their own. Their second granddaughter, Noelle Therese, was born just days before John Paul Raphael, and we knew they had faithfully and persistently prayed for us every step of the way. Chris is also an accomplished carpenter on the side. It can only have been the Holy Spirit that prompted Ralph to suggest this solution and allowed Chris to answer his cell phone immediately on that cold, Sunday morning. Ralph cried as he spoke to Chris in the funeral salon and made our most heartfelt and desperate plea. How could we even ask this? *Is there any way you could quickly build a coffin for our baby? We need it by Tuesday.*

I watched the tears slide down Ralph's cheeks as he nodded and tried to convey our gratitude and appreciation to Chris over the phone. I think now of the moments that followed in the St. George home as Chris processed this holy request and shared it with their family. It was mere hours later when Chris sent us a text and a photo, asking if it would be okay if he modeled the casket after the casket design of Pope Saint John Paul the Great, who died in 2005. It would be months before I heard from his wife, Jodi, about those few days in their home. They considered it an incredible privilege and honor to handcraft a final resting place for our boy. She told me how they wept and prayed as it was built, infusing the wood with love and hope and thanksgiving to God for this precious little child. She said it was a profound blessing for their whole family to make this act of sacrifice and love for us.

This is the power and beauty of our faith at work, isn't it? Our deepest suffering and our deepest loss become the vehicle for Christ's love, hope, and blessing to shine into the world. If I am honest, it wasn't easy for me to let Ralph call the St. Georges and ask them to build a coffin. It was so vulnerable. Our need was so great. It was such a risk. What if they were out of town or didn't feel like doing it? What if they judged us for making a preposterous request? I didn't yet have the words from the Holy Spirit that would become John Paul's legacy, but here we were in the moment, called to let ourselves be loved by our friends. We needed to be vulnerable and open our hearts to them, trusting in their goodness and trusting God to provide for us in our need. The Holy Spirit was then free to act, inspiring the St. Georges with beauty and generosity and flooding us all with peace and blessing to comfort us in our grief.

We finished our meeting with Arnold and I asked in a small voice if there was any way we could see John Paul Raphael. I don't recall the reason he said no, but we arranged for a formal visitation hour on Tuesday afternoon. We hoped Chris St. George would have the casket prepared by then and we could bring it to the funeral home and spend an hour with our little boy. Crazy thoughts filled my head as Ralph and I headed out to the car—*maybe I can just break away and run down the stairs to the basement. There has to be a basement. John Paul is here somewhere!* It felt like another betrayal of my heart to calmly and reasonably drive away.

Next, Ralph and I spoke over the phone with the cemetery coordinator at St. John's Catholic cemetery and made plans to meet with him on Monday. Every step of this process was so terribly sad. With my broken spirit and body, I had no stamina to deal with any difficulties. Just when we thought we had everything worked out, there was some concern that the gravediggers would not be able to prepare the ground because of the extremely low temperatures. The forecast called for more bad weather and the coordinator suggested we might not be able to bury him that week at all. This was unthinkable to me, and I am confident I did not respond in an appropriate way. The poor man must have had some experience dealing with the bereaved, however, as he was calm and understanding. Because of the coming storm, we moved our meeting with him up to that night and drove out in the darkening gloom of Sunday to pick out our son's burial plot.

For all my broken heart, I did remember that this was my dear husband's second time through this. In 2010, he buried his first wife in the same cemetery. We shared the same desperation to do anything to spare each other this pain. The coordinator was kind and gentle. He walked us through the plot map and was very considerate in suggesting we think about which direction each plot would be facing before we picked one out. For instance, if you stand at the foot of this grave, you will be looking at shrubs and houses and eventually a parking garage, but if you stand at the foot of these graves, you will be facing a beautiful old tree, the lawn, and the church. I would never have thought of that. We picked one of those plots and filled out the paperwork. It feels cruel to have legalities and costs associated with burying a loved one— shouldn't the grief be cost enough? —but I do respect that people need to make a living and that even death is a business. After we finished the formalities, we drove to the other side of the large lawn to the Saint John Paul the Great Memorial Garden where we would lay our sweet little boy to rest. I was grateful for the biting cold wind and the sleet beginning to fall to distract me from the reality of what we were there to do. As we stood in the grass shivering, I stared down at the plot, marked for now only by two small stone squares showing the boundaries. I gazed at the huge, barren oak tree beyond the graves. To my right, there was a boxwood hedge and a statue of the Blessed Mother. I tried to picture coming here in three days to put John Paul under the grass.

I could not.

8

LOVE AND LAMENT

The magnitude of grief comes from the enormity of love.

"Only people who are capable of loving strongly can also suffer great sorrow, but this same necessity of loving serves to counteract their grief and heals them."
—Leo Tolstoy

OVER THE NEXT TWO DAYS, the house filled with flowers and cards. Meals were delivered and would continue through the generosity of friends four times a week for three months. We received phone calls, texts, and emails from so many people, far and wide, offering their condolences. After finalizing details for the service, we wrote and shared an obituary inviting anyone who wished to attend John Paul Raphael's Mass of Christian Burial on Wednesday, January 10 at 10 a.m. at St. Theresa Catholic Church. Any remaining weather concerns evaporated and the funeral home, the cemetery, and the priest were all ready to go. The Master Singers of Virginia, a professional-quality vocal ensemble I have sung with for more than twenty years, were gracious in agreeing to sing at John Paul's funeral

Mass. It was so important to us to have beautiful music for our son's liturgy. It was an abundant blessing to hand our selections over to my friends, confident the music would be perfect.

It was very hard to deal with these arrangements, and I cried through much of it. Ralph tried to protect me by suggesting that someone else could worry about most of the details, but I did not get to mother John Paul Raphael for very long. I did not create a sunny, blue and green nursery with monkeys or puppies. I did not carefully purchase, wash, fold, and put away dozens of small outfits and blankets. But, I could do this. I could make the funeral program just right. I could order photo enlargements and a guest book for the lobby in the church. I could pick out pictures from the hospital showing John Paul Raphael in each of the loving arms that held him. My children and I could mount them on to a large poster board to have at church for everyone to see. Ralph and I picked out readings together, and I told him I wanted us to try to speak at the funeral. I didn't know what we would say or how we would say it, but this was a holy longing in my heart and of course, he agreed.

As every moment passed, I thought of John Paul Raphael. I thought of him ten miles away tucked unthinkably in some corner of the funeral home, and I counted the hours until I could see him again. We decided not to have any kind of public viewing or visitation. On Tuesday afternoon, we asked our children if any of them wanted to go and visit their brother, but only Clare, our youngest, wanted to come. We completely understood. In every way, this was painful and foreign. There was no right or wrong when it comes to whether you want to go see your dead brother at the funeral home. Ralph's mother, Olga, also came with us. She and Ralph's father had been terribly ill during the days of John Paul Raphael's brief life, and although they lived locally, they were unable to meet him. She was feeling better, however, and very much wanted to spend time with her youngest grandson. Ralph, Clare, and I drove to the other side of Ashburn to pick her up. I felt giddy and nervous but full of love. I was going to see John Paul Raphael!

We stopped at the St. George's house to pick up the casket. I was too fragile and scared to get out of the car. I didn't want to see the casket. I didn't want it to be that real and to be that close to the end. Chris and Jodi came out of the house to hug us though, and we all wept. The coffin was a work of art. It was small, roughly twenty-eight by eighteen inches. The wood was flawless with a warm maple finish, polished shiny and smooth. The design was tapered so that the head of the casket was slightly wider and taller than the foot, just like that of Pope St. John Paul. The flat top was elegantly carved with two wide grooves forming a large cross. For our baby. A simple, perfect, handcrafted resting place full of love. It was everything we wanted.

I felt nervous as we neared Leesburg. My mind raced—what if we were late? We only had from four to five in the afternoon, and I wanted every minute. John Paul had been dead for four days. One of the decisions we made was to have nothing done to his body. We knew he would have been refrigerated to slow any decomposition, but what if he looked scary? What if he looked so different that it was weird and awful and all wrong? I was shaking and my grief and longing collided with my anxiety and fears.

When we arrived, we walked tentatively into the front salon. I looked around quickly—was John Paul already here? The room was decorated like a formal living room with comfortable chairs and couches spread around. In the center of the room against a wall was a large crucifix with a kneeler in front of a small table. *That's for the body*, I thought. Then, *how can this really be happening?* Arnold greeted us presently and took the coffin from Ralph, explaining that he would place John Paul Raphael in the casket and bring him right back. I felt my heart beating wildly. Clare and Olga both seemed calm, although Clare stayed close by my side. I sat in a chair across from the crucifix and stared up at my Lord. *Only through you, Jesus. I can do all things through Christ who strengthens me.*[4]

Arnold returned and placed the beautiful casket gently on the

---

4   Philippians 4:13

table across the room from me, the lid removed. I sat there and looked over, knowing my little boy was inside. I was scared and sad. I realized that somehow in my magical thinking my heart believed that maybe this would all be better, that in some way John Paul Raphael would be alive. I turned to Ralph and asked him the impossible again. "Will you go look? I am scared." My brave husband; he squeezed my hand and walked to our son and looked down at him briefly, touching the casket. Then he looked back at me and smiled.

"He's perfect," he said.

Ralph leaned in and kissed John Paul Raphael and then scooped him into his arms. It felt oddly naughty, like we should have asked permission, but hell, no! There is no way Arnold could have expected us to sit demurely and properly looking down at our baby in there. Ralph turned and I could see the top of John Paul's familiar gray cap, his face and body obscured by the blue and white crocheted blanket I had last seen him in. Ralph's face was full of joy and peace and I knew this was going to be okay. I loved my husband so deeply in that moment for being brave when I was not and for bringing me our son. He leaned over and placed John Paul in my arms. My whole body sighed. The weight of a baby is a treasure to a mother. It is a weight we grow in our bodies and that becomes a part of our very selves. Our blood mingles with theirs, exchanging even DNA. Whenever a woman gives birth, that sacred weight held within is traded for the perfect weight in her arms and at her breast. The expectation of this holy exchange is written into the fiber of a mother. It is the fulfillment of the journey of pregnancy, the reward for every one of a mother's labors.

Pregnancy and labor are driven by primal instincts and these same instincts compel a mother to guard and protect her child with her life. As a result, my hormone-fueled maternal instinct to seek out my child and my longing to hold him had left me in brutal agony. The profound frustration of those unmet needs is a grief unique to losing an infant. But the very moment I felt John Paul Raphael in my arms, I was content. The raging beast of instinct, drive, and desperation was silenced and joy took its place. I can hear the voice of some rational critic contradicting this: "But your baby is still dead!"

Yes, he is. But we are together and I have longed for this union. For the present moment, it is enough.

I beamed down at John Paul Raphael and soaked in his perfect little face. I thought his cheeks looked the tiniest bit thinner, but there was a flush to them that surprised me. His eyes were almost all the way closed but looked very natural. I brought Blue Blankie and wrapped him in it. He felt perfect. Not cold or stiff or unbendable. I had no idea what to expect, so this also surprised me. I pulled his little arms from the blanket so I could see his fingers. I slid my finger into his grasp so it looked like he was holding on to me again. I stood and walked him gently around the room, instinctively bouncing my step as if trying to soothe him to sleep. Ralph took a picture that became one of my favorites, me standing in the front salon holding John Paul and gazing down at him, the blankets trailing down long. We look like any mother and child in that picture, no death visible from the angle of the camera.

We all took turns holding him. There were tears, but there was more joy. Olga loved meeting her tiny grandson and wept as she said hello and goodbye in the same hour. Clare was gentle but proud of her baby brother, loving him and wanting to unzip his pajamas and take a peak at the rest of him. I was cautious, not knowing for sure the impact of death on his body. But we kissed little feet tucked into dinosaur jammies. I ran my hands all over him. When there were only fifteen minutes left, Ralph and I asked Clare and Olga to say goodbye so we could have time alone with John Paul Raphael. We sat on the couch together, our little holy family of three, reunited for these brief, final moments. My panic grew. Hysteria lurked around the outside of my consciousness and whispered painful truths I didn't want to remember quite yet. *There is still tomorrow,* I reassured myself. *I will still get to come back in the morning for one last visit. I don't have to say goodbye forever and ever just yet.*

Far too soon, Arnold came in to let us know our time was up and another visitation would begin shortly. I was desperate not to let John Paul Raphael go again, but I behaved. We brought some pictures from home and his soft snuggly lamb from Christmas to leave with him in his casket. We unwrapped Blue Blankie. I soaked in his tiny body and said a prayer that he be warm. What a ridiculous prayer, some other part of me replied, since he would be returning to the freezer. We tucked the little white lamb up next to his face and swaddled him snuggly in the crocheted blanket. We brought a photo of his nine siblings and our kitty Lina and a second photo of Ralph and me kissing at our wedding. We placed these at the head of his casket where they would look down over him. Next to his head, I placed a holy card of Jesus in his Divine Mercy. Gently and with great love, Ralph laid John Paul Raphael in the casket and we each kissed him goodbye. I was dazed as Ralph guided me from the salon, my arms freshly aching with the loss of his weight and his life once more. At some point in our journey, we had started calling John Paul our "little monkey" and the monkey-imagery stuck. When we got into the car, Clare and Olga showed us excitedly what they found in the driveway right outside our van—one little tiny baby sock with a monkey on it. Clare was sure this is a sign that John Paul Raphael was still with us. I was inclined to agree.

When we returned to the house, several guests had arrived. My father and Joann returned from Philadelphia to stay with us overnight. Ralph's best friend Michael flew in from Florida. Most of our other children were there. I have no idea what we did for food; I returned to my spot on the couch, weary through and through. I know we ate. I know we checked that the programs were copied, the musicians were ready, and the kids had their clothes laid out for Mass in the morning.

After the children and my parents went to bed, Ralph and I stayed up sitting on the couch talking with Michael. I was tired and numb, but there was still one important thing to do. When we were thinking about having to plan a funeral for our baby, before he was even born, I wanted Ralph and I to try to speak. Very few people in the church would have met John Paul Raphael. Ralph and I alone were entrusted with his life and I felt called to try and capture the grace of God in our journey; to talk about our love for our baby and the gift of his life. But now it was after ten p.m., and I was empty and exhausted. I had written nothing and had no clear thoughts. My body still ached from surgery, and post-partum hormones surged through me. How could we possibly get up and speak tomorrow? What would we say? Ralph consoled me by telling me we didn't have to do it. Everyone would understand if it was too hard. "But it is printed in the programs," I countered, hollowly. But that wasn't it. I felt convicted to speak. I just didn't know what to say.

Ralph and I have a weekly adoration hour from eleven p.m. to midnight on Tuesday nights in our parish Adoration Chapel. We went that night, four days after John Paul died and eleven hours from when we would begin his Mass of Christian Burial. I took my laptop with me and sat in front of the Lord. I poured my heart out to Him and begged the Holy Spirit to come and give me His words. What could I possibly say about John Paul's powerfully short, perfect little life? What purpose was I meant to impart?

Jesus, this is your baby and your story. All of this. We have tried to give you our sufferings and joys every step of the way and to trust you beyond our own understanding. Please come and give me your words and your wisdom.

I began to write and continued for more than an hour, realizing afterwards that the words I produced were truly not my own. It was a humbling experience of grace, and I am full of gratitude to the Lord for showing up when I so desperately needed Him. The Holy Spirit spoke truth into my heart that both consoled and enflamed me, truth I would cling to for the rest of my life and that gave a shape and a mission to grieving our son. Ralph and I fell into bed close to one a.m., clutching each other and praying for the Lord to be close

as we made our way through tomorrow, our final day with John Paul
Raphael here on Earth.

January 10, 2018, was a bitterly cold, sunny Wednesday. It was
my grandmother's ninety-fourth birthday. There were mudslides in
California and an earthquake in the Caribbean. And we would bury
our son. The early days of grief were accompanied in my head by a
ticker-tape of incongruous information.

"I need to do my laundry. My baby is dead."

"Should we pick the ecru or the off-white for our baby's funeral
program?"

"Do we want daisies or carnations to drop into his grave?"

I know it sounds dramatic, but I think most grieving mothers
would find this paradox accurate, normalcy living side-by-side with
the unthinkable. It made everything feel crazy.

Ralph and I woke early and got ourselves ready for Mass. We
made sure the children were up and dressed and made plans to
carpool out to the funeral home in Leesburg to pick up John Paul
Raphael. Maggie, Andrew, Leah, James, Clare, and my mom would
join Ralph and me at the funeral home to ride in the limousine back
to the church. My father dropped Nathan at St. Theresa in order to
prepare as an altar server for Mass. Meaghan and Evan met us at the
funeral home to caravan over while Carrie and Alicia went directly
to the church. I was grateful that I woke peaceful on this difficult day.
I was excited to be able to hold John Paul Raphael again. I could not
yet consider the reality that it would be the very last time. There was
anticipation of the funeral liturgy. We looked forward to the people
we hoped would come pray for our child and support our family in
our grief. I was eager to express my mourning through music and
the prayers of the liturgical rites. I knew the music of the Master
Singers would be spectacular. Our Catholic faith has beautiful rituals
and a rich tradition of praying for the dead and blessing them on

their journey to eternity. We had the certain hope that John Paul Raphael, having been baptized and confirmed and without stain, was in Heaven. All of this brought me great comfort.

We arrived at the funeral home just after nine a.m., which allowed us about twenty minutes to say goodbye before leaving for Ashburn. John Paul Raphael lay in his casket on a table in a different salon. I felt tender and grateful to be there with so many of our children. I was full of love for them as they each navigated this challenging day in their own way. I knew our many teenagers felt grief, but at that age, it is hard to know how to respond to your emotions or to the strong emotions of your family. It is challenging to be center-stage in a sad family drama. I was proud of them for their vulnerability and willingness to enter into an experience for which none of us were prepared. Ralph and I quickly scooped John Paul Raphael out of his casket. Just like in the hospital, there were many arms waiting for their turn to hold him. We took pictures and embraced the contradiction of smiling broadly in a photo with a dead baby brother. This was the only chance we had, so we took it. The minutes went by far too quickly. When it was time to leave, the children and my mom settled in the limousine while Ralph and I prepared the casket.

Here we were, Ralph and I, alone with our little boy. Our last moment together. We whispered our love over and over into his ears. We held his perfect small body to our chests and wrapped our arms around him and each other. We swaddled him one last time and tucked his soft little lamb close by his chest. We pulled his hat perfectly down over his head. We kissed his cheeks, his eyes, and his lips and then I forced myself to lay him into the coffin. We soaked him in, memorizing the details, and kissed him again. The seconds ticked by, each of us afraid to end them. Finally, Ralph looked to me for permission and I forced myself to give the slightest nod of my head. Reverently and with great care and gentleness, Ralph placed the wooden lid over our son, closing his body in forever. He used a screwdriver to carefully screw in each of the four screws at the corners until the lid was secure.

Months and months later, when rage came, I was angry at Ralph for this very thing. I was furious that he calmly screwed on the lid to our son's casket and locked him away from me forever. Irrationally, I blamed him for making me say goodbye. I raged that he hadn't changed the ending and found a way for us to keep John Paul Raphael without it being morbid and illegal. Better yet, Ralph should have just fixed it. However faithless or crazy these thoughts seem, I was simply being human and, in my humanity, allowed myself to feel and experience the full impact of a tragic and horrifying event. Jesus is big enough and solid enough to hold the anger, grief, and rage of one very small mother. I am thankful my husband was too.

Ralph laid down the screwdriver and with great strength of heart, my dear husband lifted our son's casket into his arms, and together we walked out of the funeral home and joined our family. It was a twenty-minute drive back to Ashburn and the children kept us distracted with their chatter and the novelty of being in this surreal situation. Including John Paul Raphael and Leah's service dog, Gage, there were ten of us in the limo. The kids played with the controls and we passed around the complimentary water bottles. I am convinced that many, many people were praying for us that morning because there is no other way to explain having the strength and the grace that we did, and to feel peace and even joy in the midst of our suffering. I could see the deep sorrow etched on Ralph's face. For most of our journey, I had carried the heaviest load and he was my support. But for that day, the burden of our son was his to carry, a burden he shouldered with complete love and a father's heart full of grief vulnerably on display. Ralph would do this for John Paul, carry him home with grace and dignity, when he could not do any of the other one thousand things he longed to do with his son.

When we got to the church, there were already many cars. Mass would not start for another fifteen minutes, and I did not have the strength to do any "meeting and greeting." The children and my mother headed into the narthex to say hello to people and make sure everything else was ready. Ralph and I sat in the limo in front of the church, the tears pooling in each of our eyes. The tinted windows provided the perfect opportunity to see without being seen, and we were speechless as we sat there and watched the guests pour into the church. Coworkers, out-of-town family and friends, friends from our parish, friends from our neighborhood, friends from the gym, parents of friends of our kids, the principal and teachers from the school, nurses from Inova Fairfax Hospital, members of my choir. We wept in love and gratitude as we watched all these people here just because they loved us and they loved John Paul Raphael.

When you lose a child at any age, there is fear that they will be forgotten. But when you lose a baby that has barely even been known, that fear is even greater. My heart soared when I saw hundreds of people had sacrificed their time for our family, to show us this love and support. Each and every person who came was a blessing to us. We named them all as we saw them walk in and praised God for the profound gift of community. The Body of Christ was present and gave us the strength we needed to get out of the limousine when it was time for Mass to begin.

Peace covered me as we walked into church. The children were waiting in the narthex along with Father Guest and the altar servers, including our Nathan. As Father Guest placed the white pall over the casket, he began to pray, "In the waters of baptism, John Paul Raphael died with Christ and rose with Him to new life. May he now share with Him eternal glory." The altar servers began the procession with the crucifix raised high, followed by Father Guest, the children, myself and Ralph, the casket held in front of his chest. The words and music of the opening hymn washed over me as we walked slowly down the aisle towards the altar and our Lord, present in the Blessed Sacrament. Since Christmas was only ten days prior, the Nativity crèche still spilled around the steps in front of the altar. I saw Mary and Joseph with baby Jesus in the manger. The Holy Family, the Three Kings, and even the animals seemed to welcome us as we brought our baby to the Lord and laid him there at His feet.

Isn't this the only way to endure this life? Our hearts and our sufferings, the hearts of those we love and their sufferings? Bring them all to the Lord and entrust them to His mercy and love. I felt encouraged by Mary, standing close by in her maiden bliss, surrounded by sheep. Joseph, so strong and silent. Christ himself, so meek and mild, was surely ready to welcome our little boy. Ralph held John Paul Raphael's casket with such love and strength, the tears pouring down his cheeks as he wept openly. I held his arm and Blue Blankie and Clare held on to me. I could feel the arms of all those loved ones in that church wrapped around us as we brought the body of our baby and offered him to the Lord.

Ralph tenderly placed the casket on the small table at the end of the aisle as the words of the opening song flowed over us. *Do not be afraid, I am with you.* The Mass was glorious and beautiful. Andrew and Meaghan read from the Old and New Testament. Carrie, Maggie, and Leah each sang a verse of my favorite Christmas carol, "In the Bleak Midwinter." My mother read the prayers of petition. We received the Body and Blood of our Lord in the Eucharist. We prayed and we cried. We were held in the mystery of joy and suffering. The presence of the Lord was powerful and so we rejoiced. But our son lay dead in his coffin in the center of the aisle, and so we grieved.

After communion, the Master Singers sang a piece that had broken my heart open for months as I rehearsed it and performed it with the choir, *Even When He is Silent,* by Kim Andre Arnesen. During my pregnancy, I clung to this music and its simple but profound text. The music honors the intense suffering of this world while affirming the omnipotent presence of God. After the Holocaust, the words were found written on a wall in a concentration camp.

I believe in the sun, even when it's not shining.
I believe in love, even when I feel it not.
I believe in God, even when He is silent.

Every chord of that flawless and heartfelt performance washed over me, soothing and comforting my shattered heart, honoring and touching the loss we lamented with everyone present in that church. It was an incredibly holy and moving experience. I knew with all my being that the Lord was intimately close, holding us in His arms and holding John Paul Raphael just behind the veil, but surely within reach.

When the music ended, it was time for Ralph and me to share our message. I begged the Holy Spirit to come fill our hearts and inspire our words. We needed strength and comfort to stand in front of hundreds of people and proclaim the truth that God planted in our hearts through the life and death of John Paul Raphael. We slowly made our way to the ambo and stood there taking it all in. We were humbled as we looked out into the church. We saw our grief reflected in the faces of our friends and family, their tears mirroring ours. I stared at one tiny casket vividly proclaiming the finality of what we were there to do. I tried to memorize these images so they would be indelibly imprinted on my heart and soul. Ralph began by thanking everyone for coming. The outpouring of love and support from so many people was tangible. I don't think either of us really appreciated how our story and our son had somehow touched so many hearts. We were overwhelmed and Ralph conveyed this beautifully. He shared with great vulnerability and sadness the story of how we named our boy, the significance of each of his three names, quite a large name for one little baby. Then I shared the message the Lord had inspired during adoration:

The story of our son John Paul Raphael is God's from the very beginning, an unexpected blessing that came, I am convinced, as a result of our weekly adoration hour together and my pilgrimage to Our Lady of Guadalupe. John Paul was conceived exactly nine months after I returned. We rejoiced in God's plan, even as we knew it could be complicated convincing all our children this was a blessing.

As many of you know, John Paul Raphael died from complications of Trisomy 18, a chromosomal condition where every cell in his body had three copies of the eighteenth chromosome instead of two, making it hard for the brain to communicate well with the rest of his body. We found out about the likelihood of his having Trisomy 18 after genetic testing in August of 2017. The tests didn't say for sure, but we knew the chances were high that this baby we now longed for would not be healthy.

Many professionals will tell you that Trisomy 18 is "incompatible with life." And while it is true that most babies with Trisomy 18 don't live very long, we are so grateful that our Catholic faith calls us to go deeper. We loved John Paul before we even heard his heartbeat and, while his potential diagnosis was devastating, we knew God was calling us to trust Him with numbering his days as He saw fit. Our job was to surrender to that plan. Surrendering to the uncertainty of our baby's life is one of the hardest things we have ever done. There could be no plan. We have spent the last five months waiting, praying, and hoping for a miracle for John Paul Raphael. We know that many of you joined us in that. We love and serve a God of miracles and He is faithful. He hears our every prayer, captures every tear, hears our every plea that He have mercy on us and spare our son. But we are a family, the Leon/Good family, that knows full well that the miracle you get is not always the miracle you prayed for.

John Paul Raphael is a miracle. He was fearfully and wonderfully made. We are here to say goodbye to our beautiful son, but I want to make sure everyone knows his brief life was full of miracles. Many Trisomy 18 babies die in the womb. Or have important parts of their bodies that are unable to function. Not John Paul—a miracle. Our number one hope all along was to have John Paul born alive, if at all possible, so we could love him face-to-face, and every time we got to hear his heartbeat, it was a miracle. We watched him grow for thirty-six weeks, knowing that every one-more-day we got was a miracle. After a dire emergency last Thursday morning, John Paul was born barely hanging on. It was only after Ralph baptized him with holy water that we brought that John Paul Raphael whimpered and gave us signs of life. A true miracle. John Paul was able to breathe on his own with just a little oxygen and could drink and swallow and fill his diapers. A miracle. His presence with all of us, his little cries and the way he held our fingers, how he captured all our hearts in such a short period of time—a miracle. This beautiful, perfect, holy child. We knew all along that his life could be measured in minutes or hours or days. We got twenty-eight hours and ten minutes.

But it was total love. He was love and he brought us love and we gave him love ... 1,690 minutes of unconditional love. We know that John Paul did not suffer and he died in the arms of his mommy and daddy, surrounded by family, and listening to us all sing him home. Our miracle.

Many of you have had dinner at our house before and may remember that we end our grace by praying these words from 1ˢᵗ Corinthians: Therefore, whether you eat or drink, or whatever you do, do all things for the glory of God.[5] That was our prayer for this pregnancy. Whether or not you heal John Paul, Lord, show us how this can all be for Your glory.

We know that God formed John Paul Raphael from the very beginning and that He has a purpose for his life. And that there is purpose in his death. Our faith teaches us that John Paul Raphael, having been baptized and confirmed, is certainly welcomed into Heaven. We can trust he is watching over us and that we will see him again. But we are still on Earth and this valley of tears we are left in, this sadness and grief we are all feeling, can I make this be for Your glory?

I feel very grateful that I have not struggled with the question of

---

5   Based on 1 Corinthians 10:31.

why. I have been sad and grieving and scared but didn't wrestle with God over why this had to happen to us. A favorite verse from Proverbs carried us through: Trust in the Lord with all your heart. Do not lean on your own understanding.[6] We prayed this over and over. But I do find myself with this big question now: How? How do we do this? How can our grief be for Your glory? How can we find purpose in our baby boy's death?

I want to share two thoughts that I hope will bring even more purpose to John Paul Raphael's brief life. One, this little boy was so loved. My heart aches thinking about the lifetime of love that grew in our hearts for him in just two days. His brothers and sisters were so brave and vulnerable in opening their hearts to him and loving him and feeling loved by him. We felt love from every person that came in the room to care for him. The grace of God was so present in the fragility of his life and the nearness of his death that somehow our hearts just opened wide to love. Maybe that can be his first legacy: Let yourself be loved. John Paul didn't have to do a single thing to earn that love or deserve that love. We felt his beauty and purity as a child of God and our hearts responded to the gift of his life. Maybe we can let ourselves be loved this way, by God, by our families, by ourselves: freely, unconditionally, and abundantly because we, like our precious John Paul, have a purpose, are a gift, and are fearfully and wonderfully made. Let yourself be loved.

Second, we know that death and suffering are a part of our Christian faith; there can be no Easter Sunday without Good Friday. In the gospel of John, Jesus tells us: Unless a grain of wheat falls into the earth and dies, it remains alone; but if it dies, it bears much fruit.[7] John Paul Raphael has died, but something has also died in all of us who love him. John Paul Raphael will rest in the ground later today, and our hearts too may be in darkness as we grieve and suffer. John Paul Raphael, we believe, has been raised to new life in

---

6   Proverbs 3:5-6
7   John 12:24

Christ. But for us, there can be, with God's grace, also a tremendous harvest from this pain. If we can trust the Lord with all our hearts and not rely on our own understanding of what we thought would be best (and I promise I am talking to myself here); if we can place our own hopes and dreams into the earth with John Paul and believe with all our hearts that our faithful God is with him and with us, there will be an abundant harvest. In God's time and in his way, but God's grace will not fail. We have to believe this for John Paul's life to have purpose. This truth will help and heal us in time, especially as we see new growth or healing in our lives or in our families or in our own hearts, where there was none before.

This is the legacy I believe John Paul Raphael can offer us all. Miracles are all around us, all the time. That we can let ourselves be loved and rest in that love. And that God will bring something beautiful out of our pain and suffering if we enter into the suffering with Him and trust Him with all our hearts.

Thank you so much for being here with us today. May John Paul Raphael's life and all our broken hearts be for the glory of God and our salvation. We miss you so much, little one.

9

ALL FOR THE GLORY OF GOD

Broken, messy hearts are God's specialty.

*"Every life is noted and is cherished,
and nothing loved is ever lost or perished."*
—Madeleine L'Engle, *A Ring of Endless Light*

I AM SO PROUD OF RALPH and so grateful to the Holy Spirit for showing up and giving us the grace and strength to share that message. As his mother, it was so important for me to proclaim the value of my son's life. I had a small revelation as I stood on the altar and was able to look down at his casket. Based on the shape of his coffin, I could tell that John Paul Raphael was positioned so that his feet were closer to the altar and his head further down the aisle. For some reason, at all the funerals I had attended and all the funerals I had sung at in the past, I always pictured it the other way—the casket coming in head first and remaining that way in the aisle. But in this position, John Paul Raphael was lying on his back and could gaze straight up to Jesus on the cross, straight through the stained glass window above the tabernacle and all the way into eternity! I imagined him wiggling in there, already enjoying a glorified healthy body and shining with joy and light. I know this is not sound theology, but it brought me comfort.

A Catholic funeral Mass includes a final sacred ritual. The "Song of Farewell" is sung as the priest blesses the body with incense, slowly and reverently walking around the casket while swinging the thurible, a hanging metal container of burning incense.

> *Come to his aid, O saints of God.*
> *Come meet him angels of the Lord.*
> *May Christ who called you, take you home,*
> *and angels lead you to Abraham.*
> *Give him eternal rest, O Lord,*
> *and let perpetual light shine upon him.*
> *Receive his soul and present him to God the most high.*

The congregation sings the prayer together, entrusting the soul of the deceased to the mercy and love of God. It is truly a final and perfect farewell. The smell of the incense, the beauty of the light and the candles, the simplicity of the music paired with the profound text all affirm and declare the value of human life. We are each made in the image and likeness of God and are His beloved sons and daughters. Psalm 116 proclaims: "Precious in the sight of the Lord is the death of godly ones."[8] We are not forgotten in grief. We are deeply loved and deeply held.

After the "Song of Farewell" and a final blessing, it was time to depart. The altar servers and Father Guest led the way. Ralph picked up John Paul Raphael in his casket and with Clare at my side, the four of us made our way down the aisle as the choir sang the closing hymn. Our other children and our family followed. We were supposed to make our way directly to the limousine and head to

8   Psalm 116:15

the cemetery, but we were sidetracked in the narthex of the church. Ralph placed the casket on a side table so we could quickly hug someone before they left. And then the next person and the next person. An impromptu receiving line formed which normally would fill me with dread as an introvert, but on this day, it felt like joy. We overflowed with gratitude and grace even on this terrible occasion. You couldn't help but feel the love and joy that hung thick in the air, just like in our hospital room. I wanted to hug and say thank you to every single person and share with them how important it was to us that they came, that John Paul mattered to them, how much it mattered to us to know they would remember him and hopefully allow his life to touch theirs. We were invigorated by connecting with so many special people. There were so many meaningful moments during that time, but one that stands out for me was greeting Tia and Kris, two of John Paul Raphael's nurses. They had been at the hospital and knew our baby. They both held him and heard his cries. It was monumentally significant that we were not "just another patient" to them and they had taken their precious time to come show their support for our family and our son. They both talked about how moved they were by our family, the Mass, and our words. I felt the impact John Paul Raphael was having on others. Our family and his life could be an instrument of God's grace. I rejoiced as I considered there could be an eternal purpose to our son's life. What mother doesn't want that for their child?

Eventually, Arnold appeared by our side and made it clear we needed to move on to the cemetery. It felt awkward that John Paul Raphael had just been sitting on an empty table while we all hugged and cried, but we hadn't planned on the receiving line. Ralph lovingly retrieved the casket and we corralled the children and loaded the limo for the short drive to St. John's. The mood was almost festive, each of us relieved to have released some of the burden of our grief during Mass. I knew the work of the day was not quite done, but I too felt carried by grace, love, and support. Ralph was very quiet in the limousine and kept a solemn vigil with John Paul Raphael on his lap while the children bantered. We had encouraged anyone who desired to join us at the cemetery. My parents and our future son-in-law Evan's parents were hosting a reception within walking distance after the burial. It was a bitingly cold day, slightly overcast, but dry. Despite the warmth and comfort of our community at church, the stark winter weather and the muted gray palette in the sky were an appropriate backdrop for what came next.

As we pulled into the cemetery, I saw a large number of family and friends standing by. A canopy was positioned in the John Paul the Great memorial garden near the plot we had picked out. A few rows of folding chairs were lined up underneath. Where before two small stones bordered the plot of green grass, there was now a plywood sheet covering an open mouth of earth. We emerged from the limo and greeted and hugged again, the cold wind nipping at our cheeks. Ralph stood apart from us all, dignified and focused. He held John Paul Raphael in his casket in front of his chest, bearing the physical and emotional weight in equal measure. An informal procession moved over to the tent and we filled all the seats. Additional family and friends stood and spilled around the edges of the canopy. Ralph placed the coffin on a small table near John Paul's grave. Father Guest was already there, prayer book in hand. Our friend Johanna, the photographer, volunteered to come to the church and now the burial to provide more priceless pictures of these events. I saw her in the back of the crowd clicking away with her camera and said a silent prayer of thanksgiving for this blessing.

I have no memory of the words spoken by Father Guest during the brief ceremony. I know we prayed and cried and also laughed. The pictures show each of these. I know that when the formalities were over, Arnold wanted us to leave, but I could not. We had told him and the cemetery director that we wanted to stay there until John Paul was fully in the ground. This was not normal protocol and I think now that they had not really planned on it, perhaps hoping we would forget. Arnold came forward at the end of the prayers and started to announce the reception afterwards, but I stopped him. I held his eye with a determined look he might remember from our meeting at the funeral home and reminded him we wanted to stay while John Paul Raphael was actually laid to rest. He looked uncomfortable, and I remember him making a comment about the gravediggers not being "presentable." This made me laugh, as if the grubby attire of the gravediggers was going to ruin the day.

Arnold relented and called them over and the workers removed the plywood covering over the grave. I stared into the hole. The clean, deep cuts in the dirt so my son's body could rest below were actually quite tidy. We had reached the final moments, and I felt the now-familiar hysteria rise in me. I was desperate to stop this or change it, but could not. For the first time, but certainly not the last, I imagined climbing into the hole with John Paul and lying there, insisting the gravediggers must cover us both with dirt. Before I was ready, one of the workers hopped into the hole and gently took my baby's casket. As if in slow motion, I watched him begin to lower it. At the last second, I yelled, "Wait!"

My body could not remain still and I lunged forward to stall him. Ralph said later he thought I was going to fling myself into the grave. I tenderly knelt down and leaned forward to kiss our baby's casket one more time. The very last time. Until eternity, the last kiss. I left the print of my lipstick on the smooth wood. Ralph and Clare both came and laid their hands alongside my kiss and then John Paul went into the earth.

Ralph felt inspired to share the story of how we sang to John Paul Raphael as he lay dying. He invited us all to sing again. Music has the ability to release emotion and create connection when our human frailties won't allow for it. This was one of those times. We all needed to exhale. Ralph cracked a joke about his rustic singing voice and then everyone began to sing "You've Got a Friend," the song we sang while John Paul Raphael was dying. Johanna caught a photo of me laughing whole-heartedly, my head thrown back and a big smile on my face. Isn't this a holy mystery? Isn't this *the* mystery? That life can be so full of joy and be a valley of tears at the same time? That God can hold us as His beloved and still call us to walk a road of suffering? That Good Friday and Easter Sunday must both exist for there to be redemption? As we cried and sang, everyone came forward to drop white carnations into the earth to lie on John Paul's tiny wooden casket. It was so achingly sad and holy. I knew our baby was at peace with the Lord. I knew he would be eternally held. I just wasn't sure how I was going to be able to leave him there in the ground.

We stood vigil at his grave until everyone finished, capturing a last photo of his casket covered in white flowers. One by one, mourners paid their respects and left for the reception. Ralph and I lingered a bit, chatting and thanking people for coming. We thanked Father Guest and Arnold and then walked away. We gave ourselves permission to have a good time at the reception. After all, we were surrounded by most of our favorite people, even if it was for a sad occasion. We ate delicious sandwiches and hot potato-leek soup, drank wine and beer, and even sang a rousing rendition of "Happy Birthday" for my grandmother followed by ninety-four celebratory claps for each year of her life. The hours flew by in what turned out to be quite a lovely afternoon full of grace and fellowship. I was physically reaching my limit, however. I had put my body through more than I thought was possible less than a week after surgery and I needed to go home.

Ralph, Clare, and I wanted to go back to the cemetery one more time, anticipating the workers would have finished filling in John Paul Raphael's grave. As we got out of the car, we could see the fresh mound of brown earth. We walked slowly to the site, both because my body was aching and from the continued heaviness of the occasion. Clare clutched my arm as we stared down at the dirt. Near the head of the pile was a small metal marker with only part of his name: *John Paul Leon*. Clare laid a small clutch of flowers from the reception on top of the mound. We were all out of words and prayers and just offered John Paul our presence. As I stood hugging Ralph and apparently still not out of tears, Clare gathered a few small rocks from the upturned earth to bring home with her. The three of us made our way back to the van, a rental because ours was inconveniently in the shop. Ralph noticed how wet and muddy the rocks were and asked Clare to be careful not to get mud on the seat or floor of the van. We suggested she place the rocks on top of a white Styrofoam food container we had in the back seat that held leftovers from the reception.

As we headed home, the sky was glorious and we could tell the sunset would be spectacular. The light in the sky captivated us and instead of turning on to our street, Ralph parked at the bottom of the hill by our house where we often walked to see the sunset. The three of us got out to go sit on the stairs of the hillside as the colors in the sky unfolded. I could feel God's presence as the light and the clouds played together. This awe-inspiring sunset was another beautiful consolation on the hardest of days. Already I could hear my grief starting to hiss louder and louder within me: *How could you leave him there in the ground?* I tried to let the peace of the moment calm my tired mind and body.

As the colors faded, we made our way back to the van, and Ralph gently helped me into the front seat. As I clicked my seatbelt, Clare exclaimed, "Mom! Ralph! Look!" She lifted her hands to show us the rocks she had gathered from John Paul Raphael's grave. They were perfectly clean. Not a speck of dirt or mud remained on them anywhere. There was no dirt on the floor or the to-go box. It was as if they had been scrubbed and made new. The three of us were in awe of this small but mighty miracle. What a consolation for our beautiful little girl who watched her baby brother die and whose heart was broken along with ours. What a clear sign that, in faith, we are each scrubbed clean and made new in the presence of God; that John Paul Raphael enjoyed the privilege of being a new creation with our Heavenly Father. All three of us saw those dirty rocks from the cemetery. There could be no denying the transformation, and we praised God for bringing us one last, generous miracle of His presence on this long, painful day.

10

THE GRIEF BEAST

There is freedom in facing your worst fears.

"A single person is missing for you, and the whole world is empty."
—Joan Didion, *The Year of Magical Thinking*

MY EYES OPENED SLOWLY on Thursday, January 11. It was all over. I had no idea how to live this day or any of the others that would come after it. Frankly, I still wasn't sure I wanted to. It would be a simple day. The last of our family left. The kids were back in school and had playdates and rehearsals to keep them busy until dinner. Ralph and I would spend the day side by side, our mutual pain flowing between us. It was hard to accept that the doing was all done. It was both comforting and terrifying to consider that maybe the only thing I had to DO for the next year was survive.

I laid in bed far longer than I should, not able to get up yet and help Clare and Nathan off to school. I prayed silently and then looked at my phone. Facebook showed me a beautiful post from a friend with the perfect words to soothe my heart and remind me we are not alone.

Although this precious, little man lived on this earth for only a short time, every single second was about love and weighing only four pounds, he changed our world. Like so many, I will forever remember John Paul Raphael; his darling face, his beautiful name, and how he brought together thousands of people and prayers reaching across Ashburn and beyond. As this family humbly begged for our prayers, social media worked at its best as his nine siblings and so many others reached out to their circles of love and support and we watched as prayers were answered and miracles happened. My heart breaks and I know I will never understand the pain his beautiful mother and father must feel, but I do know that heaven has a new saint and this precious soul will live forever and ever, Amen. I believe our true mission in life as mothers is to do this very thing; welcome the souls God sends us and love them all the way to eternity. Now that is purpose. For each of us is planned, each of us is loved and each of us is necessary.

Tears fell and my heart soared. On this morning after, I was not the only one remembering John Paul Raphael. Saying his name. I wanted to say it over and over again. I wanted to hear other people say it. To see it written. John Paul Raphael. I remembered the perfect, holy moments during the funeral Mass yesterday when Ralph and I stood clinging to each other on the altar and spoke our love and grief over losing John Paul Raphael. And my beautiful, holy husband weeping as he told the story of his name.

Your daddy has loved you so perfectly, John Paul Raphael. He chose your name so beautifully. He carried your ultrasound picture in his shirt pocket every day you were in my womb. He packed your special blanket and your Duckie for our trip to Italy and whenever we left town. He carried you so bravely in his arms as you lay in your casket. He guarded and protected you, desperate to shield you from death, but at the very least, he held you in his arms until the bitter end. He carried you so beautifully down the aisle at church, crying openly, and laid you before the altar. I pictured you in your casket gazing up at the Lord. If we had taken the lid off, maybe we could see a sneak peak of you with your glorified body, wiggling and smiling at Jesus. You are the luckiest baby to be loved by your daddy. He has the biggest and most beautiful heart I know. Maybe from Heaven you can see just how much I love him and you.

Ralph and I spent the morning on the couch looking at pictures of our baby. We counted down the minutes until 10:33 a.m., one week after he was born. At the precise time, we played one of his special songs and I took the first of fifty-two Snapchat pictures, the day and hour stamped on to the image. "One week old! We love you, JPRL!"

One week before, at this very moment, I was still in joy. Every Thursday at 10:33 a.m. until every Friday at 2:43 p.m. would forever remind me of 1,690 minutes of joy with John Paul Raphael alive with us, being passed from arms to arms. Every Thursday night would remind me of his one perfect night asleep on my chest, with his daddy sound asleep in our cocoon of the hospital bed.

My thoughts quickly spun into grief. I didn't touch his face enough or kiss his cheeks enough or run my finger under his perfect, soft chin enough. I already felt the raw desperation of early grief. I am so grateful that we lived the hours of John Paul's life without anxiety and fear, but now I look back and scream at myself that I didn't do enough. Did I take for granted that we would have more than one night? *Please, God, couldn't I go back and have one more night?* I am so thankful that I barely slept and got as many minutes awake with John Paul Raphael as I could.

I love you I love you I love you, my perfect little boy. Please come back.

We stayed on the couch most of the day. I iced my swollen breasts and let my body rest. In addition to the emotional toll from the day before, my post-surgical body was worn out. I took two naps. We listened to John Paul Raphael's music. I read online about losing your baby and how to cope and grieve. I ordered a stuffed monkey to make into a weighted comfort animal. There was nothing we could ever do to fill the emptiness in our arms, but according to my research, a little four-pound, one-ounce soft monkey might help a tiny wee bit. I visited an infant loss website and felt very brave for trying to put words to our experience for the first time, then posting it to share. After spending months reading so many stories, we now had our own.

Despite doing almost nothing, I was profoundly weary from enduring the day. I tried to pray before bed and I begged God to open my eyes to the rich harvest I hoped would come from the death of our beautiful son and from our suffering. I called upon the Lord to show us His face because otherwise we would be lost. I remembered a phrase I often used during the years of my divorce when life also felt painful and out of control: *I want I want I want.* Now, like then, my inner voice was a litany of things I wanted but could not have.

I want to go back to last week so that I can live again the perfect beauty of his 1,690 minutes. I want all the clichés—to do it all over again. To just have him back. To have one more day. I want John Paul in my arms drinking the milk out of these sore breasts. I want him here wrapped in his blue blanket while I rub his back. I want tiny baby clothes and burp cloths all over the house and the laundry left undone. I want to be so tired from walking him in the hall while he cried instead of sleeping. I want to see him with his daddy again and watch him grow up to be a holy man like he is. I want to see and feel my baby in my dreams. I want. I want. I want.

Jesus, have mercy on us. Forgive me my ingratitude. Help me surrender to your holy will. I am sorry for being ungrateful, Jesus, but it wasn't enough. I will try very hard with your grace to accept 1,690 minutes and make it enough for a lifetime.

But what I wouldn't give for one more minute holding him in my arms. For the rest of my life, every time someone asks me: Do you need anything? Can I get you something? What do you want? *Only you, my baby.*

I awoke Friday, January 12 with my arms aching, desperate for something I could not reach. John Paul Raphael had been gone one whole week, the most painful week of my life. The empty hole inside me threatened to consume me with its hunger.

Before I was even out of bed, Clare arrived full of tears. She had gone to bed the night before clinging to me and crying. She felt worried and stressed about everything, she said, which seemed like an appropriate reaction given everything she had been through. She would be leaving that afternoon with her brothers to spend three days at her dad's house and she didn't want to go. Poor Clare's beautiful ten-year-old heart was grieving so much. She was desperate for John Paul to live and come home with us, and his loss was more than she could handle. Ashley, the child-life specialist at the hospital, could not have done more to support and prepare Clare. We were so impressed by the resources and the attention we received from Inova Fairfax Hospital during our three days there. Ashley helped by spending hours with Clare in order to distract her from the intensity of emotion and help her to begin to process her brother's death through books and art. She helped us with our memory-making projects at the hospital. Most of all, she made Clare feel seen and validated her feelings during a time Ralph and I were not emotionally available to meet her needs.

After Clare left for school that morning, I turned to Ralph for comfort just as Clare had turned to me. It was very difficult to be strong for Clare in her sadness. I was drowning, but I needed to find a way to help her while she was drowning as well. I had no idea how to do that without Ralph holding me up while I tried to hold Clare. I knew we only survived those days on the grace of the prayers of so many loved ones. It had to be grace because there was no human explanation for how we managed to "go on." I was exhausted from ten minutes of trying to be strong for my daughter and relieved that she could only tolerate her grief in small doses. It occurred to me that our older children found a way to process their emotions without needing our help. I am both grateful for and saddened by the necessity of this.

Later that morning, I asked my mom to come over and help me tidy up and put away clothes in Clare's room. It brings Clare joy and peace to organize and personalize her room. The disarray reflected the chaos of the last week. I could give this act of love to my daughter to soothe her heart. After everything we had been through, it felt disorienting to do something as mundane as organizing Clare's drawers and clothing. Part of my spirit rebelled, but I held a newfound tenderness for my living children and needed to show them love now more than ever. I couldn't do anything else to love and serve John Paul Raphael here on earth, no matter how desperately I wanted to, but I could help my sweet Clare feel more peaceful in her room.

After we finished and my mom left, I sat on Clare's bed in her quiet, clean room and spoke aloud to the universe. "My name is Elizabeth Leon. I have six children." I spoke their names and their ages out loud because I needed to make John Paul Raphael feel more real. He came and went so quickly, sometimes he didn't feel real.

Oh, my dearest baby, you were SO REAL. You were flesh and blood and little bird cries and love and skin and breathing and diapers.

My thoughts spiraled back through the traumatic events, the echo so loud in my head. *My baby my baby my baby.* I read on a website that "preoccupation with your baby" is a normal part of grieving infant loss. Good. Because all I wanted to do was remember holding him and touching him and feeding him. I just wanted to look at his pictures and his videos and remember. Maybe I could find a magical way to turn back time so that he was no longer gone. My mind somehow believed this was possible. I recalled author Joan Didion writing in *The Year of Magical Thinking*[9] that she continued to leave her deceased husband's shoes out for almost a year, in case he needed them. One impact of traumatic grief is that it takes a very, very long time before the loss and the new contours of your life even begin to make sense.

"I am Elizabeth Leon, and I have six children." I said it over

---

9   Joan Didion, *The Year of Magical Thinking* (*Vintage*: 2007).

and over again. I didn't have to say "one is in heaven." I still had six children. In fact, I had seven including my one little miscarried soul. But for so long I had only birthed five children and now it was six. Six. This made me smile until the hurt caught up.

Still crying, I joined Ralph in our room and settled into the soft chair by our bed to pray at 10:33 a.m. I forced myself to shower and get dressed for the day. I was heavy and moved slowly through my daily routine, accompanied by a silent interior assault from the grief beast: *"How can you be acting like everything is ok? Why aren't you screaming?"* I longed to climb back into bed. I wanted to take a pill. Several pills. I wanted the dark, drugged refuge of sleep. Fueled by the powerful drive of maternal love, I forged ahead and brushed my teeth, combed my hair. Nathan would be home soon from a half-day at school, and I longed to spend time with him. Seventh grade is not easy on anyone, and Nathan and I had been having a rough year. In addition to normal adolescent challenges, he was beginning to process anger and sadness about the divorce and the fact that he could not see his dad as much as he wanted. But Nathan, with his deeply empathetic heart, was so sweet and loving with me, even while I could tell he was hurting too. He'd come to me the day before and put his head on my lap several different times and let me love him. "Mom," he said, "I think that losing your child must be the worst thing anyone could ever have to go through." *Oh, my sweet boy.* I was deeply touched by his compassion, but so sorry that he learned this truth while having a front row seat to his mother's grief.

When Nathan got home from school, Ralph, Nathan, and I had a simple lunch and then decided to play some games. Games are Nathan's love language. We played four rounds of Yahtzee. It was a welcome relief from my intense emotion to do this simple, normal thing with our son, though I have no idea what the word normal meant anymore. "Normal" had eluded us for quite some time. The last normal day I remembered was May 9, 2017. Maggie and I were driving home from Virginia Tech after moving her out following her freshman year. On Interstate 81 North I got the phone call from my ex-husband that our other daughter was in the emergency room having a mental health crisis. Three weeks later I found out I was pregnant. Ten weeks after that we got John Paul's diagnosis. I could not imagine how life would ever be normal again. It occurred to me in that moment, one week after our son died, that at this moment, the best I could hope for were moments of normal—moments when, for some brief period, the Grief Beast had been fed and now silently slept.

In those early days, I came to know grief as a ravenous beast. Every part of my interior life was taken over by this angry, raging, demanding, ugly creature. His presence consumed me as he screamed and stormed in my heart and soul. The only way to calm him, even the slightest bit, was to give him what he wanted RIGHT NOW. But of course, I couldn't do that. Our small boy was forever gone. Instead, I tried to soothe the beast's ravenous appetite with meager substitutes. Silence, crying, writing, showering, sobbing, walking, sleeping, remembering, curling up in a ball—these all had an opportunity to soothe the beast. I spent almost every day that first month doing those things with Ralph. It was the only way to survive. I quickly understood my frail humanity and the limits of my body and soul. I could only function around Ralph or my children, and if there was too much stimulation, I couldn't function at all. The average everyday tasks of my life seemed impossible. Before losing our son, I thought that a newly-bereaved person might really appreciate help, whether cooking meals, mowing the lawn, or driving their children around, but I didn't grasp that they would *need* it. I couldn't yet comprehend that in fresh grief, the body actually stops functioning. Now I knew that the brain could simply shut down. I stopped sensing my environment and could not complete a thought or a sentence. Hours went by and I had no recollection of what I had done. Often, I didn't even know where I was or what I was doing. I so desperately needed to be cared for, and I was blessed to have Ralph next to me for the first month. That he could help me through my grief was not a measure of his own grief. Ralph ached and missed his son too. But the combination of God's grace, his perspective as a doctor, and his experience as a man who has already walked through grief enabled him to be my rock, day in and day out.

As I finished Yahtzee with Ralph and Nathan, I started to unravel. The beast shouted at me, *"Ok, fine. I can behave for twenty or thirty minutes, but that is it. Your time is almost up!"* My anxiety grew rapidly and my heart now rebelled at the simplicity of playing a game with my child.

Without warning, grief erupted and demanded a reckoning. *WHAT DO YOU THINK YOU ARE DOING? DO YOU REALLY THINK YOU CAN PRETEND TO BE NORMAL?* I had felt peaceful playing with Nathan, but, in the blink of an eye, I couldn't do it anymore. I faked my way through the end of the game. I tried to prevent Nathan from sensing my unravelling, but grief bubbled up like nausea. I fled the kitchen and buried myself under the covers of my bed, sobs escaping before I even was at the top of the stairs. Ralph joined me shortly and held me as wave after wave of grief crashed over me, neither of us knowing how long the tsunami would last.

When the storm subsided, we lay exhausted on our bed. This time the only thing that motivated me to get up was the clock. I wanted to be with John Paul Raphael at his grave at 2:43 p.m., the time of his death one week earlier. We gathered a few small mementos and headed to Leesburg. I felt my heart beat faster as we took the first of many drives to visit our son lying in the ground. Trying to reconcile what was real with what I was capable of processing as truth left me disoriented. Clinically, I existed in a stupor, as if I were post-anesthesia and still had a limited mental capacity. *Wait, what? My son is in the ground? He lived? He died? He was real but is gone? Am I also in the earth yet?* How could I wrap my head around my son's death and accept that this truth was now my reality? This confusion was contrasted by my macabre excitement at going to visit my dead baby. I longed for him so desperately that it didn't matter that it would not be anything close to what I really wanted.

Visiting a grave was a new experience for me. I set a high bar for myself on that first visit by thinking, "I want to bring him something special every time I come!" It was easy that day with a house still full of flowers. We pulled a bouquet of small white roses from a vase and wrapped a ribbon around them before we left. I brought a small angel statue from a flower arrangement from my grandfather's funeral, along with a short letter to John Paul Raphael.

As we walked to his gravesite at the cemetery, Ralph glanced at the thick clouds and hoped aloud, "Maybe the sun will come out at 2:43." I saw the mound of fresh dirt from a distance. My anxiety grew as we came close and stood above him, looking down at the small grave marker. Ralph spread a blanket on the wet ground and we sat side by side. Looking at that mound of dirt, I pictured his tiny, perfect, cold body tucked in his coffin, down there alone. I was frantic to dig through the dirt. I knew I could reach him! I could hold him and curl up next to him and have the gravediggers cover us both with dirt this time. *Please, God. There has to be a way I can still reach him.*

As the clock ticked closer to 2:43 p.m., Ralph and I began to pray the Divine Mercy Chaplet. We watched the clouds cross the sky as we prayed for God's mercy on us and on our son and our family. We finished our prayers at 2:44 p.m. and the sun suddenly broke through. It was a startling and glorious moment. The light shone brightly on our faces and we felt hot even in the January air. John Paul Raphael's grave marker sparkled like diamonds in the sunlight. Warmth spread through me and I felt the peace that surpasses understanding.[10] Ralph and I clutched each other's hands and soaked in the comfort pouring over us, tears still rolling down my cheeks. The sunburst lasted for about a minute and then the clouds closed and the shadows returned.

---

10   Philippians 4:7

My skin tingled. We were in awe of our Glorious God and the clear gift of His presence. We began to pray out loud, praising and thanking God for the gift of the sunlight, His sure sign of His everlasting presence, of John Paul Raphael's presence with Him in heaven, and the brightness and perfection of God's love that we can barely begin to comprehend. Ralph and I thanked God for our baby and for the time He gave us with our son. We praised the Lord for showing up so clearly that we could not miss it.

I thought of Psalm 8:5. "*What is man that you think of him, and a son of man that you are concerned about him?*" And not just a son of man, but ME. Who am I that you think of <u>ME</u>? I let myself be loved in this. What a gift. Another miracle from John Paul Raphael and Jesus.

Ralph and I were tender and quiet on the ride home. We listened to our playlist and wept. My dearest husband's heart opened wide as tears poured down his cheeks. It sounds terrible, but I never love him more than in moments when the tender vulnerability of his love is there for me to see and hold, our sadness big and loud together.

There were many kids home when we returned. Clare was back from a playdate and read in the family room. James and Leah had finished with activities after school, and Andrew had returned from a day with his girlfriend. We felt the grace of God's presence still with us and enjoyed a peaceful dinner with the five of them. Our dear friend brought pizza from our favorite delivery spot. We ate together, and Ralph and I drank wine and played another dice game with Nathan, filling up his love tank again and hopefully displacing some of his grief. Shortly after that, Leah, James, Nathan, and Clare left to spend the weekend with their dad. Maggie had left after the funeral to return to Virginia Tech, and Andrew needed to leave the next day for the University of Virginia. We were thankful for their time at home and for their help during their winter break from school, but I also looked forward to the quiet when Ralph and I would have the house to ourselves while the younger four were at school the next week. My grief demanded solitude and it took enormous amounts of energy and strength to be a mother to my other children right then.

At some point on this long Friday, a package arrived from Laura Ricketts, our bereavement doula. Despite all our preparations together, bad weather kept her from the hospital. I opened the box and pulled out a luxurious soft blanket and a plush teddy bear holding its own bear baby. She enclosed a note that said: "*Something to hold when your arms feel empty and something to wrap around you when you are in need of comfort.*" My tears fell. This dear woman knew grief in a deeply personal way because these gifts and words were painfully perfect. I immediately wrapped the blanket around me and clutched the silly soft bear to my heart as I wept and said his name over and over in my head. *John Paul, John Paul, John Paul.* Laura's gentle, thoughtful love was exactly what I needed during a time when nothing was right and would never be right again. I clutched the blanket and teddy bear along with Blue Blankie. Ralph and I finally headed to bed at the end of that first week. I tried to process that John Paul Raphael was forever with me and forever gone. With my limited capabilities, all I could manage was a heartfelt plea: *Please come back.*

There was a brutal intensity to the tidal wave of grief during that first week. I found comfort in all the flowers and cards. There was a rush of momentum and vitality, even in death. But after that? The mail stopped. The flowers died, leaving a sweet stench in the air. The cruel days of early grief began to blur together.

Normal barged its way back into our lives, a presence I did not recognize or care to meet. I hated that word. I didn't want anything "normal" right now. There was nothing normal about the inescapable, crushing weight of loss. How could the absence of something be so heavy? I struggled to find adequate words to convey the experience. Shattered. Disoriented. I felt agony. Complete emptiness. Crushing sadness. They were all insufficient. The truth was fiercer: I didn't want anyone or anything if it was not my baby. If Jesus had opened a door in the veil separating Heaven and Earth right then and asked, "Will you leave it all to be with him? Can you come right now?" I would have run all the way to John Paul Raphael and not looked back.

This was a new life I didn't want. The old life was out of reach, and I was angry and resentful of its reminders. I wanted to scream at each day as it rolled out on the conveyor belt of time. I wanted to go back to the holy bubble of January 4 and 5.

"The burden is crushing me," I thought daily without any sense of being dramatic. My grief demanded attention. It insisted on being recognized and tended. I stumbled through my early grief without any idea how to live my life or how to carry on, other than knowing that the sun would rise and set and, somehow, I would have survived another day. Ralph and I spent January mostly sitting on the couch in the family room, a memorial to John Paul Raphael spread out on the table before us. A basket of condolence cards, a scented candle, the framed photos from the funeral, the poster board collage from the church were all within reach. My comfort objects— Blue Blankie, my heavy green security blanket from the years after my divorce, and the new blanket and teddy bear from our doula. *It all went too fast*, I cried in my head every day. I gave the Lord my shattered heart over and over again. I clung to the truth that He is a faithful God and that He is so close in our suffering. John Paul was not lost and we were not lost. I remembered, somehow, to thank Him for all of it, and the song of my thanks and the lament of my heart mingled daily.

February 1 arrived and I couldn't turn the calendar. My perfect baby boy would forever be January. The last bit of my hope for his life lived in January. His birth, the sacred, perfect bubble of his 1,690 minutes in the cocoon of our hospital room. His death, his funeral, and burial. The agonizing, beautiful intensity of his life and his loss and the early days of meeting grief. The fiercely strong memory of John Paul Raphael still in my arms, breathing on my chest. Ralph home with me every day and the daily arrival of cards and flowers. Time frozen in honor of this sweetest child. All January.

February meant his due date. It meant my husband going back to work and everything being "over." February was not "cute and pregnant" but just fat. February was betraying my baby by leaving him behind. February was having to re-learn my life without him. I wasn't ready. I stared at a long bleak road of calendar pages and seasons and was afraid I would never be able to find John Paul there. I wanted January back.

February 2 stormed in, John Paul Raphael's due date and also First Friday. As a bereaved mother, each of these dates, these invisible milestones, however painful, are all points of connection with the child I lost, moments to pause and remember. To let myself grieve a little deeper and feel a little more. I went to pray in front of the Blessed Sacrament in the chapel at St. Theresa. I sat with Blue Blankie across my lap, an unfamiliar calm in my heart. I brought every empty space within me, the giant hole left by one small baby.

I bring it all to you, Jesus, and lay it at your feet. I climb into your lap and bury my face in your soft, white robes. I drag a ladder to your Cross on the hill of Calvary as you hang there in your own suffering. The wind whips through my hair. I climb up the ladder and stand there next to you. It is a desolate place, this Calvary. The valley of tears stretches before us, vast and endless. The rust-colored mountains and the gravel and dust of a thousand years covers everything. I close my eyes and breathe. The smell of salvation, the hope of eternity fills my lungs. Is it possible, this life of love, loss, and longing, of emptiness and overflowing? It is possible with you. I am comforted just standing by your side, the juxtaposition of this surprising peace while blood drips from your sacred heart on to the nape of my neck. Jesus. Always the way. Always the answer.

I lift my face to your face and see your eyes—the bottomless well of eternity, liquid brown love pouring over me. I am pierced in love by your gaze. I close my eyes and the sun breaks through, warming my face as I am held tightly in your love, your arms still bound by nails, the nails I hammered in with my own doubt and sin.

"I am empty," I whisper to you. My arms. My womb. My hope.

I hear you answer in my heart. "I know. I will hold and carry your baby for you. Will you hold and carry some of my death and suffering? And in carrying it for me, bring souls to my Sacred Heart. Souls I long for. Souls I will use your beautiful child and your broken heart to reach."

Forgive my doubt, forgive my fear, I pray. Forgive the weakness of my humanity. I long for you, my Jesus, and I long for my son. He is wrapped in your arms, held in your love so that I know in my longing for one I am also longing for the other. In finding one, I am finding the other. In holding one, I am holding the other.

Somewhere during these weeks of early grief, the counting began. Always a tally—how old would John Paul be and how long had he been gone? At first, I counted days, then weeks. Every week I stopped at the double vigil and sat with him, cried with him, and played his songs: 10:33 a.m. Thursday and 2:43 p.m. Friday. I was crazy about this—planning ahead and turning down invitations to make sure I was somewhere I could take this time to hold my grief and remember, memorializing it with a time-stamped Snapchat. The first week I missed 10:33 a.m. I was devastated, convinced I was forgetting our baby. I was unforgiving of myself until I found a way to offer myself compassion and understanding. I tried to see missing that small moment as a sign of healing, but guilt immediately followed. I didn't want to heal. I just wanted to remember and stay back where my son was. Healing meant moving on and away. It would take many months to see it any other way. The Snapchats continued all year, a small memorial of remembering and honoring our son. *Twelve weeks gone, twenty-five weeks gone, Happy six months JPRL.*

On March 30, we got a call from the cemetery director that

John Paul Raphael's headstone had been placed at his grave. One of the early chores in grief is selecting a headstone. The cemetery had recommended a monument company to help us. Designing his memorial actually brought me joy. We had little opportunity to parent John Paul Raphael, so it was meaningful to Ralph and me to craft a lasting remembrance that definitively declared his existence to the world. In addition to giving his name and his birth and death dates, the headstone proclaimed: *Beloved son and brother. All for the glory of God.* In time it would become a place of refuge when I was afraid of moving forward without him. The solid stone reminded me that he was here, he was real, and he mattered.

When May arrived, John Paul Raphael and I were together again as we crossed into the memory of time we'd shared. He came to life in my memories. We lived June together last year, the last day of school, the Fourth of July, and one glorious September when I first felt him move in the morning light of Venice. There was joy in this, and I marked each milestone silently in my heart. *Last year on this day I was still pregnant; I was still pregnant when I . . .*

Repeat. Repeat. Repeat. I wondered if I could postpone grieving while I focused on reminiscing. How's that for magical thinking? Every joy was still layered with sorrow. There was no denying the tragic, undeserved ending.

In my loss research, I read about how the body knows organically the impact of these silent memorials even when the brain may not completely process them. I felt that during Memorial Day weekend as I plunged more deeply than normal into sorrow. I unraveled in grief for several nights in a way that felt like Week One all over again. And maybe in a way it was. It was my first experience looking back to remember our baby—looking at a pregnancy test in a dumpy CVS and then getting Slurpees to celebrate. Maybe I was looking back at that innocent, pregnant version of myself from last May 29 and grieving her, too. She couldn't see what was coming.

I've thought a lot about "before" when it comes to grief and death.

Isn't that one of the natural responses when we lose someone? *I want to go back*. The bereaved may find themselves living in the past in hopes that somehow, they can rewind the clock and go back to the time before their loss. When a baby dies, it is tricky because if you go too far back in time, you erase their life. Of course, I wanted to go back, but only as far as May 2017. Any further back and I lived in a world where John Paul Raphael *never* existed and that is worse than living without him. I wanted to go back just far enough that I could relive every moment of my physically and emotionally challenging pregnancy and spend more time with my baby. I wanted every bit of his thirty-five weeks and six days in my body and every drop of the 1,690 minutes of his life. I even wanted the twenty-two hours after he died when I held his perfectly still body close against mine in the hospital and the hours of our final goodbyes at the funeral home. It was not enough. It could never be enough.

I read a beautiful memoir by Elizabeth McCracken called *An Exact Replica of a Figment of my Imagination*[11] about her unexpectedly stillborn son. She shares precisely my own experience of floundering after the loss of John Paul and the somewhat unique nature of grieving a baby. She describes on page ninety-seven the unnerving reality of going back to life after the death of her son:

"Our life as usual. We picked out restaurants, opened a bottle of wine at 6:00 p.m. if we were cooking at home. On the one hand it was comforting and even lovely... and on the other hand the very usualness, the loveliness, the freedom to do what we wanted, was a kind of torture: look at your unencumbered selves. After most deaths, I imagine, the awfulness lies in how everything's changed: you no longer recognize the form of your days. There's a hole. It's person-shaped and it follows you everywhere, to bed, to the dinner table, in the car. For us what was killing was how nothing had changed. We'd been waiting to be transformed, and now here we were, back in our old life."

---

11   Elizabeth McCracken, *An Exact Replica of a Figment of my Imagination* (BackBay Books, 2010), p.97.

Back in our old life. Waiting to be transformed. So much the same and at the same time nothing would ever be the same again. Like the author's title: an exact replica of my previous life and yet so intrinsically different that I was still finding my bearings.

11

IN THE LAND OF THE LIVING

The darkness of grief can lead to peace, purpose, and joy.

*"Give sorrow words; the grief that does not speak knits up
the o-er wrought heart and bids it break."*
—William Shakespeare, *Macbeth*

LEARNING ABOUT JOHN PAUL RAPHAEL'S condition introduced a whole new world we wished we never knew existed. In addition to carrying fear and anxiety about what might or might not happen, we needed to explore and understand many practical aspects about this most horrifying of experiences: having your baby die.

No one wants to land in this foreign country. No one. But if I had an 87.5 percent chance of ending up there, I wanted to read the guide book and try to learn the language. It would help me to study the road maps and have a small sense of control in a situation where we really had none. It took a tiny bit of terror out of the great unknowns that lay before us.

With a tender, trembling heart I took to the internet and entered the heartbreaking world of infant loss. I wept as I read story after story of grieving mothers and fathers. I poured over the Trisomy 18 family page and paid close attention to how long each baby lived—seconds, days, weeks, the few who lived longer, the many who died before birth. I read about baby coffins and cuddle cots. It was all devastating, but I was empowered to learn about beautiful, meaningful ways we could love and welcome our baby, even if he was only here for a brief time or even stillborn.

One of the things I wondered about the most was what it would feel like for *me*. I knew so many phrases from my research: earth shattering, heartbreaking, soul wrenching, life altering. But when the guillotine fell in *my* life and *my* heart was cut out, was there anything at all that could take away the pain? It is a devastating truth that in my experience, the answer was no. Not really. Prayer brought me solace, and when I am strong, my faith gives me hope, but few things lessen the intense loss of losing a child.

This is where our monkey comes in. Monkey has the softest brown fur and weighs precisely four pounds and one ounce, the exact weight of John Paul Raphael. Monkey is also almost exactly the same length as our baby and therefore fits perfectly in the nightgown that John Paul Raphael wore for most of his brief life. We brought Monkey home the week after we buried John Paul Raphael when my arms burned and ached the most in their emptiness. He is an incredible comfort to hold; his head fits in the palm of my hand exactly like John Paul Raphael's did. The small heft of his body fills the same pressure points in my arms and on my chest as my baby's did. We even wrap him in Blue Blankie sometimes and spray him with the Italian sandalwood cologne to help us feel closer to John Paul.

I am a little shy about Monkey. If you have not been in my shoes, I imagine this could sound a little crazy. We have several children that think so. But Monkey is a gift to Ralph and me. It brings consolation to hold him. Until his seams started to fray from the added weight inside him, I slept with him every night curled up against my chest in the cozy night-nursing position that is so delicious with a newborn. Monkey fills about .01 percent of the emptiness that John Paul Raphael left in our lives, but when every breath hurts, a bereaved mother will take what she can get.

I first read about the idea of a weighted comfort animal during my forays into the online world of infant loss. Several families shared stories of comfort bears ordered from a company called *Molly Bears* and I watched videos of weeping parents sharing the impact of their personalized bear. The idea of a weighted toy or blanket emerged from research primarily based in autism and other sensory conditions. The weighted blanket or animal provides a calming effect based on deep pressure therapy and is shown to reduce anxiety and increase comfort and security. These are all beneficial to newly bereaved parents. Plus, there is the perfect weight of your beloved baby in your arms. And your body remembers. I knew I would want one. I filed the website away in my brain and we continued along our path, ready to welcome our son in whatever way God allowed.

In those blurry days after John Paul Raphael's funeral, I pulled up the Molly Bears website and started looking. I was very disappointed to learn it took months and months to receive a personalized bear, but I also realized I didn't really want a bear. I needed a monkey. I was grateful to have a meaningful distraction in those early days, and Ralph and I began to figure out how to make our own weighted stuffed monkey. I started by looking at site after site of stuffed monkeys. I figured this would be the easy part. I ordered a brown monkey that said it measured fifteen inches, thinking this would do. Next, I watched several YouTube videos on how to make your own weighted animal, including what kind of pellets work best for filling and how to open and close up the seams. Ralph and I shopped for four pounds of plastic beads and a seam ripper while we waited for the monkey to be delivered.

After the first monkey arrived, I compared his small size to the four bags of pellets. Hmm. Turns out "fifteen inches" was from top of the head to tip of the tail, and I doubted this would work, but we gave it our best try. We headed to our local grocery store to begin our operation, needing to make use of the large digital produce scale for an accurate measurement. We sat at a table in the coffee shop and I only cried a little as we opened the monkey's seams, pulled out most of his stuffing, and crammed him full of heavy beads. Cram as we might, we could only get that monkey to weigh one pound six ounces. My Godmother, an excellent seamstress, was in town that weekend so we headed her way with our monkey so she could close him up. He was adorable and very sweet to hold, but he was definitely not John Paul Raphael. We gave him to Clare and went back to the internet.

I found a company that made luxurious stuffed animals, including monkeys, that came in medium, large, huge, and really big. Not wanting to make the same mistake, I ordered the huge and the really big, hoping one of them would work. We restocked our pellet supply and waited for Amazon. When the packages arrived, we enjoyed a good laugh! The "huge" monkey was about the size of a small bulldog and the "really big" monkey was half the size of Nathan, our thirteen-year-old! Take three. We returned them both and bought the "large." It was perfect. We headed back to the store with our supplies and started over with the seam ripper. We pulled out as much fluff as we could and used a small cup as a funnel to fill the monkey with beads. However, even stuffed as full as we could make him, he still only weighed three pounds. I was starting to lose heart.

Keep in mind that everything about this was emotional, nothing about it was rational, and I was at a popular local grocery store. In my magical thinking of grief, I did not think I could possibly survive without this monkey being perfect. Ralph came to the rescue and suggested a trip to the sporting goods store. While I stayed in the car holding the full-to-overflowing-not-yet-sewn-up monkey, he went in to hunt for a solution. He returned just a few minutes later with the perfect answer—giant metal fishing lures. We headed back to the grocery store and removed enough pellets to make room for six, six-ounce fishing lures. We had to leave Monkey on the produce scale at the end and add beads slowly, but eventually we did it! Success. My so-patient doctor husband fished out his needle and thread and carefully finished the operation. When Monkey was put back together, Ralph gently placed all furry four pounds and one ounce of him into my arms.

Unless you have been on this agonizing journey, there is no way to describe the solace of this moment. Pregnancy is meant to end with a baby in your arms. It was twenty-nine days after I gave birth, twenty-eight days since John Paul died, and twenty-three days since I last held him. My squishy tummy and leaking breasts announced that I was a postpartum mother. Every hormone and instinct drove me to want to hold my baby. The need was primitive and primal. In the absence of that baby, in the giant vacancy left by John Paul Raphael's death, I was profoundly disoriented, as if the very planet had tilted off its axis. I thought, in that micro-moment before Monkey rested in my arms, of my joy in returning to the funeral home four days after John Paul Raphael's death. My Christmas-morning excitement was fueled by an instinctive, desperate yearning for my arms to be filled with my baby. Desperation in a bereaved mother resembles insanity, and I feel bound to any mother who has convinced herself she can be reunited with her lost child.

With Monkey snug against my chest, I cried and cried. For the briefest of mystical moments, I could pretend, I could *will* myself to believe that all was right with the world again. For one minuscule breath, we could be whole, John Paul Raphael and I. Later at home, we dressed him in the nightgown that John Paul Raphael wore and put Monkey on our bed. He stayed there for months and months until he began to leak beads and was moved to the chair by my nightstand. Frequently, I tuck him on my lap. When I am sad and longing, I hug him to my chest. Each night as I sleep, I still pull him and Blue Blankie to my heart. I didn't need him as urgently after the first year, but Monkey was a salve to my broken heart when it was most needed. When my father visited some weeks after Monkey arrived, I explained it all to him and brought Monkey down to share. I can still see the look on my dad's face when he picked monkey up. He could feel John Paul, I could just tell. He could hold his littlest grandson again in that brown furry body. I saw the way he closed his eyes and held his breath, remembering. A sacred longing flashed across his face. It was not at all enough, but it would have to do.

The house was extra quiet that fall with our three middle children off at college and only the younger three at home. I took advantage of the extra time to myself and indulged in a three-hour lunch with my dear friend, Erin, who also was grieving the loss of her son. This was a balm to my soul. Grief is so often either uncomfortable for others or ignored. It is something I feel I have to hide. It was a gift of peace to sit with my friend and know she knows. I didn't have to say anything, and she knew.

We had not spent much time together since her son died, and I was profoundly touched to see her at John Paul Raphael's funeral. Both then and during our lunch meeting, I sensed her profound transformation. It was not just the loss of her son, but of her carefree spirit, the loss of naiveté or invincibility or the illusion of safety. I recognized this change because I knew it in my very own soul. Could others see it in me too? Was there a shadow of sorrow in my eyes or a stillness like the depths of the ocean?

From the outside, I think I seemed fairly normal. I got up and got dressed and went to Mass. I exercised and cleaned my house and saw friends over lunch. The inner me was very different, however. I needed more time and quiet space to live my life. For every hour

I was "out and about," I needed another hour of calm to give my sadness the attention it demanded. To feel whatever my mind and body needed to feel that day. My friend reaffirmed this critical component of grief, especially after the brutality of the first months subsided. I needed to listen to my body and accept what came next, whether it was silence in my head and heart or numb stillness or tears that erupted and opened the cavern of grief, the waves still so powerful they knocked me down.

I understood intuitively that returning to who or how I was before was no longer an option. I tried to let go and learn to recognize the new me. Broken. Always in two pieces and two places. The whole world felt cosmically changed, even though no one else seemed to notice. I went through the motions of normalcy, but I was always carrying the secret that the world was radically different. At any moment the floor might open beneath me and transport me to my other self in another place where grief and love live together and where I feel closest to my baby and closest to God.

If I am being honest, I would choose to stay in this other place if I could, not because I don't want to live, but because this other life, my other reality, feels more real to me than the regular world most of the time. In fact, it is this place—the place in our souls of deep intensity and connection, joy, faith, communion, and suffering—that is the place of sacred, whole-hearted, holy living. I want to always be there. I just don't know how to be there and in the rest of my life at the same time.

Sometimes I miss her, my former self that didn't know about living in two different realities. Missing her feels like a betrayal of the treasures I have mined in this sorrow, though. Sure, that woman didn't carry this pain, but she also didn't hold a new understanding of life and death and have a deeper intimacy with the Lord. She was always trying so hard to prove herself, so afraid still of loss and failure. She didn't have the freedom of falling into her worst nightmare and being held aloft on the other side. I know I am right where I need to be, but when I feel worn out from the burden of love, it is tempting to want to go back to some selfish, safe, narrow version of my life. But John Paul Raphael doesn't exist there. He is only here with the joy and pain together. So I accept my new perspective, even though it means sometimes feeling disconnected with my day-to-day life. I know that to love the Lord and my son with my whole heart means the comforts of this world, however lovely, will never truly satisfy.

I had come a long way eight months after John Paul died. I felt like I was putting together a familiar jigsaw puzzle that had fallen apart. The large pile of pieces was daunting, but I knew what the puzzle looked like. I felt relief completing the edges, defining the shape of my heart again. I functioned at this stage for many months—looking "all together" on the outside and slowly doing the work of putting piece after piece together on the inside. I was surprised, however, to discover that many of my puzzle pieces were brand new. New shapes, new sizes, smaller or bigger than they were before. They were more complex and had more intricate points of connection. I thought I was doing so well, but now I understand that if my heart was once a hundred pieces, it was now 1,000 and I was nowhere close to fitting them all together.

I struggled that fall as the seasons changed again. I had experienced this change of seasons as a grieving mother twice before—winter to spring, spring to summer, but this felt different. John Paul Raphael had been gone nine months. The weight of grief had not lightened and was now settling in and pressing down. My body squirmed—shifting, softening, and strengthening to make space to hold the weight of it within me. I forced myself to go through the seasonal motions and put out the pumpkins and the leaf garland. The pages of the calendar turned and the seasons changed, but my season of grief stayed put. The weather ebbed and flowed, but the weight of grief remained. Like the forever love I carry for my son, love is a forever season.

The weight of grief can still make me stumble, but the length of grief leaves me breathless. Decades of grief stretched ahead of my husband and me. There was no way to put it down. No way to get a break from it. The grief was just there, a forever season that reminds me of a movie my children loved, "Elmo's Christmas." Elmo wished for it to be Christmas every day. But boy, that Christmas tree and garland didn't look so fresh after thirty-eight weeks. Still, the crazy truth was that I didn't want to escape my grief. Not really. I knew grief was just love without the beloved. The transitive verb without the direct object. And never would I ever go back to a life where John Paul Raphael himself had not existed. But I was so, so tired inside.

My grief was challenged not just by the passing of time but also by the arrival of a season of joy when two of our daughters got engaged. This presented another new hurdle: the desire to be present and live joy and excitement with them while still hunched with the weight of sorrow. The snaky whispers of shame swirled around me. *Really? You are STILL so sad? It's been eight months or nine months or ten months? You aren't OVER this yet? Why are you being so dramatic about it all?* No one said this of course, but in my moments of weakness and emotional fatigue, I sometimes accused myself. When I did, I wrapped my arms around my heart and reminded myself of truths that grew from self-compassion. I gave myself permission to just be in this season. To still be sad. To still need so much space and breath to grieve. To be a season of joy on Sunday and to spend Monday crying in bed. To feel excited to lead my Bible study and to go to the gym every day and yet stare blankly in the grocery store or weep because it was 2:43 p.m. on a Friday. It didn't have to make sense. It was all one big messy season, and I didn't know when it was going to change. Death and life so beautifully close.

Blankie was still my comfort, the soft blue plush blanket that held John Paul Raphael every moment of his life. It was my companion as I slept and went to Mass or to stores or lunch with friends. I judged myself for this sometimes. The bossy part of me that still cared what other people thought hissed: *How long are you really going to carry that around?* But I shushed her and held Blankie tighter. This too was a season—needing the physical comfort of this blanket in my arms. The smell of sandalwood sprayed freshly on to the soft blue cloth every few days. Something to hold and carry when I could not have him for whom my heart longed.

At the dentist one day, I put Blue Blankie comfortably across my lap. The hygienist commented on it right away.

"Did you bring your blanket?" she chuckled in her Caribbean accent. "Are you cold?"

"We lost a baby in January," I replied quietly. "It helps me to carry it around."

"I'm so sorry," she said, and I expected that to be it. It tends to be a conversation stopper. I refuse to feel bad for sharing my uncomfortable truth, but mostly, people don't know what to say next.

After she finished getting my tray prepped, she paused and said, "Do you want to tell me about your loss?"

Oh, my heart. Those nine words were a priceless gift to an invisible, grieving mother. They floated in the air and landed gracefully on my tender, vulnerable spirit. *You see me,* I thought. *You recognize and hear that something is not right with me. You have wisdom to suspect I may carry a giant, invisible wound and you don't want to make it worse by not acknowledging its presence. You are not afraid of me or my baby. You are brave enough to ask.*

I treasured this.

You see, this child that is not here anymore, this baby I cannot hold? He is still alive to me. Alive in how I think of him all the time, long for him with every breath, ache for him in all I do. He is gone with brutal finality and yet not gone at all. He is present to me in the massive baby-shaped hole that was blown out of the center of me. In the early days of grief, the enormity of that emptiness overwhelmed me. It covered every part of who I was and how I felt and what I could do or where I could go and if I could speak. It altered my identity so that I felt like an imposter most of the time. I wanted to announce to the world, "If I walk into the gym or the school office, I might appear to be the person you know and remember, but *I am really NOT*."

I was awkward and uncomfortable once it was no longer possible to hide in the safety of my home. My day-to-day responsibilities required that I return to the land of the living in some way, shape, or form. I felt naked and exposed. As much as I longed to be asked how I was doing, I was still scared of sharing my emotions with others. Would I be able to talk about my baby and still breathe? I expected the weight of my grief and the cavern of my barren arms to repel people around me, for them to step away and hide their eyes.

My experience was very different. People didn't see. They didn't notice. They didn't ask. And it wasn't that I wanted attention, but I felt so profoundly abnormal that it was hard to understand why people *weren't* staring at me, why there weren't children whispering innocent questions to their mothers and pointing shy fingers at my strangeness. With the exception of my few dearest friends, there were no questions and no reason to talk about John Paul Raphael at all. The silence burned me, and I felt invisible everywhere I went. In order to function, I worked hard every day to appear normal and do the normal things required of me. The cavern of emptiness and the giant monster of grief I carried everywhere were ever-present, but somehow so imperceptible to others that I must have been a master of illusion.

In a moment of clarity, I finally understood the custom of dressing in black and an official "period of mourning." When you walk around wearing black mourning garments, you are not invisible. Your clothing announces to all those around you: *Please treat me with care. I am not okay. I am not currently the person I was and I may never be again.* Mourning attire would give me permission to skip social events or avoid idle chatter in the checkout line. It would explain why I might be standing immobile by my car, staring into space. It would remind you why I have not answered your text, called you back, or signed up to bake cupcakes. I would actually love a mourning veil to cover my tears and my red, swollen eyes.

As the months passed, my fragile grief brain was tested over and over. Sometimes, I had time to warn Ralph that a breakdown was coming. There were often too many challenges and changes for my tender heart to just roll with it all gracefully. At Clare's back-to-school night, I delivered an all-star performance playing the Perfectly Normal Mother and then dissolved into tears in Ralph's arms upon returning home. Big, ugly, grieving-mother sobs poured out of me for an hour. Grief still comes out of the blue like this, startling us both. It was now possible to carry out most normal events in my life, but not without a challenge to my system. I was still learning how to carry a gaping hole in my heart and needed practice to live my life in all its joyful, painful complexity.

Only those who have "been there" really understand the secret truth about grief: Most people want to talk about it. I longed to talk about my baby. I longed to hear his name and say his name. Grief is a ravenous beast and was only satisfied when I brought John Paul Raphael to life in my mind and heart. I realized as the weeks ticked painfully by that I didn't get to talk about him because no one asked. Out of respect or ignorance or fear of upsetting me, I didn't know. I understood and was not angry; I am not sure I would have known what to say or do either. But the longing to bring John Paul Raphael to life and to know he lives not only in my heart and in the heart of my husband was so deep.

Being a bereaved mother is all about unfulfilled longings. One of the easiest ways to bring a tiny bit of relief is to speak our child's name. Write his name. Text his name. Make a pretty marker drawing out of his name. You don't have to worry about upsetting me or making me cry. I am going to be upset and cry whether we talk about my baby or not. If you bring up my loss and ask how I am feeling or just say you are thinking of my child and say his name—please know you are helping me. It is a relief and a gift. It brings me comfort to tell you about my loss.

Sometimes, even now, before we fall asleep at night, lying face to face in our bed, either Ralph or I will say, "Tell me about our baby." We follow a ritual of speaking his life to each other. *His name was John Paul Raphael. He was born at 10:33 a.m. on January 4, 2018, and weighed four pounds and one ounce. He was eighteen inches long. He lived for 1,690 minutes. He had the softest skin and a cry like a little bird . . .* Warmth spreads through me as we bring him to life in the love we share. We proclaim, if only to each other, that he was real and his life mattered.

12

UNCERTAINTY AND UGLINESS

Sometimes we need to be wild and fierce.
God is big enough to handle our rage.

"There is a sacredness in tears. They are not the mark of weakness,
but of power. They speak more eloquently than ten thousand
tongues. They are the messengers of overwhelming grief,
of deep contrition, and of unspeakable love."
—Washington Irving

FOR MOST OF US, uncertainty is unwelcome. As humans, we have a need to strategize to maximize security and minimize danger. There is peace and comfort in the ability to predict and prepare for future outcomes. But the perception of control is a house built upon sand. Even as a woman of faith, I sometimes pray for my needs while still secretly believing my good deeds—or my lack of bad deeds—will influence the outcome. I shamelessly, if subconsciously, bargain with God: If I try to do the right things, He will surely bless me. I remind God that I have already suffered enough. Yet the truth is that in these moments I am bowing to the idol of self-reliance and the myth that I can control the outcome of my life.

Many people live a long time before this veil of illusion disappears, and they confront the truth that we are mostly powerless. Yes, we can do some things to shift the odds or to lower our chances of certain hardships, but much we can never see coming. The cancer diagnosis. The unfaithful husband. The freak accident. The job loss. The unwelcome prenatal diagnosis. When life as we know it changes, we are plunged into the unwelcome territory of uncertainty and suffering.

"What's going to happen?" *I don't know.*

"What can I do?" *Nothing.*

"How can I fix this?" *You can't.*

"How will this end?" *We just have to wait and see.*

Powerlessness is a painful place. From the moment we received John Paul Raphael's possible diagnosis, we entered this land of uncertainty. We loved our baby with all our being but had NO ability to control the outcome of his life. We chose not to confirm his possible diagnosis through amniocentesis, not just because it risked his security in the womb, but also because it wouldn't answer the real questions that burned in my heart. Would it tell us if he had Trisomy 18 for sure? Yes. But it couldn't answer the questions that really mattered: *Will my baby be born alive? How long will he live? How will it feel to have him die in my arms? How will we ever go on?* These deep questions filled the space under my need to know for sure. Only time could answer them, and we were forced to live in a raw, unprotected reality where my worst fears might come true.

We also felt powerless as we accompanied our daughter through her battles with mental illness during the same twelve months we carried and mourned John Paul Raphael. Our daughter struggled with self-harm and anxiety attacks that left her hospitalized multiple times. In many ways, that year felt like a struggle to keep John Paul Raphael *and* our daughter alive. Teenage suicide is a devastating, shocking outcome to the deep inner pain in a child. We worked tirelessly to get her every bit of help available, but at the end of it all, I had to learn a harsh truth: I could not keep my daughter alive. No amount of hard work, striving, or monitoring on my part could keep her from finding a way to end her life if she chose to. All I could do was love her, sacrifice for her, keep showing up for her, and pray it was enough. The uncertainty was brutal.

Intense pain surrounded me day in and day out. It often left me breathless and panicked, unable to get out of bed and grasping for solutions or a way to escape. As Ralph and I surrendered to God's plan and abandoned ourselves to this journey (I mean, really, what other choice did we have?) we begged the Lord for hope, comfort, faith, and trust. And He showed up. His presence, His hope, His love carried us in His arms when there was no other way to get through the day. I see now this was the beginning of my calling as a new vision and a new way of living took shape within me.

There is a vibrant intensity to my faith when I am at my most desperate and broken. When all the shields are down and I can no longer pretend that I can change or fix a situation, I am like a little child. *Let the little children come to me*, the Lord tells us.[12] When I remove my own agenda (my noisy, insistent plans that cannot possibly change, my fears for what may or may not happen to me or to my family) and come to the end of myself and my very best efforts, I can be found. When I surrender and expose my heart to the Lord, His grace pours in. I am filled to overflowing by this total abandonment to Divine Providence, and I am transformed.

I found true freedom when my own worst fears came true and I survived. And not just survived, but increased somehow. I became something more than I was before.

Journeying with the suffering is often a challenge for others. There is a societal tendency to blame the sufferer, not out of malice or ignorance, but out of a primal need to convince ourselves that this

---

12   Matthew 19:14

tragedy couldn't happen to us. There can also be an effort to "tidy up," to minimize or limit the suffering others are going through.

While I would never wish sufferings on anyone, I am so grateful for the imprint of His heart that the Lord leaves on us in our pain. We are not alone. We are held in and through our suffering. I am completely His beloved daughter. This is brutal and beautiful surrender. If we learn to run into uncertainty, and not from it, our greatest fears can lead to freedom. As I learned to stop thrashing and fighting when life did not turn out as I thought it would, I became a better version of myself: kinder, softer, more loving, compassionate, and gentle. More understanding and available to other people in their pain. More generous in praying for and serving others.

I was learning to let myself be loved.

This was not a graceful process. From the moment we received John Paul Raphael's diagnosis and understood the limitations of our son's condition, I became reacquainted with grief. Grief forced itself into our world and prepared to stay. I knew grief already. You don't get to be forty-five years old in this broken world without any grief. Grief from my parents' divorce. Grief from my own divorce. Grief at the pain in my children's lives. Grief over my miscarriage. Grief over a child's mental health struggles. Grief from the loss of grandparents, a nephew, a cousin. Grief that several important relationships were not what I longed for them to be. Grief from the loss of expectations I had for my own life.

But grief from the loss of my child? I never wanted to know this kind of grief.

Grief was on the list of things I worried about during my pregnancy. My child was going to die. I didn't know exactly when, but we had every reason to expect it in minutes, hours, or days after his birth. Months if we were lucky. I loved my baby so much already. My love grew along with his tiny body until it filled my whole being just as he filled my womb. When that love exploded into the world on January 4, 2018, it hung thickly in the air like clouds, drenching us with its purity and holiness—no longer just my love, but Love Himself was with us through our son in the freshness of his life and the expectation of his death. The cost of this love was grief.

For every measure of love I had for my son, there was an equal measure of grief coming after his death. I am learning this painful and liberating truth on my journey. Grief and love are indivisible in their very nature. There is no grief without love. The greater the love, the greater the grief. As long as I love my son and we are separate, there will be grief.

Because I feared grief so much, I researched everything I could about it during my pregnancy. I read memoirs on child loss. I searched out blogs of families with sick babies who were going to die. I spent hours reading about children with Trisomy 18 to glean whatever wisdom or coping skills I could from their experience. Without realizing it, I pre-managed my grief. I convinced myself that learning about loss would take away its power.

Ralph and I didn't always see eye-to-eye on this. I tried to explain it by comparing my research to the trip we took to Italy during my pregnancy. Foreign travel can be daunting. In order to fully embrace Italy when we were there, I needed to be prepared. I made reservations, researched the sights, and scheduled some tours. I scoped out good restaurants and read guide books. My preparation gave me much to look forward to and helped me relax once I arrived. If I could learn about the details ahead of time, then later, I could just enjoy the moment.

Trisomy 18 was also a foreign country. If I could research the experience of losing my baby, it would help me live those moments well when the time came. And you know what? I was right. Mostly.

When John Paul Raphael died, grief hit me like a tidal wave. Life changed instantly and brutally. As the months passed, we survived, and I naively thought I had grief figured out. I knew the ins and outs of navigating this agonizing road, and we were getting through it. Then, ten months after John Paul's death, my dear cousin Martha delivered her first child. After a weekend meeting and holding her newborn daughter, Celia, I began to disintegrate. The foggy depression I had been living with grew a razor-sharp edge. I felt prickly and brittle. I was snippy, irritated, and angry most of the time. I would soon realize I had not, in fact, learned all about grief.

These feelings came to a head one evening when my husband shared a clueless text he received from a female coworker who had recently delivered a little boy after experiencing life-threatening complications. She texted Ralph to thank him for his support during her pregnancy and ended with the line: *"It must have been your prayers that saved my baby."*

Instantly, I named the emotion that had lurked inside me for weeks: Rage. That rage now had a target. There is no way to sugarcoat the firestorm of emotion that roared through me. Angry, violent thoughts and ugly words filled me. *"I want to kick that woman in the face,"* I thought savagely. I was shocked at this vicious and brutal reaction, but it was true. I ranted and screamed. How dare she suggest that my husband's prayers saved her baby! Don't you think if his prayers were going to save a baby *they would have saved ours*? I was a madwoman.

It didn't take long for a still small voice in me to recognize my rage was not truly directed at this new, grateful mother. This is one reason it took so long for rage to show itself. Rage, like anger, seeks a target. Shooting an arrow into the air is nowhere near as satisfying as launching it fiercely into *something*. When John Paul Raphael died, though, I had no bullseye. I wasn't angry at God or the doctors or the hospital or Ralph or myself or even John Paul. There was no one at fault, no blame to place. Yet, the rage still arrived, barreling through me in violent spasms. For weeks I raged as the ugly grief inside me forced itself out and incited a rebellion against the unacceptable truth that my son was dead. I wanted to act as unreasonably and irrationally as that reality felt.

In one frenzied moment, I grabbed a Costco-sized box of cornbread mix and hurled it to the ground in my kitchen, desperate to find relief. Its unsatisfying THUD heightened my craziness. I grabbed the next thing I could find, a two-cup Pyrex measuring cup, and hurled it on to the hardwood floor. The sound of its crash and the explosion of thousands of tiny pieces of glass were EXACTLY what I needed. YES. It absolutely matched the chaos inside my heart.

I began to create a "Smash Pile." I gathered any chipped or unwanted breakable items and piled them on the bench in my kitchen to await the next round of rage. When it slammed into me, I grabbed a pile of dishes and stalked through the snow and ice on the back patio to the cement steps coming up from the basement walkout. Like a crazy woman, I hurled piece after piece into the stairwell, relishing how they broke into shards and fragments. The strong motion and intensity of using the muscles in my arm with force was perfect, the effort and the release satisfying. The cold air in my lungs made me feel alive. The sound and sights of the destruction comforted and calmed me.

On another day, I felt flooded with emotion after a conflict at home and found myself quickly incapable of regulating my feelings. Rage roared through me. I fled the house and drove to the Potomac River, stalking in twenty-degree temperatures and high winds down to the riverbank, areas of ice crunching beneath my feet. Wild insanity grew within me. I looked at the rushing water and longed to be swept away. Not to end my life, but to end the feelings that engulfed me without hope. I found a huge branch and thought that cracking it against a solid tree trunk would bring me the relief I so desperately craved. I was outrageous as I picked it up and swung with all my might. The actual physics of the equation caused me great pain and my feeble body simply absorbed the force I was hoping would end in the satisfaction of splintered wood. As a last resort, I howled into the wind and water. There were no words, only a guttural, raw, raging lament.

One day my rage fueled an argument with Ralph. I tried to flee the intensity of my heart by hiding out in our basement bedroom. I curled up in the dark under the covers with a pillow over my head, sobbing and wailing. When Ralph came in to try and soothe me, I screamed at him. I raged at him to GO. GET OUT. JUST GO. JUST GOOOOOOO. My wails left me vacant and drained. What I really wanted to scream was *just bring him back*. When I was empty, Ralph was beautiful and gentle and gathered me into his arms as I cried.

I barely recognized myself during this time. There was no rational explanation as to why I would rage at a particular moment, but I felt confident that many people found rage to be a part of the grieving process. I believe I needed to fully experience rage in order to move through my grief in a healthy way. But why now? Why was I so angry ten months after John Paul died?

After working with my therapist, I learned that in my longing to trust God during our journey with John Paul Raphael, I minimized the human reality of what we were facing. In trying to be prepared for what John Paul Raphael's death might be like, I managed to normalize the unthinkable. In order to cope with the unimaginable scenario that he would die in our arms, I over-imagined it in order to feel a sense of control. When the time came, I *was* prepared. I *was* able to savor the hours we had with him without fear or panic and did not have to worry about making decisions. But I over-prepared to such an extent that the agony of what we endured hadn't fully impacted me yet, even ten months later.

Clinically, the rage was my body's attempt to integrate my intense interior emotions with an equally intense exterior experience. Wanting to smash, hit, and break things; the need to curse, yell, and scream; even shocking thoughts of violent actions—these were all part of my body processing a traumatic and horrifying event, an event I apparently had managed to convince myself was not so horrifying.

It took a newborn baby to awaken my heart. As I held my cousin Celia, I replayed John Paul Raphael's death in my mind. He was alive and pink one moment, and green and dying the next. John Paul was loved just as much as Celia. What if she were to just stop breathing here in my aunt's living room? What if she were to turn green and die and we were powerless to save her? I imagined Celia's death over and over. It would be horrifying. Devastating. Traumatic. Life-altering. I knew with complete clarity that to lose Celia like that would rip her parents open with a pain that no person should ever have to endure.

Well, there you go. Without my conscious mind connecting the dots, my heart managed to. If losing Celia was all those things, then so was losing John Paul Raphael. I now understood the rage. It was righteous rage that screamed that losing our son was not fair, and we did not deserve it. It was the rage of love against death that was never meant to be a part of life. It was rage at the enemy of our souls whose insidious lies exiled us in this valley of tears.

Ephesians 4:26 tells us, "Be angry and yet do not sin." I took to heart the words that came from John Paul Raphael: Could I let myself be loved in the raw ugliness of grief? In despair, in the violence and hatred of death, and in the struggle to be hopeful? Even here? I see now that as a woman of faith, I put pressure on myself to "grieve well" when in reality, I just needed to grieve. Giving myself permission to feel rage was essential to my grieving process, but it was also dreadful and humbling. I am grateful that with God's help and my husband's presence, I did not hurt myself or others. Self-compassion keeps me from judging myself for how I processed our devastating loss. In order to heal, I need to be truthful and authentic about the surprising intensity and ugliness of my journey. I know nothing that I felt was a surprise to the Lord or would ever scare Him away.

Let yourself be loved in your own darkness. Give yourself

permission to feel your story deeply in your heart. Don't make it neat and tidy. Sometimes we need to be wild and fierce. I have found that my crazy places are an invitation from God to pay attention to a part of me that needs love, compassion, or comfort. The Lord wants to walk with me there, wherever it leads, even to a pile of shattered dishes and a throat sore and raw.

13

RADICAL ACCEPTANCE

What if the worst thing and the best thing are really the same thing?

"Radical acceptance rests on letting go of the illusion of control and a willingness to notice and accept things as they are right now, without judging."
—Marsha M. Linehan

WE TRAVELED TO SCRANTON for Thanksgiving again that year. My grandparents' home would be sold soon; this could be our last holiday there. It was a bittersweet holiday in and of itself, but there was more for me. I couldn't stop thinking about last year. Still pregnant. Still hopeful. Still with my baby. My heart still in one piece. Thinking about that other version of myself, my heart cried: *I want to go back. I want one more dinner feeling you kicking away in there. I want one more ultrasound to see your sweet belly. I want one more kiss.*

I worried about this for weeks, our first real holiday without John Paul Raphael. What did I need? How would I feel? What would help me find more joy than grief or lighten the weight of sadness just a little bit? I didn't even know. I moved more slowly. I was quieter. I felt brittle and broken, then peaceful and calm. I worked very hard to be present to my feelings and not try to manage them. I returned to the words of a friend that had become a lifeline: *So this is what grief feels like today.* No pressure, no expectation, no judgment on myself. Only radical acceptance of myself and the organic path of grief unfolding in me. I wept when I read her words, knowing they came from a heart that deeply understood the unexpected and unpredictable journey of loss, a path that is dark and confusing to navigate. Her wise words gave me permission to be gentle and kind to myself. To let myself be loved in a season when I didn't know what I needed. *So this is what grief feels like today. So this is what the first Thanksgiving feels like.*

As we gathered for Thanksgiving dinner, some thirty of us, my throat tightened with anxiety. The hum of sadness in my mind intensified. I held Blue Blankie in my lap and looked at the many dear loved ones gathered in the large Victorian dining room, a room where I have loved and eaten and laughed for every one of my forty-seven years. My place at the table this year was the most-hallowed chair vacated by my grandfather when he died. My grandmother sat in her traditional spot to the right. Our six youngest children were there along with my mother, aunts, uncles, and some cousins. How was it possible to hold fullness and emptiness at the same time? My cousin Sarah laid a gorgeous and abundant table, each napkin holder lovingly personalized. "I am grateful for Elizabeth." "I am grateful for Ralph." I felt the painful absence of one tiny napkin holder. *I am grateful for you, John Paul Raphael,* I whispered in my heart.

Before dinner, Ralph stood across the room and called the whole family together in order to say grace. Family grace is a ritual I cherish. My heart leaped because instantly, I knew what I needed. Ralph would offer a blessing and then he would say some beautiful words about family and those we love who were not with us. He would honor the poignant absence of my grandfather Papa, then our baby, and many others we missed for one reason or another; he would speak briefly about our gratitude for the gift of our little boy's life and end by saying, "John Paul Raphael, pray for us!" like we always do. In this small way, I would feel the presence of my son.

Except he didn't. None of it. He read a lovely poem by Robert Louis Stevenson and then said, "God bless the chefs!" I stood frozen as my heart broke and my tears flowed. Devastated and alone, grief surged out of me. Why didn't Ralph mention John Paul? How did he not know I needed to hear John Paul Raphael's name proclaimed? To not have him forgotten? Why didn't he also need this? These laments quickly slid into self-pity. *Why did my son have to die? Am I the only one who even remembers him? Will it ever feel better?*

Ralph saw my tears from across the room and rushed to my side. I knew my feelings would hurt him, but there was no way to hide my disappointment. "I needed you to talk about him," I sobbed. "I needed you to say his name. I am so heart-broken that you didn't even say his name."

I have no doubt that Ralph's heart also broke when I shared my sorrow. I wasn't angry and I didn't blame him, but I still felt so let down. I knew I hadn't shared anything with him that might have helped me at this first holiday. I didn't even know what I needed. But it was a double-heartbreak, both for my son and from my husband.

I remembered radical acceptance. Bereaved parents needed to radically accept the grief that the other is experiencing, or not experiencing. I needed to radically accept that my grief and Ralph's grief might be very different on a given day or for a given season. It was complex to understand that while we were both on a grief journey, it was not possible to always keep pace with each other. That moment during grace was an opportunity for me to radically accept Ralph. I had to give him total grace to feel what he was feeling, while also accepting that I needed something completely different. These were not easy waters to navigate during an emotional holiday season that encompassed the "first-everything-without-our-baby."

After more tears, a few needed hugs from dear family members, and some private prayer, the rawness of my disappointment faded, and I could finally forgive Ralph for just being human and doing the best he could, like the rest of us. Ralph and I talked later, and we understood it would help us to slow down and be more aware of special opportunities to recollect John Paul Raphael. We were still learning so much about love and loss.

I remembered a word I learned many years ago—*eucharisteo*. It is the Greek word for "thanksgiving." Author Ann Voskamp focuses on this word in her book *1000 Gifts: A Dare to Live Life Fully Alive*. She describes *eucharisteo* as not just being thankful for all our beautiful blessings. It is also the hard, brutal thanksgiving that we surrender to with blood, sweat, and tears, a thanksgiving we groan because we accept it is the only way to survive.

1st Thessalonians 5:18 says, "In everything give thanks; for this is the will of God for you in Christ Jesus." In everything. Always. In this moment. Even if it is tragic. Even if I am sad. Because "in everything" can't be later. It has to be now. I preached this to myself over and over. *The Lord is loving me in my sorrow and in my loss. Although it is a mystery, I am more the woman I need to be through this suffering. I trust that in my scars, I look more like Him.*

It is a wild act of faith to give thanks for pain and suffering. *Eucharisteo* changes my perspective. It burns and bleeds, but saying thank you for all of it brings joy to the Lord and opens me to the possibility of joy as well. Without thanksgiving, we shrivel. Our hearts harden and our fists clench. We stubbornly hold on to our own view of life instead of releasing and surrendering ourselves to God's plans. I remember now how much I have to practice this. I have to relearn how to give thanks for all things at all times.

During this first holiday season as a grieving mother, I tried to let these truths fill my heart. Slow me down. One lesson grief taught me is that I was usually moving too fast. I love slowness now. I give myself the gift of time. I try to live with margin in my schedule and to give myself space to breathe. To find God in the present moment. Let Him love me, heal me, and bring me my son in the depths of my heart.

By the time we faced our first Christmas without John Paul Raphael, I had learned in some measure to hold joy and sorrow at the same time. I reflected how the Christmas story began with an invitation from Gabriel to Mary. In faith and trust, she responded "yes" to an invitation she didn't fully understand but that plunged her instantly into the presence of God—total communion and intimacy with Him as He began to form within her. *Emmanuel.* God with us.

I contemplated this mystery again but no longer from a safe, shiny distance. I felt very close to the Christmas story that year with all the hardships and sufferings that go along with saying yes to God. During Advent, I looked deep into the eyes of baby Jesus and heard His invitation. *Will you come close? Will you trust me? Can I be enough for you? Will you let yourself be loved by me?* I said yes again and again, even though during some seasons, like in the Christmas story, a yes can be very painful.

That Christmas, we were blessed to have all nine of our living children home with us, plus two fiancés and a boyfriend. Christmas Eve was a miracle of family joy. Fourteen of us filled the large sectional and the armchairs of the family room and we played games, finished our advent devotions, and enjoyed having the kids exchange their "Sibling Santa" gifts. We put on our Christmas-best and went to eight o'clock Mass at St. Theresa. We set up the piano and the guitars and the microphones and shared our talents with our parish by providing the prelude carols and all the music for the liturgy. Our traditional raucous carol-singing filled the van on the way home as we tried to squeeze in a few more Christmas lights. We took priceless photos of our time together: a mother and a father, their many children, one dog, one cat, and one stuffed monkey wrapped in a soft blue blanket.

The joy of Christmas Eve overflowed into agony Christmas morning. Ralph and I woke early and the tears flowed between us, both clutching Monkey and Blue Blankie. We didn't mean to hide the depths of our sadness from the children, but it was most often in these quiet moments when all the doings were done that we had the space to open our hearts and let the grief come pouring out. On that tender Christmas morning, Ralph wept too as we remembered and shared our longing for our son. The agony was worse that week. Something of the light outside and the Christmas tree and the smells and sounds of the season collided deeply inside me. My emotional muscle memory triggered the rawness of the wound when John Paul Raphael was first ripped away.

When we were ready, noses red and eyes swollen, we dressed and stuffed the stockings we were too tired to fill the night before and headed down to our children and the joy of Christmas morning. We carried our blanket and our broken hearts. There was laughter and love and cinnamon rolls. Plenty of prosecco and gifts and later dominos and beef tenderloin. We received an ornament commemorating John Paul Raphael's first Christmas in heaven and a bracelet reminding us that we will always remember our little boy no longer here. Our Christmas baby, born on the eleventh day of Christmas and gone on the twelfth. For years, our family tradition during the Christmas season was to truly celebrate all twelve days of Christmas by singing before every dinner, one verse of "Joy to the World" and then the "Twelve Days of Christmas," adding one additional verse each day all the way to the eve of Epiphany on January 5. How could we sing it ever again? It felt like a death march. I desperately did not want to get to the Twelve Drummers Drumming. *Can we please just stop at Eleven Pipers Piping?* I was desperate. *Please.*

This is the mystery of Christmas. Christ invites us to draw so close that we feel him both in the joy and in the pain. He wants to show us with love that His journey was joy and pain and if we unite our lives to Him, ours will be too. But He is Emmanuel, God with us in the love and in the sorrow. He endured it all for us and holds us as we too endure. His love is enough. He can be trusted to hold us and carry our love to our son. I fight for this and struggle to live this truth in faith. It is hard to live with gratitude in joy and pain, trusting they are both His love story, but I find my Savior and my son most when I live them both together.

After living through the onset of rage and the holidays, we arrived at John Paul Raphael's first birthday and the anniversary of his death. I had no idea what to expect from myself during these two days. Grief rose to the surface, but there was also unexpected peace. We had already lived through the worst, and the memorial of these days provided an opportunity to honor and remember John Paul more publicly than normally felt appropriate. January 4, 2019 fell on a Friday, and Ralph took the day off from work. We had a calm, quiet day planned. We went to Mass in the morning and then drove to the cemetery with a collection of large birthday balloons and a festive fountain of streamers. We brought Monkey wrapped in Blue Blankie and lay a ground cloth on the grass next to John Paul's grave to be by his side at 10:33 a.m. We prayed and cried and listened to some of his special songs. We went out to lunch at our favorite deli and spent the afternoon together at home. After dinner, we celebrated with the kids by having ice cream cake and singing "Happy Birthday." The children were happy to go along with our remembrance, but otherwise did not seem affected. We were touched to receive flowers from my sister-in-law and a lovely angel wind chime from my Godmother to remember John Paul. We received a few texts from friends.

I had worked hard not to put expectations on anyone. While it is always a balm to my heart for someone to reach out and remember John Paul, I also know that life goes on. I cannot hold resentments or have unreasonable expectations that our memorials will be meaningful to anyone but Ralph and me. As I closed my eyes in bed that night, I was full of thanksgiving for our son and grateful to feel more peace than sadness. We went back to the cemetery on January

5 at 2:43 p.m. I took time that day to put together a slideshow of John Paul's funeral and burial. Re-entering those poignant and painful days with a purpose was healing and restorative. I shared it on social media and emailed it to our family, glad to have something "new" to share. Then it was January 6 and we had done it. We had survived the first year.

Like I knew they would, the days continued. The months passed. From conversations with other broken mothers I knew or articles I read online, I expected the second year of grief to be worse. *How could that be*, I kept wondering, *when I feel like I barely survived the first year?*

I soon understood. The first year of grief was a forest fire, a raging inferno. It completely absorbed the landscape of my life. It flattened me with its intensity and power. In the second year, I lived in the devastation left by the fire. I navigated a barren landscape. Everything felt dead. Even the scientific knowledge that a forest fire brings regeneration and new life felt hollow. As of yet there was no apparent growth in the charred debris.

The first year of grief was a tidal wave. It crashed in, all momentum and motion. I was swept away and could barely breathe as I surrendered to its churning power. It engulfed me and altered everything about life as I knew it. But, there was activity and there were decisions to make and mourning to do. The months were shrouded in a dismal vibrancy that was tragic but had a progression. The first year was an arc of survival from the day we lost him until the anniversary of that terrible day. And somehow there were words. Words flowed from me bringing purpose and healing and the promise of meaning and significance from the pain.

The second year was brittle and harsh and gray. The tsunami of grief and words that once consumed me dissipated and I was left exiled in a wasteland of depression and anxiety. On some days I was "fine" and could live my life in a way that kept most people from recognizing that I was just going through the motions. I barely visited the cemetery or listened to our special songs or looked at John Paul's photos because it was just too painful. And it didn't change anything. Instead, I sat numbing and flipping and scrolling and eating and stuck. I was mute and could not write. Darkness that was once manageable grew doubly dark. A flat, hopeless depression arrived in year two. It was stillness without peace. I missed the passion of the forest fire and the tsunami. They were destructive, but at least they felt alive. They forced me to react and respond. The depression that settled on me was an endless expanse of emptiness without purpose or promise. The deepest darkness was the discouraging prediction that since my love for my son wouldn't change, the agony of this loss would not either.

I may sound a bit dramatic; I would probably have accused myself of this before it became my life. But I need to be courageous and tell the truth. Grief's impact slammed into me. It had a trajectory that led me to rage. And there, after rage, the place I found myself was full of edgy anxiety on the loud days, bottomless sorrow on the quiet days, and on the worst days, despair.

I think most people in my day-to-day life would find this all a bit surprising. I assure you, I didn't hide deliberately. I value honesty and authenticity in relationships more than most people, but frankly, grief is tiresome and often I was tiresome even to myself. As much as I needed support and understanding, in order to survive, sometimes I needed to pretend to be normal. Many times, my charade worked and I enjoyed hours or days of relief from the wasteland and found peace and contentment, and even joy, in my life and with my family. There was much to be joyful for: two extraordinary weddings for two of our daughters, launching another daughter to a new city and venture, and many other unpredictable and ordinary miracles.

But part of the heaviness of the second year was the growing realization that the weight of loss I carried was not going to go away. I knew it would change. I knew I would change. My depression demanded isolation and this helped me process and accept just how drastically my heart and the landscape of my life were altered. Forever. And to grieve that too.

I understood there was a line between healthy and unhealthy depression and anxiety around grief. I moved across that line regularly, but I was hopeful that being able to finally put words to my darkness would illuminate it enough to keep me on the bright side a little longer each day. I found a rhythm as I integrated grief even more fully into my life. Depression and anxiety invited me to self-compassion and radical acceptance of my own story. I practiced not judging myself for how much I hurt or for how unproductive I was. I knew I was never alone, even in the bleakest moments, and tried to keep hope as the anchor of my soul.

It still surprises me that John Paul Raphael feels as alive to me as the day he was born. I thought maybe his memory would fade like the festive intensity of Ralph's and my wedding reception. I am so grateful I was wrong. I feel him here breathing on my chest. I hope someday that brings me comfort and agony, not just agony. I trust that my baby lives with the Lord and that in ways I cannot see or understand, our love for each other transcends all boundaries and thus lives on; that the magnitude of my grief comes from the enormity of that love; and that with God's grace these charred sufferings will someday birth a new forest within me.

14

THE NEW YOU

We cannot wait until suffering has ceased to try and seek joy.

"The reality is that you will grieve forever. You will not 'get over' the loss of a loved one; you will learn to live with it. You will heal and you will rebuild yourself around the loss you have suffered. You will be whole again but you will never be the same. Nor should you be the same nor would you want to."
—Elisabeth Kübler-Ross, *On Grief and Grieving*

SEVERAL MONTHS AFTER John Paul Raphael's death, Ralph and I re-watched the movie *Arrival* in which the main character receives the gift of seeing the future from a visiting alien species. With this gift comes the knowledge that the child she will have someday is destined to die as a teenager from a rare disease. She has a beautiful response to this dark and painful news: *Despite knowing the journey and where it leads, I embrace it, and I welcome every moment of it.* Her words echo in my head as I think about my own journey with child loss. Yes! I said those same words to myself over and over as we lived without our baby. We embraced the life of our child even knowing the limitations. I would do it all over again just for those 1,690 minutes. I hold this conviction deeply without any doubt. But I challenge myself—why? Why was it worth it? Why is it still worth it? How does this even make sense?

Eight months after John Paul died, Ralph and I were asked to tape an interview with a small news show in Hazleton, Pennsylvania to talk about our baby and the impact of his life and how his story could be an encouragement to those facing a difficult prenatal diagnosis or a crisis pregnancy. I was grateful to have a chance to share John Paul Raphael's story. But what of the pain? How could I tell someone a lifetime of loss and agony was actually worth it?

The interviewer made many pointed comments about how pro-life we were to carry our pregnancy to term, but having John Paul Raphael was never a pro-life issue for me. He was my son. Waiting for his arrival, I already loved him. I grieved hearing the news that he might not be healthy enough to stay with us for a long time. But I never made a choice. The choice was made when I fell in love with my husband. I dreamed of having a baby with Ralph before we even conceived John Paul. I understand that my perspective is shaped by my deep commitment to my Catholic faith, but we never chose John Paul Raphael's life. God chose him for us.

In fact, living through a physically and emotionally difficult pregnancy gave me deep compassion and an understanding for why another mother or father would want to just end it. The months of uncertainty and fear were brutal. Living powerless to the outcome of your child's life is fierce. Waiting for the ax to fall is terrible. I appreciate the temptation for some women to want the agony of the unknown to just be over. I see now how those decisions are made, especially if you don't have a supportive relationship or a faith background to guide you.

Without a support system to encourage and remind you of the

value and purpose of your baby's life or the value and purpose of your own suffering, I understand how many women reach the painful conclusion to terminate their pregnancies. My heart breaks for them and their babies, especially because I do not believe there is any escaping the grief of losing a child.

I am so thankful God prepared me to embrace John Paul Raphael's life. Not just spiritually and morally, but psychologically too. I knew my core values: honesty, faith, and courage. I want to live a whole-hearted life. I want to be all in. To do that, I need to live my values. I need to live honestly, faithfully, and courageously. I don't want to get to the end of my life and have regrets about my integrity and my character and whether I lived my life in line with the values I hold dear. I also understood that I couldn't turn off pain in my life without also turning off my ability to feel joy and happiness. If I wanted to live a whole-hearted life, I had to have the courage to open myself to the suffering in front of me. But in doing so, I also opened myself to the possibility of finding purpose, joy, meaning, and even happiness through that suffering. Or in spite of it. Or maybe even because of it.

That was my foundation when I found out I was pregnant and that John Paul Raphael very likely had Trisomy 18. I wanted to experience my baby's life whole-heartedly, courageously, and faithfully. He was God's baby and our baby. He was God's story and our story. He was a gift to us and I did not want to get in the way of that. That meant I had to open myself to the possibility of pain. But because I did that, I also opened myself to joy, hope, purpose, and meaning. And love. *Oh, the love.*

I know there are many women who are currently or will be in the position of receiving terrible news about their baby. It is on my heart to share my deep conviction that *your baby will be enough to make the pain worth it.* It may be impossible to imagine right now. The obstacles or fears or challenges of your pregnancy may seem enormous, insurmountable even. There may be no hope of a happy ending and only the promise of great hardship and suffering.

You may not be able to imagine how to change your life in order to welcome this baby. It may not seem possible or worth it to put your body through what it needs to go through in order to grow this child and allow his or her life to unfold in its natural way.

I know from holding my own perfectly imperfect son in my arms, though, that these littlest babies are pure love. They come dewy from Heaven and they offer themselves to us as a gift of pure innocence and love, trusting they will be loved and cared for in their helplessness. And I am sure they love us too, not just because they need us as mothers to give them the gift of life, but because we are their parents. Their love comes to us in a wordless, intangible way, but it is powerful. If we are open to it, there is a transformation that occurs in this exchange of love. If we give all of ourselves and all of our hearts to our babies, our babies are enough. Whether they are born still or you get to number your time on Earth with them in minutes, months, or years, our babies and the love they bring and the love they inspire in us are enough to make it worth it.

Loving and grieving John Paul Raphael transforms me and expands me when I open my heart to his life and lean in to the lessons from his loss. Yes, there is pain. There is suffering. These are heavy and not to be underestimated, but they are less than the joy and the love, and my hope to be reunited with him some day. And I am more. I am more of the woman I am meant to be when I open myself to the love and the lessons that come from the life and death of my child. I am kinder, more compassionate, and more empathetic. I am gentler and more understanding. I am more willing to love others because I no longer take time for granted. And yes, I cry more too, but because my heart has stretched to hold this pain, it can swell and magnify the love and the joy. I am learning to surrender to the unknown and the uncontrollable and to find peace and freedom, despite my external circumstances.

The reality is that when we enter into parenthood, there are no guarantees. We can't help having hopes and dreams for our child.

Some of us know before birth that our particular story is going to be different than we expected. Some of us can go five, ten, or twenty years before the path we imagined for our child is altered. It is always a risk to love our children, but the return is worth it.

Grief is a tricky companion. Sometimes now, months and years later, my emptiness and loss are as great as those first few hours and days, and I long for someone to take care of me again. To give myself permission to announce that today, it is simply too much to carry. I cannot do it. I need help. I need to get back in my bed and have someone hold me and stroke my hair and say, "I am so sorry that it hurts so badly," and then bring me soup and let me play sad music. Once I am strong enough to carry my grief down the stairs and out the front door, once I shower and put on real clothes and begin to re-enter the world, there is an assumption that I should be strong forevermore. That I am not allowed to have another day when I Just. Can't. Do. It.

I am blessed to have a dear husband who has been patient and steadfast during our journey. He has missed work to care for me or has come home again and again when I needed him. I am lucky to have friends that are understanding and patient as I continue this rough ride. I have a few dear family members that give me time, space, and acceptance as I learn to keep living.

I remember sitting with a beautiful couple I have known for years. They lost their sixth child to Trisomy 18 almost thirty years ago. They came over in those first blurry weeks of loss and sat with us on our couch and let us cry as we shared our story, and they cried as they told us about Mark Francis and his brief, beautiful life. They were blessed with almost six weeks with their baby before he surprised them with a final breath and left them in their own devastating loss. The husband said of their dark and terrible grief: "We had to figure out how to live through this. To live with it. We had to realize this might not be the worst thing that ever happened to us." Now they have buried a second son—gone at forty-nine from colon cancer, leaving a wife and two beautiful children. What a brutal, honest lesson from that father's suffering: *This pain may not be the worst thing that ever happens to me.* My heart breaks for them because, of course, burying a second child is far worse than burying just one.

Those words wash over me, those words of a father that still cried over his lost baby thirty years later: *This may not be the worst thing that ever happens to me.* Is John Paul's death the worst thing that ever happened to me? *Of course it is,* I think quickly, but it is an immediate conundrum. John Paul Raphael was beauty and love. He was a gift and left a profound legacy. How could this be the worst thing that ever happened to me?

A dear grieving friend shared her wisdom: *"It's all so hard. But I am so grateful for the truths that I now know. Which also makes me mad for being grateful because somewhere it makes me think, wait, does that make me grateful my son died? It's a bit of a mind-bender, but I hold something deep inside that sets me apart from other people (or maybe I should say from my former self) and it's not just grief or profound loss. It's something that warms my soul and sustains me when I channel it. I pray that you come to know that feeling too someday."*

I feel it. I feel the profoundly purposeful gift of life and death, love and suffering. It expands my heart, and I hope, in some way, helps the light of Christ and the love of God to shine more brightly in and through me.

I remember when I used to think my house had to be perfectly clean in order to invite friends over. And with five small children, it never was, so I never did. Eventually, I learned to get over it and just let people into my mess. I try to apply the same philosophy to my truest self: Do I think I have to be healed and "together" or to have things figured out? Am I supposed to not be needy or have problems in order to invite people into my heart?

The world needs us to be our true selves now. Our families and communities need us to live authentically, honestly, and bravely now. We need to step forward every day with who and how we are—to present ourselves to our loved ones with the gifts of our imperfections, struggles, and losses. If we show up authentic, real, and messy, we give others the permission to do the same. The Lord longs for us. He doesn't want us to think we have to change or fix or perfect ourselves before we approach Him. He loves us most when we are at the end of ourselves. When I realize I do not have it going on and I have a desperate need to be rescued from pain or loss or my very self, He is there. Broken, messy hearts and lives are His specialty.

This kind of radical self-acceptance is part of my journey to let myself be loved. You and I, we are a gift to the world just as we are right now. Our thoughts, our dreams, our talents, our prayers. Our wounds and whatever great mess there is in our lives, our hearts, or our families. Whether we feel like things are falling apart or coming together, God has a purpose and plan for this season. Maybe it is wisdom, or maybe it is just the reality of time marching on, but I'm not willing to wait any more to be "okay" or "enough." Surviving the loss of my son lit a fire inside me, a renewed conviction that with God's grace, I can rest in who and how I am right now. I can hope this mess will change and heal. Maybe this mess is the new normal. Either way, when we rest in the truth that we are loved by the God of the Universe, we can have the courage to be our true self in the world. At the end of it all, I am His and that is enough. I am so thankful for His grace and the gift of my baby to lead me to learn to love myself.

I remember the early days of grief when I read the words from Matthew 11: "Come to me all who are weary and burdened, and I will give you rest. Take my yoke upon you and learn from Me for my yoke is easy and my burden light."[13] My heart rebelled fiercely. Your yoke is easy and your burden is light? Losing my baby is not light. This yoke of death is not easy.

And yet, I am still called to pursue joy. To pursue love. To pursue

---

13   Matthew 11:28-30

peace. To have hope. This is the legacy of Jesus, his gift to us through the Holy Spirit. He tells us in the Gospel of John that he wants our joy to be full and complete. Psalm 16 says that "in His presence is fullness of joy." Psalm 89 says that, "In your name, they rejoice all the day." Philippians 4 gives us a double dose: "Rejoice in the Lord, always; again I will say, rejoice!" Joy seems not just a feeling to be sought after but a command we are given. How, I wondered, was this even possible in the valley of tears with all this grief and the hardships of life and the losses and disappointments we face? It was too hard. I was still stuck in some other passages. Psalm 42 says, "My tears have been my food day and night." Psalm 6 reads: "I am weary with my sighing . . . my eye has wasted away with grief." How was I expected to find joy?

I go back to those two perfect days, January 4 and 5. What was my focus? What did I do? I surrendered to God's plan. I invited Him into the experience. I let myself be loved by Him while we held our baby. I trusted that I was not alone. I had hope and total confidence that my whole journey was with God and towards God. And perhaps most striking for me, I was completely in the present moment. I wasn't lingering in past hurts and fears. I wasn't racing ahead to what pain and suffering lurked around the next corner. I was right there, right then with God and with whatever He had in store for that very moment, that very day.

Is that part of the secret? To give ourselves the gift of freedom found only in the present moment? To stop dwelling on past hurts and disappointments or quaking in the face of an unknowable future? To just let ourselves be loved right now?

Part of what I am learning through John Paul Raphael is the enigma of both/and. It is the mystery of living both Good Friday and Easter Sunday at the same time. It is being grateful for the bloody sacrifice of the Crucifixion because of the beauty of the Resurrection, while accepting there is no resurrection without death. It is living the perfect joy of John Paul Raphael in my arms while still knowing the next breath could be his last. It is laughing at a hilarious movie and feeling the silent stab that my baby will always be dead. It is loving my family with all my heart, but with open hands now, knowing there are no guarantees. I can be both suffering and joyful. In fact, I am called, however hard it may be, to be joyful IN my suffering and because of it. We cannot wait until suffering has ceased to try and seek joy.

However challenging that proposition may sound, it has actually been a great comfort to me. As a wife in a second marriage, the painful impact of divorce in my life and in my children's lives cannot be changed. As a bereaved mother, although my grief has changed over time, the loss of missing my child will always be with me. If I had to eradicate all that pain in order to ever be joyful again? Impossible.

These are great mysteries. I barely feel qualified to speak of them at all, except that they are part of my story. I did find joy again in my marriage to Ralph. I am feeling joy at times after John Paul Raphael's death. In fact, I have been so stretched and changed by these experiences of suffering that joy, when it comes, is even greater.

At first, this joy was discolored by guilt: *How can I possibly be feeling joyful today? How can I be happy? Why am I peaceful? Did I not love my baby enough? Am I not mourning enough?* I even worried that my grief was "done" and wouldn't come back. That terrified me because the pain was the place I felt closest to John Paul Raphael. I need not have worried. The sorrow is never gone for very long, but now lightness and peace flow in too. A new pattern emerged: In my deep sorrow I cling to God. This leads me to rejoice in His presence. I hurt. I run to Him. He is close. He brings joy. Repeat. I harvest the wisdom that lies hidden here: I can be thankful for the pain because it leads me to the Lord.

How does this work with our beloved baby? We were hoping for days and weeks with our son, not minutes and hours. We are thankful for his short and shining life and also full of grief at having to let him go. Will abundant blessings come from our suffering, our loss, his life, and his death? Even now it feels too close, too blurry to see the fruit of the pain. I have faith that it will come. Even miracles may come from John Paul Raphael's intercession from Heaven. It won't ever take away the pain of missing him, but in God's time, I have faith we will reap meaning and purpose from what we have sown in tears.

I miss you, John Paul Raphael, but I rejoice at the gift of your life and feel hopeful in the mission of your death. I am grateful for the calling I am discovering in my own heart. I am being remade in this time of healing and re-birth. As I learn to live without you, sweet boy, the Lord is close and He invites me to live a whole new kind of life, both in and out of this world, trusting the nearness of His presence and yours. It is a long road we will walk together in this life, you and I— your silent, invisible presence as real to me as my other children. I will carry your memory and the immense love of a mother for her child; I will spread your mission and learn to let myself be loved. You will carry me in a way I cannot see or understand but still believe is true. Loving and losing you was not the worst thing that ever happened to me, little one. The worst thing would be to have never loved you.

I prayed endlessly for a miracle and my own happy ending when my first husband left. I was convinced the Lord would do that for me. There was no miracle. *"Or was there?"* my heart whispers. Was the miracle His presence? That God never left my side and led me to something even better? I see that now. But how could I ever imagine then that divorce would be the path to a richer and more joyful life? That it would lead me to Ralph and our crazy family? That divorce actually led to John Paul Raphael? I remember the words I spoke at John Paul Raphael's funeral: The miracle you get isn't always the miracle you pray for. What if, this time, the miracle wasn't that John Paul was healed, but that I was?

The beauty and purity of our deepest sufferings is that through them, we abandon ourselves to God in a way we never would otherwise. In my mourning, I was empty. My journey would be, could only be, God's since I had no resources of my own to sustain me. Every crying baby or cute newborn would always remind me that I was nothing and had nothing of my own after the death of John Paul. I am entirely dependent on God to walk me through my story and show me what He wants for me through my suffering and in my joy. I trust that God is with me and will never let me go. His presence is the pearl of great price.[14]

It is a divine paradox that it took the death of my son to bring me the peace that surpasses all understanding.[15] I relied so desperately on the nearness of God that, in time, His presence cultivated my longing to pursue Him in all I do. I was slowly transformed and came to see John Paul Raphael's life and death as an invitation from God to let my own heart be healed. I am forever grateful we chose to love our son. My understanding of suffering and of my own human frailty are priceless. I have a stronger connection to the Lord and to Eternity and I have learned to surrender and live without fear. These are treasures. What if the worst thing and the best thing are really the same thing? It reminds me of some lyrics I wrote several years ago: *Every scar that I have makes me look more like You.*

Grief is a dark and terrible journey, but it is a love story that led me to freedom. Wild, beautiful freedom that allows me to throw back my head and laugh, even in the face of death. *You did this, John Paul Raphael. You and Jesus. You broke my imperfect heart open so perfectly through the brilliance of your life and the enormity of my love for you. You gave me courage to fight through darkness to bring my broken heart wholly to the world as a beacon of hope that peace, purpose, and joy are found in and through our pain. Miracles are all around us if we only have hearts to receive them. Show us how, little one. All for the glory of God and our salvation. Amen.*

---

14   Matthew 13:45-46
15   Philippians 4:7

ACKNOWLEDGEMENTS

MY GRATITUDE GOES FIRST to all of those who helped us welcome and hold John Paul Raphael in the land of the living, especially Dr. Moustafa Hassan and Dr. Kathy Wolfe whose assessments guided our care decisions. We are grateful to the dedicated professionals at Inova Fairfax Hospital whose expertise allowed John Paul Raphael to be born alive: Melissa Eatherly and the Fetal Care Center who coordinated our care seamlessly; Mona, who took the initiative to find my phone and camera and take priceless photos and videos in the moments after John Paul Raphael was born; Dr. Alex Kline who arranged special accommodations for our unique situation; Ashley, Kris, Natasha, Lynne, Teresa, and Monique whose gentleness and compassion soothed our broken hearts; and finally, Tia Pettit, John Paul Raphael's nurse who cared for him and our family so beautifully and vulnerably during our hospital stay. Her warm mother's heart made the unbearable slightly more bearable. Thank you to Johanna Waisley for giving her time and talent to provide professional photography at the hospital and during John Paul Raphael's funeral Mass and burial. Thank you to Laura Ricketts of Filumena Birth & Bereavement who prepared us to welcome John Paul Raphael with beauty and joy. Our heartfelt thanks to CJ and Jodi St. George for being willing to stop everything and craft a work of art to hold the beautiful body of our son. Thank you to Matthew Ho, Kathy Farmer, Carolyn Dignan, and the many members of the Master Singers of Virginia, whose music filled the church with radiance, glory, and beauty during the Funeral Mass. Our gratitude goes to our entire parish community and school who held our family, especially our children, with tenderness and love during this beautiful, heartbreaking time. Thank you to Father Richard Guest and Father Stefan Starzynski for serving us with their priestly vocation, prayers, and presence. Thank you to every person who took time to honor our loss and pray with and for our family on January 10, 2018. Your presence was a true gift to Ralph and me.

I am grateful for and devoted to the Holy Spirit for inspiring me with John Paul Raphael's mission to *let yourself be loved* and for calling me to write this book. My deepest gratitude to Erin Gallagher and Tom and Diane Fields for vulnerably sharing their own journey losing a child and inspiring me to share our story with courage and honesty. Thank you to the early readers who provided invaluable feedback and encouragement when I was still full of doubt: Erin Gallagher, Kate Moore, Jeanette Engel, Beth Moschetto, Kim Mares, Laura Dumouchelle, Frank Felsberg, Elizabeth Torresson, and Vincent Buono. Thank you to Sarah Triano and Meaghan Leon who coached me through the final details. Thank you to Emily Jaminet, Rachel Lewis, and Kathleen Gallagher, personal mentors whose support and experience have been invaluable on this journey. Thank you to my launch team for your dedication and commitment to helping me birth my book into the world. I am so grateful to each of you.

I am grateful to the entire Koehler Books family for believing in me as a writer and partnering with me to birth my book: my editor Kristin Davis who handled my words with kindness and care, Miranda Dillon, Joe Coccaro, the design team, and John Koehler for his unending positivity and encouragement.

To old friends and new friends who have walked with our family during the last four years: Every meal, every act of kindness, every prayer held us up in ways you will never know. We are profoundly grateful.

To our big crazy family—thank you Tom, Jen, Sydney, Mom, Dad, and Joann for coming in a blizzard to meet our baby, knowing every minute mattered. Thank you for holding down the fort and bringing the children back and forth to the hospital over and over again. It was a blessing to know they were all well cared for. To our dear children—Clare, Nathan, James, Leah, Andrew, Maggie, Carrie, Travis, Alicia, Drew, Meaghan, and Evan—your presence, love, support, tears, photos, videos, hugs, cards, and gifts meant the world to Ralph/Dad and me. We are so proud of your courage in bravely and vulnerably loving your little brother and opening your heart to loss again. We love each one of you more than you will ever know.

To my dearest husband, Ralph. This is your story too, and I am honored that you trusted me to tell it. You have been steadfast through our whole marriage, but exceptionally so through our journey loving and losing our beautiful son and during these last years as I have birthed John Paul Raphael's story into the world. Thank you for being strong when my strength failed me, and for holding me up and drying my tears over and over again. No one has ever loved me like you do. To the end of my days, I will hold on to one perfect night.

And finally, John Paul Raphael. Who knew a little baby could have such a big voice? Thank you for leaving a message of love for the world through your short and shining life. I am so grateful to be your mother, so abundantly blessed to know you, hold you, love you, and carry out your mission. Thank you for teaching me to let myself be loved. I can't wait to see you again.

ABOUT THE AUTHOR

ELIZABETH LEON is a Catholic author, speaker, and musician from Ashburn, Virginia. She has been a leader in ministry and faith formation for more than twenty-five years and desires to inspire others to find freedom and healing through Christ. Her gift is her willingness to be vulnerable and love with a heart wide-open despite the brokenness of divorce, death, and abuse. She and her husband Ralph are the parents of ten children, five of hers, four of his, and their son, John Paul Raphael who died in 2018. She is a frequent speaker at women's events in Northern Virginia and is pursuing a master's degree in social work at George Mason University. You can find her online at www.elizabethleon.org or www.letyourselfbeloved.com.

Questions for Going Deeper

Chapter One: New Beginnings, Second Chances
- In what ways are you surprised by the path your life has taken?
- What are your dreams or unspoken longings?

Chapter Two: Our Little Boy
- When have you felt overwhelmed by the anguish of uncertainty?
- How have you relied on your community for support? How have you been able to support others?

Chapter Three: Holding on to Hope
- Have travel, beauty, or art been meaningful to you in your journey?
- What events in your life have caused your heart to stretch and grow?

Chapter Four: The Shadow of Death
- How do you comfort yourself when you feel uncertain or scared? When did you learn to soothe yourself?
- When have you had to shift from your plan to God's plan?

Chapter Five: Miracles
- What miracles can you see around you?
- Can you reflect on a time when a profound disappointment became a source of blessing?

Chapter Six: Sacred Surrender

- Have you allowed yourself to fully experience love and grief simultaneously?
- In what ways can you imagine bringing beauty into painful moments?

Chapter Seven: Stunned and Shattered

- How has death or loss impacted your journey?
- How have the words or actions of others brought you comfort in hard times?

Chapter Eight: Love and Lament

- Are you able to be vulnerable with your community? Why or why not?
- How do you allow yourself to lament – to verbalize mourning or grief?

Chapter Nine: All for the Glory of God

- Can you recall an experience that was full of grace? How did it affect you?
- Can you identify moments when God has called you to bring grace to others? How did that feel?

Chapter Ten: The Grief Beast

- How has your personal journey required you to face your fears?
- How are you able to make space for grief when it arrives unexpectedly? Can you recognize and manage triggers?

Chapter Eleven: In the Land of the Living

- How have you experienced goodness in the midst of suffering?
- How do/did you care for your body and spirit after your loss? What is/was most helpful?

Chapter Twelve: Uncertainty and Ugliness

- How have you experienced being powerless in your life?
- Do you give yourself permission to be angry? What helps you manage intense emotion?

Chapter Thirteen: Radical Acceptance

- How do you practice self-compassion and radical acceptance?
- Can you allow yourself to grieve at your own pace? Can you let others in your life grieve at a different pace than yours?

Chapter 14: The New You

- In what ways has grief changed you? How does it feel to consider your grief as a love story?
- How can you let yourself be loved right now, today?

Playlist for Child Loss and Grief

- "All of Me" by Matt Hammitt
- "Baby Mine" by Bette Midler
- "Beautiful Boy" by Coleen McMahon
- "Godspeed (Sweet Dreams)" by The Chicks
- "Gone Too Soon" by Daughtry
- "Gracie's Theme" by Paul Cardall
- "He Will Carry Me" by Mark Schultz
- "He's My Son" by Mark Schultz
- "How He Loves Us" by Me in Motion
- "I Will Carry You (Audrey's Song)" by Selah
- "I'll Think about You" by We Are Messengers
- "Keep Your Eyes on Me" by Tim McGraw & Faith Hill
- "Lullabye (Goodnight, My Angel)" by Billy Joel/The King's Singers
- "Need You Now (How Many Times)" by Plumb
- "Redeemer" by Paul Cardall
- "Remember Me" by Mark Schultz
- "See You Again" by Carrie Underwood
- "Slow Down" by Nichole Nordeman
- "Somewhere Over the Rainbow" by Israel Kamakawiwo'ole
- "Tell Your Heart to Beat Again" by Danny Gokey
- "There You'll Be" by Faith Hill
- "When I Pray for You" by Dan + Shea
- "Winter Bear" by Coby Grant
- "You Can Close Your Eyes" by James Taylor
- "You've Got a Friend" by James Taylor

Books and Resources for Child Loss, Grief, and Trisomy 18

Books

- *The Broken Way* by Ann Voskamp
- *An Exact Replica of a Figment of my Imagination* by Elizabeth McCracken
- *Expecting Adam: A True Story of Birth, Rebirth, and Everyday Magic* by Martha Beck
- *A Gift of Time: Continuing Your Pregnancy when your Baby's Life is Expected to be Brief* by Amy Kuebelbeck & Deborah L. Davis, PhD
- *Holding Silvan: A Brief Life* by Monica Wesolowska
- *I Will Carry You* by Angie Smith
- *Letters to Gabriel: The True Story of Gabriel Michael Santorum* by Karen Garver Santorum
- *Letters to John Paul: A Mother Discovers God's Love in her Suffering Child* by Elena Kilner
- *Loved Baby: 31 Devotions Helping you Grieve and Cherish Your Child after Pregnancy Loss* by Sarah Philpott, PhD
- *Once More We Saw Stars* by Jason Greene
- *One Thousand Gifts: A Dare to Live Fully Right Where You Are* by Ann Voskamp

- *The Power of the Powerless: A Brother's Legacy of Love* by Christopher de Vinck
- *Rare Bird* by Anna Whiston-Donaldson

- *Tear Soup* by Pat Schwiebert & Chuck DeKlyen
- *Unexpecting: Real Talk on Pregnancy Loss* by Rachel Lewis
- *Waiting for Gabriel: A Story of Cherishing a Baby's Brief Life* by Amy Kuebelbeck
- *Walking with God through Pain and Suffering* by Timothy Keller

Resources

- Brave Mamas Facebook support group, Rachel Lewis www.facebook.com/groups/bravemamas
- Filumena Birth and Bereavement, Laura Ricketts https://www.filumenabirth.com/
- Let Yourself Be Loved, Elizabeth Leon www.letyourselfbeloved.com
- Mommies Enduring Neonatal Death (M.E.N.D.) https://www.mend.org
- NIDCAP Federation International https://nidcap.org/
- Now I Lay Me Down to Sleep https://www.nowilaymedowntosleep.org
- Perinatal Hospice and Palliative Care https://www.perinatalhospice.org/
- Red Bird Ministries https://www.redbird.love/
- Share Pregnancy & Infant Loss Support http://nationalshare.org
- Still Standing Magazine https://stillstandingmag.com/
- Support Organization for Trisomy (S.O.F.T.) https://trisomy.org/
- Trisomy 18 Foundation https://www.trisomy18.org

CPSIA information can be obtained
at www.ICGtesting.com
Printed in the USA
BVHW030732130122
626133BV00018B/199

PAPER CREATIONS: PAPER AIRPLANES

Norman Schmidt

Sterling Publishing Co., Inc.
New York

6   8   10   9   7   5

PUBLISHED BY MAIN STREET, A DIVISION OF STERLING PUBLISHING CO., INC.
387 PARK AVENUE SOUTH, NEW YORK, NY 10016

© 2005 BY STERLING PUBLISHING CO., INC.

THIS BOOK IS EXCERPTED FROM THE FOLLOWING STERLING/TAMOS TITLES:
BEST EVER PAPER AIRPLANES © 1994 BY NORMAN SCHMIDT
SUPER PAPER AIRPLANES © 1994 BY NORMAN SCHMIDT

DESIGNED BY KRIS TOBIASSEN

MANUFACTURED IN CHINA
ALL RIGHTS RESERVED

ISBN 1-4027-3034-9

Contents

Flight

People have been obsessed with the idea of flight ever since they looked into the sky and saw birds soaring gently overhead. Mythical stories in many cultures around the world have flying creatures of all sorts, including human beings. When did the reality of human flight begin?

Archeologists in Egypt have discovered a small wooden bird, carved from lightweight sycamore wood, that has a very aerodynamic shape. This small wooden bird is unlike any real bird because its tail has both horizontal and vertical surfaces, just like present-day airplanes. It is not known whether this was a toy, a weather vane, or a small model of some larger craft.

There are other examples of flying toys, such as the Saqqara bird invented by the Greek philosopher Archytas in about 345 B.C. It was a small wooden dove attached to an arm that allowed it to "lift off" in wavering flight. It is not known how the bird was propelled. At about the same time, the Chinese philosopher Mo Tzu constructed what was possibly the first kite, which is simply a tethered airplane. Some Europeans made wings of wood, cloth, and bird feathers, strapped them to their arms, and jumped off high buildings. In 1020, Eilmer "the flying monk" did this, and attained some success with flight, but broke both his legs in the attempt. In the 1500s, the artist and inventor Leonardo da Vinci made many drawings and models of different kinds of aircraft, including the parachute. Another story from the 1700s tells of a French locksmith named Besnier who, with wings strapped to his arms and legs, jumped from a tall building and glided over neighboring houses.

The development of kites continued, and they became the forerunners of free-flying airplanes. European inventors and scientists used them to carry out experiments in aerodynamic forces. Such experiments led to the first free-flying airplanes of Sir George Cayley in the 1790s. They demonstrated the principles of flight as they are understood today. In the 1850s Sir George's coachman was among the first people to fly in an actual airplane. The stage was now set for the development of controllable airplanes.

Construction

When carefully made, the paper airplanes in this book are super flyers. They can be built using the paper included, or ordinary 20 or 24 lb bond copier paper measuring $8^1/_2$ inches by 11 inches (21.6 cm by 27.9 cm). Bond paper is lightweight, easy to cut and fold, and easy to fasten together. It is available in a variety of colors (black paper may have to be purchased at an art store). Since a paper airplane's lift and thrust are limited, every effort must be made to keep drag at a minimum. Every surface not parallel to the direction of travel (wings, nose, and canopy) adds drag, so the neater and more accurate your construction, the better the plane will fly. Clean and accurate cuts and crisp folds are a top priority.

MEASURING AND CUTTING

Use a sharp pencil to mark the measurements and draw firm, accurate lines. Cut out pieces with a sharp pair of scissors or a craft knife and a steel-edged ruler. A knife makes a cleaner cut. When using a knife be sure to work on a proper cutting surface.

FOLDING

Always lay the paper on a level surface for folding. Folding is easier along a score line (an indented line on the paper made with a hard pencil drawn along a ruler). There are only four kinds of folds used in making the airplanes in this book. They are mountain folds, valley folds, sink folds, and reverse folds. Where multiple layers are folded, run your fingers back and forth along the fold, pressing hard to make a sharp crease.

GLUING

A glue stick works well for paper airplanes. Follow the instructions for gluing. Cover the entire contacting surfaces that are to be joined. If there are multiple layers, apply glue to each of the sheets. Glue should be used sparingly, but use enough to hold the parts together. Where multiple layers are being joined, you may need to hold the pieces for a few minutes until the glue sets.

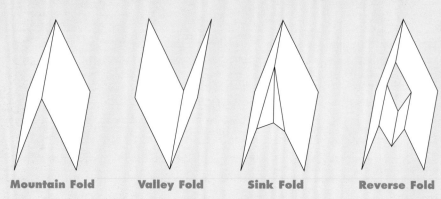

Mountain Fold   **Valley Fold**   **Sink Fold**   **Reverse Fold**

A **MOUNTAIN FOLD** and a **VALLEY FOLD** are actually the same kind of fold. Both are made by folding a flat piece of paper and sharply creasing the fold line. The only difference is that one folds up (valley fold) and the other folds down (mountain fold). They are distinguished only for convenience in giving instructions.

To make a **SINK FOLD**, begin with paper that has been folded using a mountain (or valley) fold and measure as required across the folded corner. Then push in the corner along the measured lines, making a diagonal fold. Finish by creasing the folds sharply.

To make a **REVERSE FOLD**, begin with paper that has been folded using a mountain (or valley) fold and measure as required, down from the top and in from the edge. Then cut along line from the top (heavy line). Push cut piece in, as shown. Finish by creasing folds sharply.

Trimming for Flight

Air is made up of small, solid, evenly spaced particles called molecules. Everything in the universe is made up of molecules, but air molecules are quite far apart compared with those that make up metal, wood, or paper, and they are easily separated when a body moves through them. The molecules are piled up in a thick layer from the ground, and this is called the atmosphere. It forms part of the space around us and the sky above us. This layer of air molecules (atmosphere) exerts pressure on everything in the world, and it is this pressure that makes flight possible. The shape of the airplane affects the molecules as they move across the airplane's surfaces, increasing or decreasing air pressure, determining the flight characteristics of the plane.

No paper airplanes are perfectly straight. And they are easily bent. Shown on page 8 is an example of trimming using the rudder. Airplane A flies straight

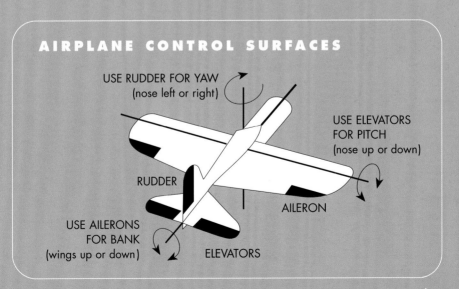

AIRPLANE CONTROL SURFACES

USE RUDDER FOR YAW
(nose left or right)

USE ELEVATORS
FOR PITCH
(nose up or down)

RUDDER

AILERON

USE AILERONS
FOR BANK
(wings up or down)

ELEVATORS

because air flows smoothly along its surfaces. It needs no trim. Airplane B yaws to its left because the air on the left is deflected by the bent fuselage, increasing air pressure on that side. The rudder is used to compensate. Airplane C again flies straight because it has been trimmed so that the deflected air on the left is opposed by air being deflected by the rudder on the right. But airplane C does not fly as well as airplane A because it is creating much more drag.

Before making any trim adjustments to a paper airplane that you have just constructed, be sure you are releasing the plane correctly for flight. Always begin with a gentle straight-ahead release, keeping the wings level. Hold the plane between thumb and forefinger just behind the center of gravity. As your technique improves, you can throw harder, adjusting the trim as needed. But remember, all planes do not fly at the same speed.

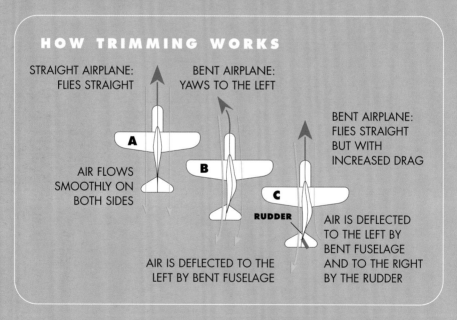

HOW TRIMMING WORKS

STRAIGHT AIRPLANE:
FLIES STRAIGHT

BENT AIRPLANE:
YAWS TO THE LEFT

BENT AIRPLANE:
FLIES STRAIGHT
BUT WITH
INCREASED DRAG

A

B

C

RUDDER

AIR FLOWS
SMOOTHLY ON
BOTH SIDES

AIR IS DEFLECTED TO THE
LEFT BY BENT FUSELAGE

AIR IS DEFLECTED
TO THE LEFT BY
BENT FUSELAGE
AND TO THE RIGHT
BY THE RUDDER

NOTE: Fly Safely. Some of the airplanes in this book have sharp points, so never fly them towards another person. If you fly the airplanes outdoors they may go farther than you expect. Be sure they do not go into the street where you will have to retrieve them.

Flying Tips

Don't be discouraged if on first flight your paper airplane "corkscrews" and crashes. Flying paper airplanes is a delicate balancing act. Only when everything works in harmony—wings, horizontal tail, vertical tail, and control surfaces—is successful flight achieved. With each paper airplane that you build, aim to improve the construction. When carefully made and trimmed, the paper airplanes in this book are super flyers. But remember, the performance of each airplane differs. Experimentation is necessary in order to achieve maximum performance. This is part of the fun of flying paper planes.

Folds that are not neat and crisp add drag to the airplane. This will decrease glide performance. Sloppy folds can also result in twisted airplanes. Inaccurate gluing does not help matters. A twisted plane is sure to "corkscrew" badly (see below). The importance of careful folds cannot be overemphasized.

Airplanes must be symmetrical—one side must be just like the other. On both sides wing and horizontal tail sizes, shapes, and thicknesses must be the same. Also make sure that the control surfaces on one side are the same sizes and are bent the same amount as on the other side.

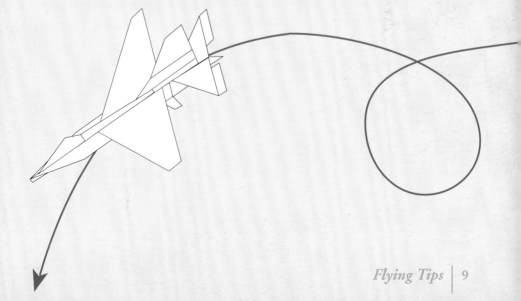

Make sure that the dihedral (upward slanting of wings and tail) is adjusted correctly. In each design, refer to the last step of construction for suggestions. Sometimes experimentation with a different dihedral (or none at all) will be successful. Dihedral provides stability; however, too much dihedral has a destabilizing effect.

Some of the airplanes in this book have secondary control surfaces (flaps). Secondary control surfaces need special attention. If they are bent down slightly, lift is increased. If they are bent down 90°, drag is greatly increased and the nose will pitch down. Additional up elevator is needed, increasing the angle of attack but also increasing drag. Trimmed in this way an airplane does not glide very far. In full-sized airplanes, this trim is good for landing. Experiment with different settings of the secondary control surfaces. Adjust carefully for best results.

Paper airplanes are not baseballs. They cannot be thrown hard. To launch, hold the fuselage lightly between thumb and forefinger near the point where the plane balances. Throw with a firm forward motion, keeping the nose level, pushing the airplane more than throwing it. With a bit of practice you will discover just how hard each of the planes need to be thrown under different conditions.

PITCH TRIM

Although the paper airplanes in this book are built to resemble a bird or powered aircraft, they are obviously all gliders. For thrust they must convert altitude into airspeed. The pitching axis is very important in determining airspeed. Once properly trimmed, an airplane will always fly at the same speed. If the airplane zooms toward the ground, bend the elevators up slightly to raise the nose.

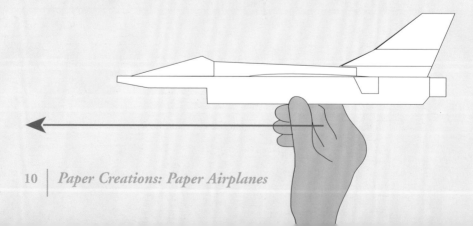

If more speed is needed, as in an outdoor flight, less up elevator will produce the desired result.

ROLL TRIM

Providing the wings are not twisted, the wings should remain more or less level in flight. If one wing drops, bend the aileron down slightly on that wing and up slightly on the other wing.

YAW TRIM

If the plane still has a tendency to turn, bend the rudder slightly opposite to the direction of the turn.

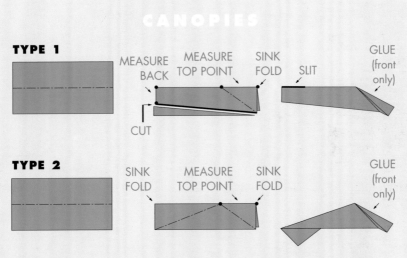

STEP 1 Measure and cut paper to dimensions specified for the particular airplane. Lay paper flat in a horizontal direction. Fold in half horizontally, using a mountain fold.

STEP 2 With the paper folded in half as in Step 1, measure top point and draw lines. For type 1, sink fold (see page 6) the front corner and cut on heavy line. For type 2, sink fold front and back corners.

STEP 3 Press flat to finish the canopy. Only the front end should be glued.

Egret

BACKGROUND INFORMATION

This airplane is called the "Egret" because of its slender shape and long nose. It is a delta (triangle) wing design. The plane looks like a flying triangle. Delta wings are used in slow-flying planes such as hang-gliders and high-speed planes such as the Concorde, which carried passengers faster than the speed of sound. Delta wings will probably be used in future planes that will carry passengers into space and back.

The Egret is constructed similarly to the common paper airplane that everyone makes. But because of this model's carefully measured shape, it can attain a very smooth and flat glide. Make sure that its shape is properly adjusted, with vertical tails straight up and down. Hold it between thumb and forefinger, launching it gently straight ahead.

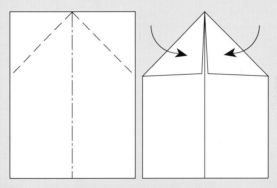

STEP 1 Lay paper flat in a vertical direction. Fold paper in half vertically using the mountain fold. Unfold. Then valley fold the upper corners to the center crease.

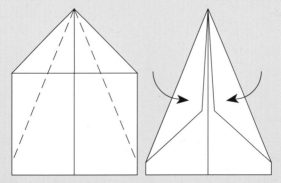

STEP 2 Valley fold the upper diagonals along broken lines to meet the center crease.

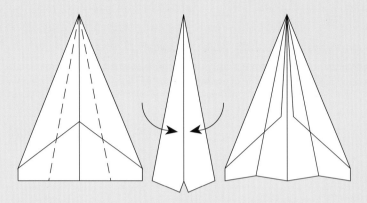

STEP 3 Valley fold outer edges along broken lines to meet the center crease. Unfold, as shown.

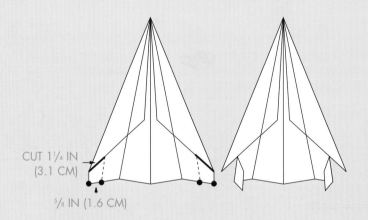

CUT 1¼ IN
(3.1 CM)

⅝ IN (1.6 CM)

STEP 4 On each side, measure along diagonal edge of the paper, as shown by heavy line, and cut. Measure along bottom edge, in from each wing tip, and from this point, draw a line to the end of the cut. Valley fold along this line to make vertical tails.

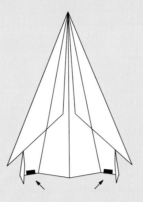

STEP 5 In the locations shown, measure, cut, and fold the elevators.

ELEVATORS ½ in x ¼ in (1.3 cm x .6 cm)

NOTE: In the instructions, control surfaces (elevators, ailerons, rudder) are shown in black. The cuts are always ¼ inch deep on ends only, but widths vary. Their dimensions are always written as follows:

1 IN x ¼ IN (2.5 CM x .6 CM) OR
½ IN x ¼ IN (1.3 CM x .6 CM)

GLUE

STEP 6 Glue folds only at the center of fuselage. Flip airplane over. Adjust shape so that when viewed from the back, the airplane makes a shallow upside-down W, as shown.

Pipit

BACKGROUND INFORMATION

This airplane is called the "Pipit" because of its small size, just like the bird by that name. This paper airplane has small wings for its weight, which makes it a fast flyer. It can be thrown hard. It is well suited for flight both indoors and out.

The Pipit is a compact little airplane folded entirely from one sheet of paper. It can be constructed without control surfaces. For trimming adjustment, bend the entire airplane. If thrown hard, it will fly not only fast but far. For launching, hold it between thumb and forefinger.

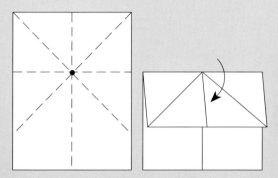

STEP 1 Lay paper flat in a vertical direction. Fold paper in half vertically using a valley fold. Unfold. Then valley fold diagonally so that right upper edge meets the left outer edge. Unfold. Repeat, folding down left upper edge. Unfold. Using the intersection of the creases as a reference, valley fold upper section of the paper along broken horizontal line, as shown.

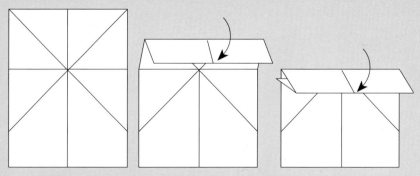

STEP 2 Unfold paper. Valley fold top edge to horizontal crease. Valley fold again along horizontal crease.

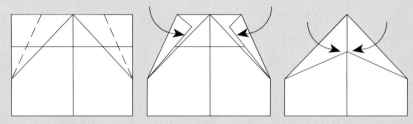

STEP 3 Using a valley fold, bring outer edge to meet the right diagonal crease. Repeat, folding over left edge. Then valley fold the diagonal creases.

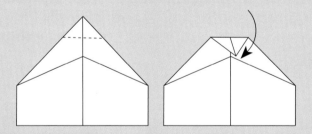

STEP 4 Valley fold tip down to meet crease, as shown.

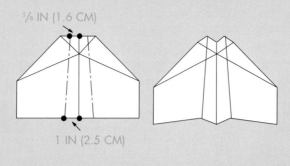

⅝ IN (1.6 CM)

1 IN (2.5 CM)

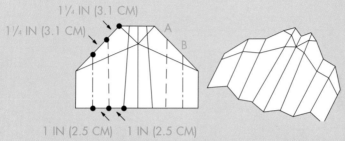

1¼ IN (3.1 CM)

1¼ IN (3.1 CM)

A

B

1 IN (2.5 CM)   1 IN (2.5 CM)

STEP 5 On each side of vertical center crease, measure and draw lines as indicated. Then mountain fold along drawn lines, as shown. Measure and draw the next two sets of lines, on each side. Valley fold line A and mountain fold line B on each side, as shown.

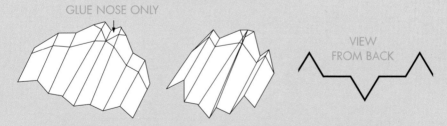

GLUE NOSE ONLY

VIEW FROM BACK

STEP 6 Glue nose only, and let back flare open. Adjust so that, when viewed from back, it makes a shape as indicated.

Swallow

BACKGROUND INFORMATION

This airplane is called the "Swallow" because of its deeply forked tail, which resembles that of the bird. When airplanes were first invented, many different kinds of tails were tried. This is an interesting looking airplane. It can soar in a gentle breeze.

The Swallow is also folded completely from one sheet of paper. It can be constructed without control surfaces. For trimming adjustment, bend the entire airplane. For launching, hold between thumb and forefinger. Launch this airplane gently. Fly it indoors or out.

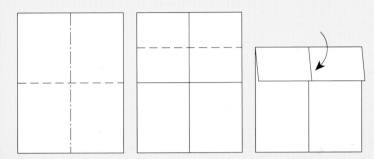

STEP 1 Lay paper flat in a vertical direction. Fold paper in half vertically using a mountain fold. Unfold. Valley fold the paper in half horizontally. Unfold. Then valley fold the top to meet the horizontal crease.

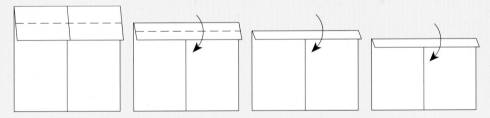

STEP 2 Valley fold the top again to meet the horizontal crease. Then valley fold top again, to meet the horizontal crease. Finally, refold the original horizontal crease.

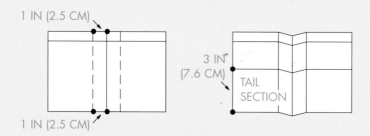

1 IN (2.5 CM)

3 IN (7.6 CM)

TAIL SECTION

1 IN (2.5 CM)

STEP 3 On each side, measure from center crease and draw lines, as shown. Valley fold along these lines. Unfold. Measure from bottom along side and draw a horizontal line.

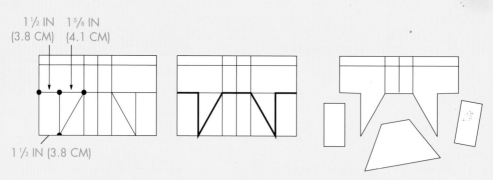

1 ½ IN (3.8 CM)

1 ⅝ IN (4.1 CM)

1 ½ IN (3.8 CM)

STEP 4 Measure and draw lines on tail section, as shown. Cut out along heavy lines, as shown. Discard cutouts.

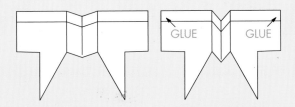

STEP 5 Reshape the airplane by refolding the vertical creases. At each wingtip, glue folded-over portion of the wing's leading (front) edge. Glue no more than 1 in (2.5 cm) from each wingtip.

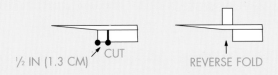

½ IN (1.3 CM) CUT

REVERSE FOLD

STEP 6 Measure, draw, and cut along heavy line at back of fuselage, as shown. Reverse fold to make the vertical tail (see page 6).

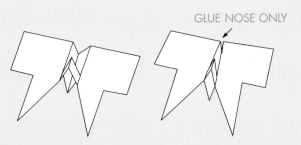

GLUE NOSE ONLY

STEP 7 Apply glue to the nose only, leaving the back to flare open. Adjust the wings so they are level in flight.

Condor

BACKGROUND INFORMATION

This airplane is called the "Condor" because of its large broad wings. This design is a variation on a flying wing. Unlike conventional airplanes, this design has no horizontal and vertical tail. Winglets are incorporated into the wingtips, which provide both horizontal and vertical stability. Like all flying wings, it is sensitive to pitch control. The wide wingspan makes it quite fragile, and it should be launched gently straight ahead. It is not a windy weather airplane.

TECHNICAL INFORMATION

Condors have large feathers at their wingtips for control. Instead of feathers, this airplane has winglets. Because of its wide wingspan, this paper airplane is fragile where the wings meet the fuselage. Adjust the winglets and bend the airplane for trim adjustment.

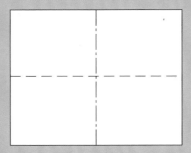

STEP 1   Lay paper flat in a horizontal direction. Fold paper in half vertically using the mountain fold. Unfold. Then valley fold in half horizontally. Unfold.

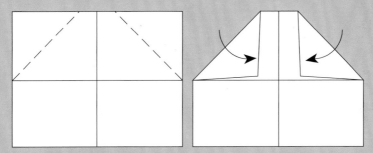

STEP 2   On each side, valley fold diagonally so that the outer edges meet the horizontal crease.

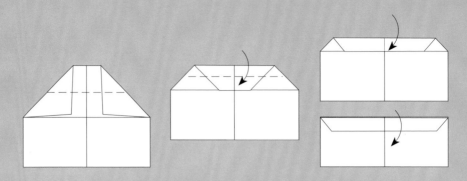

STEP 3 Valley fold along broken lines so that top edge meets the horizontal crease. Valley fold again, so that top edge meets the horizontal crease. Then refold the original horizontal crease.

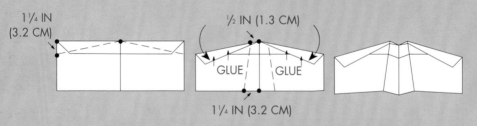

1¼ IN (3.2 CM)

½ IN (1.3 CM)

GLUE   GLUE

1¼ IN (3.2 CM)

STEP 4 On each side of vertical crease, measure and draw diagonal lines. Valley fold top outer edges along these lines. Glue folded-over triangles to form the leading (front) edges of the wings. Then measure and draw vertical lines, as shown. Valley fold along vertical lines to form the fuselage.

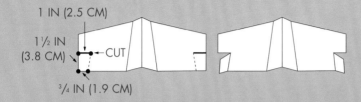

1 IN (2.5 CM)

1½ IN
(3.8 CM)

CUT

¾ IN (1.9 CM)

STEP 5 Flip the airplane over. On each side, measure and draw lines for the winglets. Make horizontal cuts on heavy lines. Valley fold, as indicated, to make winglets. Make a canopy type 2 (see page 11).

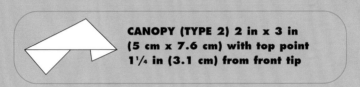

CANOPY (TYPE 2) 2 in x 3 in (5 cm x 7.6 cm) with top point 1¼ in (3.1 cm) from front tip

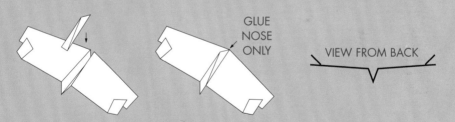

GLUE
NOSE
ONLY

VIEW FROM BACK

STEP 6 Apply glue to inside of nose only, and insert canopy. Align with nose. Adjust the shape so that the wings have a slight dihedral angle (upward slant) and the winglets slant upward, as shown.

Biplane

BACKGROUND INFORMATION

One way to improve lift without making large wings is having two sets of them, one above the other (biplanes). The box-like construction of these airplanes made it easy to cross-brace the lightweight wooden frames with wire for strength. In 1903 Orville and Wilbur Wright put an engine into a biplane and became the first to attain sustained powered flight. Biplanes were used for most of the air battles of World War I, which began in 1914. Fighter biplanes were highly maneuverable although difficult to handle. Some examples are the Spad 7, Sopwith Camel, and Fokker 7. Biplanes are now used where small, durable, and maneuverable airplanes are required. Crop spraying is a good example. This paper airplane is modeled on early biplanes.

TECHNICAL INFORMATION

Biplanes have stubby noses and short wings and tails, making them sensitive to pitch and roll because the distances from the center of gravity to the control surfaces are small. The planes require careful trimming.

If the airplane zooms nose down to the ground, bend the elevators up slightly to raise the nose in flight.

This may cause the nose of the plane to pitch up sharply. As a result, the air no longer flows smoothly over the wing surfaces but separates into eddies and the wings stall. To solve this problem bend the elevators up less.

If the elevators are not bent at all and the nose still rises, don't bend the elevators down to correct the problem (a plane should never fly this way). Rather add a bit of extra ballast to the nose.

If the plane veers to left or right, bend the aileron up slightly on the wing that rises and down slightly on the wing that falls. Also bend the rudder on the vertical tail slightly, opposite to the direction of the turn.

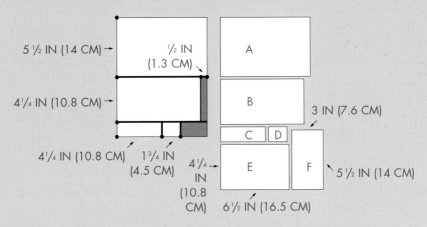

STEP 1 Measure and cut the various pieces from a sheet of bond paper, as shown. Two additional pieces (E and F) are needed, as shown.

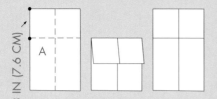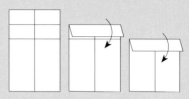

3 IN (7.6 CM)

STEP 2 Lay piece A flat in a vertical direction. To make the fuselage, fold in half vertically using a valley fold. Unfold. Measure and valley fold horizontally, as shown. Unfold.

STEP 3 Valley fold the top to meet the horizontal crease. Then refold the original horizontal crease.

VIEW FROM BACK

STEP 4 Valley fold each side so that outer edges meet the center crease, as shown.

STEP 5 Fold each side again using a mountain fold, so that outer edges meet center crease at back. Then adjust folds so that paper looks like an upside-down W, as shown.

GLUE

GLUE

GLUE

STEP 6 Unfold fuselage completely. Refold, applying glue to all contacting surfaces, as shown. Make sure fuselage is straight. Do not glue nose yet.

STEP 7 Lay piece B in a horizontal position to make the lower wings. Fold in half vertically, using a mountain fold. Unfold. Fold in half horizontally, using a valley fold. Unfold. Then valley fold so that top edge meets center crease. Fold again so that top edge meets center crease. Refold original horizontal center crease.

1 5/8 IN (4.1 CM)

1/2 IN   3/4 IN
(1.3 CM) (1.9 CM)

STEP 8 Unfold completely. On each side, measure and cut diagonally, as shown. Refold. Apply glue before refolding original horizontal center crease only. The folded-over part is the bottom of the leading edge (front) of the wings.

STEP 9 On each side, measure and valley fold, as shown.

STEP 10 Lay piece E horizontally to make the upper wings. Fold in half vertically, using a mountain fold. Unfold. Fold in half horizontally, using a valley fold. Unfold. Then valley fold so that top edge meets center crease. Fold again so that top edge meets center crease. Refold original horizontal center crease.

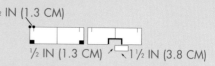

½ IN (1.3 CM)

½ IN (1.3 CM) 1½ IN (3.8 CM)

STEP 11 Unfold completely. On each side, measure and cut diagonally, as shown. Refold. Apply glue before refolding original horizontal center crease only. The folded-over part is the bottom of the leading edge (front) of the wings.

STEP 12 On each side of upper wings, measure from each wingtip and mark attachment points for lower wings, as shown. Cut out center piece on trailing edge, as shown. Make ailerons in locations indicated.

AILERONS ½ in x ¼ in (1.3 cm x .6 cm)

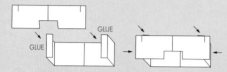

¾ IN (1.9 CM)   ⅝ IN (1.6 CM)

STEP 13 Applying glue, fasten upper and lower wings together, as shown. Make sure both leading edges face the same direction.

STEP 14 Use piece C to make the horizontal tail. Valley fold in half vertically. Unfold. On each side, measure from outer edges, as shown, and cut along heavy lines. Then, on each side, measure from center crease and mountain fold, as shown. Make elevators.

ELEVATORS 1¼ in x ¼ in (3.1 cm x .6 cm)

¼ IN (.6 CM)   ¾ IN (1.9 CM)

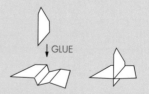

STEP 15 Measure and cut leading edge along heavy lines, as shown. On trailing edge, make rudder.

RUDDER ¾ in x ¼ in (1.9 cm x .6 cm)

STEP 16 Apply glue to inside of horizontal tail and insert vertical tail, aligning trailing (back) edges.

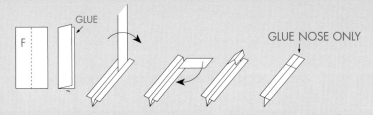

GLUE

GLUE NOSE ONLY

F

STEP 17 Use piece F to make the nose cowl (ballast). Valley fold piece in half vertically. Glue halves together. Applying glue to one side, insert F into nose and wrap entirely around fuselage, as shown. Then glue fuselage together at nose only.

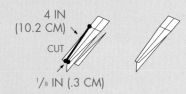

4 IN
(10.2 CM)

CUT

¹/₈ IN (.3 CM)

STEP 18 On each side, measure and cut fuselage back along heavy lines, as shown.

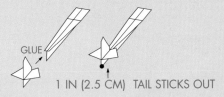

GLUE

1 IN (2.5 CM) TAIL STICKS OUT

STEP 19 Applying glue, slide the tail into the back of the fuselage.

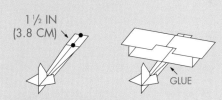

1½ IN
(3.8 CM)

GLUE

STEP 20 Measure from front of fuselage and mark front of wing position. Glue wings in place, as shown.

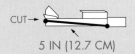

CUT→

5 IN (12.7 CM)

VIEW FROM BACK

STEP 21 Measure and cut back of fuselage, as shown. Adjust dihedral (upward slanting of wings and tail) to finish airplane.

X1 Experimental

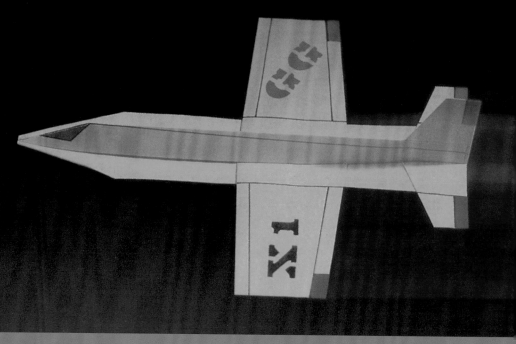

BACKGROUND INFORMATION

Some people believed that the speed of sound was a barrier that would never be crossed. But designers did not abandon their quest. They shaped an airplane like a 50 caliber bullet, which was known to travel faster than the speed of sound. This experimental plane was the stubby-winged Bell X1. It was called "Glamorous Glennis" after the pilot's wife. While this plane did not have swept-back wings, it successfully "broke the sound barrier" for the first time in 1947. Thus began the building of a long series of X planes used for experiments in ultra-high-speed and high-altitude flight.

The X15, for example, flew 8 times the speed of sound to the edge of space at an altitude of 70 miles (112 km) in 1956. This paper airplane is modeled on the Bell X1.

TECHNICAL INFORMATION

What we hear as different sounds are actually differences in air pressure that strike our eardrums. These waves of air (called sound waves) travel at about 760 mph (1,224 kph). An airplane traveling at that speed creates a tremendous pressure ridge because so many air molecules are piled up ahead of its leading edges. What makes it so dangerous is that as speed increases, the ridge of pressure moves farther back over the wings and begins to affect the control surfaces which are on the trailing edges. Airplanes that successfully fly faster than the speed of sound must be designed so that the pressure is deflected in such a way that it does not affect aircraft control. Thus, their noses are pointed and their wings are thin, and either tapered or swept back. The planes must also be built strong enough to withstand the pressure. When supersonic airplanes break the sound barrier, they create a loud booming noise (like a clap of thunder), as heard from the ground.

The speed of sound is also called Mach 1, twice that speed Mach 2, three times Mach 3, and so on, in honor of the scientist Ernst Mach.

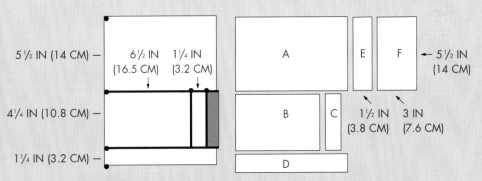

STEP 1 Measure and cut the various pieces from a sheet of bond paper, as shown. Two additional pieces, E and F, are needed, as shown.

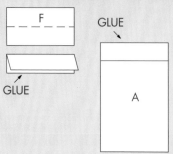

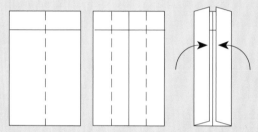

STEP 2 Use piece F to make nose ballast. Lay flat in a horizontal direction and valley fold horizontally. Glue halves together. Then glue to piece A, as shown.

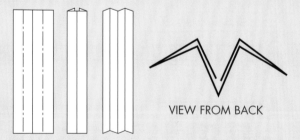

STEP 3 Lay piece A flat in a vertical direction. To make the fuselage, fold in half vertically using a valley fold. Unfold. Then valley fold each side so that outer edges meet center crease, as shown.

VIEW FROM BACK

STEP 4 Fold each side again using a mountain fold, so that outer edges meet center crease at back. Then adjust folds so that paper looks like an upside-down W, as shown.

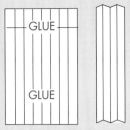

STEP 5 Unfold fuselage completely. Refold, applying glue to all contacting surfaces, as shown. Make sure fuselage is straight.

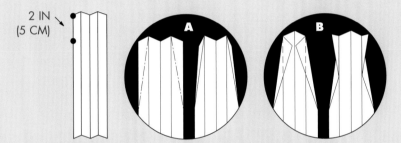

2 IN (5 CM)

STEP 6 On each side, measure from top (front of fuselage), mark, and mountain fold along broken lines, as shown in enlarged view A. Then flip over fuselage. On each side, valley fold triangle along broken lines, matching fold line to existing crease, as shown in enlarged view B.

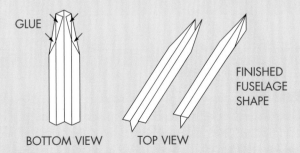

GLUE

BOTTOM VIEW

TOP VIEW

FINISHED FUSELAGE SHAPE

STEP 7 Glue triangles. Hold in place until glue sets. It is important that the fuselage stay straight. Do not glue nose yet.

STEP 8 Lay piece B horizontally to make the wings. Fold in half horizontally, using a valley fold. Unfold. Fold in half vertically, using a mountain fold. Unfold. Then valley fold so that upper edge meets center crease. Fold over again along original center crease.

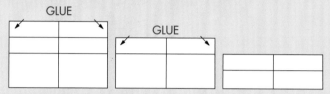

STEP 9 Unfold completely. Refold, applying glue to no more than 1 in (2.5 cm) from outer tips, as shown. The folded-over part is the bottom of the leading edge (front) of the wings.

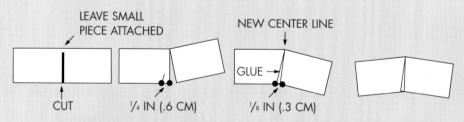

STEP 10 To taper wings, cut along center heavy line from trailing edge (back), leaving a small piece attached at the leading edge. Then measure and make a mark on trailing edge, as shown. Align pieces to the mark. Glue. Measure and draw a new center line.

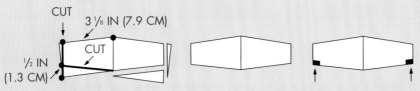

STEP 11 On each side, measure and cut, as indicated by heavy lines. On the trailing edges of wingtips, make ailerons.

AILERONS ½ in x ¼ in (1.3 cm x .6 cm)

STEP 12 Use piece C to make the horizontal tail. Valley fold in half vertically. Unfold. On each side, measure from center crease, as shown, and mountain fold. On each side, measure and mountain fold leading edge along broken lines. Glue. Make elevators on trailing edges.

ELEVATORS ¾ in x ¼ in (1.9 cm x .6 cm)

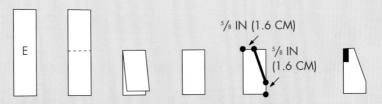

STEP 13 Lay piece E vertically to make the vertical tail. Valley fold in half horizontally and glue halves together. Measure and cut along heavy line, as shown. Make rudder on trailing edge.

RUDDER ¾ in x ¼ in (1.9 cm x .6 cm)

GLUE

SLIT 1¼ IN (3.2 CM)

D

STEP 14 Finish the tail. Apply glue to inside of horizontal tail and slide vertical tail in place, aligning at trailing edge.

STEP 15 Use piece D to make the canopy (see page 11). Make slit in the back of canopy.

**CANOPY (TYPE 1) 1¼ in x 8½ in (3.2 cm x 21.6 cm)
Top point 1½ in (3.8 cm) — Back is straight**

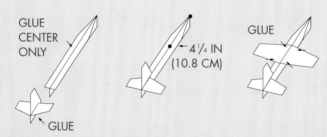

GLUE
CENTER
ONLY

4¼ IN (10.8 CM)

GLUE

GLUE

STEP 16 Apply glue to inside center only of fuselage. Then apply glue and slide tail into fuselage, aligning at trailing edge. Measure from front and mark for wing position. Glue wings to fuselage.

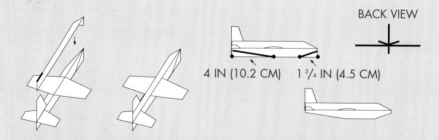

BACK VIEW

4 IN (10.2 CM)   1¾ IN (4.5 CM)

STEP 17 Apply glue to inside back of canopy and front tab of canopy. Insert tab into fuselage. The vertical tail fits into slit. Align at nose. To finish, measure and cut front and back of fuselage along heavy diagonal lines, as shown. Adjust dihedral (upward slanting of wings and tail).

Nighthawk

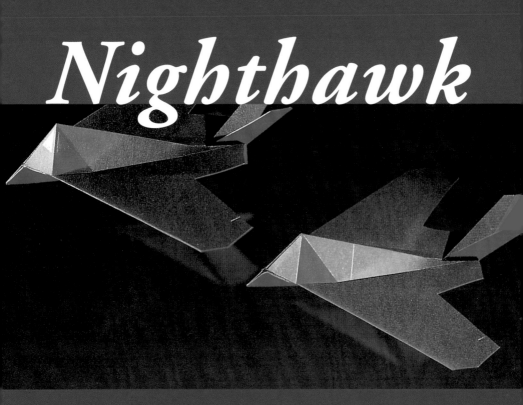

BACKGROUND INFORMATION

This airplane is called the "Nighthawk" because it is modeled on the Lockheed F117 Stealth, which is used primarily for nighttime military operations. It is not a fast airplane, but it is highly maneuverable. The unusual shape of the F117, together with its black color, are what make the airplane difficult to see, even by radar. This paper model has fine flying characteristics.

TECHNICAL INFORMATION

This is an unconventional airplane design. For the most realistic appearance, this paper airplane should be made from black paper. This model does not have a standard canopy, and care must be taken in shaping it. The airplane can be trimmed for level flight or aerobatic flight. Fly it indoors or out. For launching, hold between thumb and forefinger.

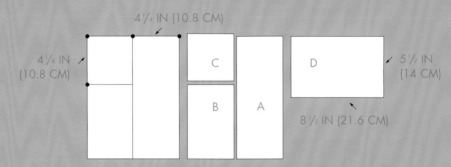

STEP 1 Measure and cut three pieces from a sheet of 8 ¹/₂ in x 11 in (21.6 cm x 27.9 cm) paper. One additional piece is needed, as shown.

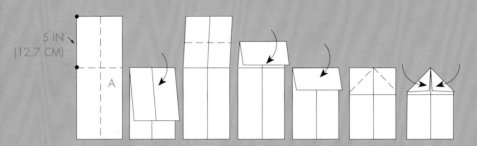

STEP 2 To make the fuselage, fold piece A in half vertically using a valley fold. Unfold. Measure from top, as shown, and valley fold horizontally. Unfold. Then valley fold so that the upper edge meets horizontal crease. Refold the original horizontal crease. Then on each side, valley fold diagonally so that top edge meets center crease.

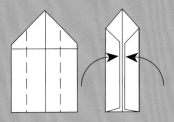

STEP 3 Valley fold each side so that outer edges meet center crease, as shown.

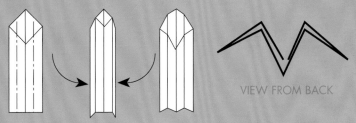

VIEW FROM BACK

STEP 4 Fold again using a mountain fold, so that outer edges meet center crease at back. Then adjust folds so that paper looks like an upside-down W, as shown.

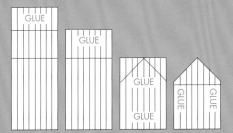

GLUE

GLUE

GLUE

GLUE

GLUE

GLUE

STEP 5 Unfold fuselage completely. Refold, applying glue to contacting surfaces, as shown. Make sure fuselage is straight.

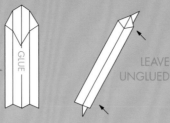

STEP 6 To finish fuselage, glue center of fuselage, leaving 2 in (5 cm) at the nose and 1 in (2.5 cm) at the tail end unglued.

STEP 7 Use piece C to make the twin vertical tails. Fold in half horizontally using a valley fold. Glue sides together. Valley fold vertically. Unfold.

STEP 8 On each side, measure from center crease and mountain fold. Unfold, as shown. On each side, measure and draw lines, as shown.

STEP 9 On each side, cut on heavy lines, as shown. Make rudders (see page 15). Adjust creases, as shown, and glue at center.

RUDDERS ³/₄ in x ¹/₄ in (1.9 cm x .6 cm)

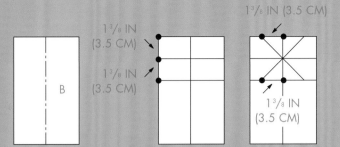

STEP 10 Use piece B to make the canopy. Fold in half vertically using a mountain fold. Unfold. On each side, measure and draw lines, as shown.

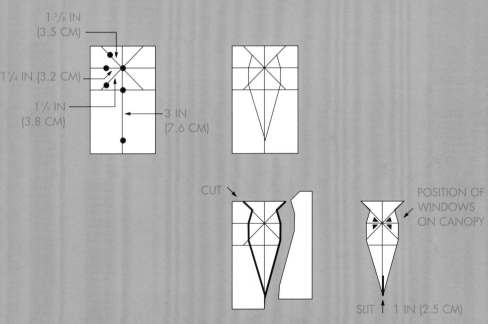

STEP 11 On each side, continue measuring and drawing lines. Then cut along heavy lines to make canopy outline, as shown. Make a slit at the bottom.

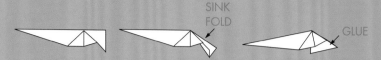

STEP 12 To finish canopy, mountain fold along diagonal and horizontal lines. Unfold. Fold again along original center crease, as shown. Then sink fold the front (see page 6). Glue front only.

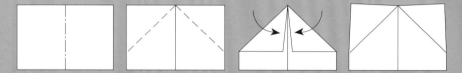

STEP 13 Use piece D to make the wings. Fold in half vertically using a mountain fold. Unfold. On each side, valley fold diagonally so that top edge meets center crease. Unfold.

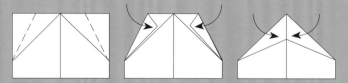

STEP 14 Fold diagonally using a valley fold, so that outer edge meets diagonal creases, as shown. Then fold again along original diagonals.

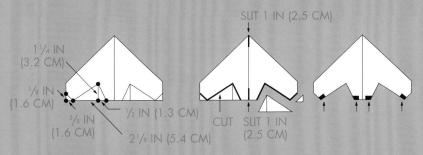

SLIT 1 IN (2.5 CM)

1¼ IN (3.2 CM)

⅝ IN (1.6 CM)

⅝ IN (1.6 CM)

½ IN (1.3 CM)

2⅛ IN (5.4 CM)

CUT

SLIT 1 IN (2.5 CM)

STEP 15 Flip wings over. On each side, measure and draw lines. Cut along lines and make slits at the top and bottom, as shown. Make elevators and ailerons (see page 15).

AILERONS ELEVATORS ½ in x ¼ in (1.3 cm x .6 cm)

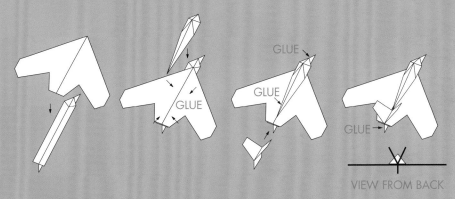

GLUE

GLUE

GLUE

GLUE

GLUE

VIEW FROM BACK

STEP 16 Glue wings to the fuselage, aligning at the trailing (back) edges. Make sure that the wings are centered and at right angles to the fuselage. To mount the canopy, apply glue to the bottom front tab and the back of the canopy. Slide front tab into the fuselage, aligning with the diagonal front of the fuselage. Make sure the slit at the back of the canopy is centered on the fuselage. Canopy should fit snugly to the wings. Applying glue, slide tail into back of fuselage, aligning trailing edges.

F18 Hornet

BACKGROUND INFORMATION

The F16 was used as a land-based fighter aircraft, but there was no equivalent sea-based fighter. Therefore the F18 was built in the early 1980s as a medium-sized multitask maneuverable military aircraft capable of both sea and land operations. This plane is commonly called the "Hornet." It has tapered wings and a conventional horizontal tail, but with two canted (tilted) vertical tails located between the wings and horizontal tail. The F18 is used by the U.S.A., Canada, Australia, and Spain. This paper airplane is modeled on the F18.

TECHNICAL INFORMATION

The F18 is constructed mostly of aluminum, with parts of its wings and other surfaces made of composites. It has two afterburning turbojet engines that can propel it at almost twice the speed of sound when traveling at high altitudes. This airplane is both a fighter and an attack plane, and it can be fitted with a wide variety of armament for both air-to-air and air-to-ground military tasks. Like the F16, it has a missile rail at each wingtip, with space under the wings for other armament and extra fuel tanks. Besides its military role, this plane is also used as an aerial display airplane at air shows.

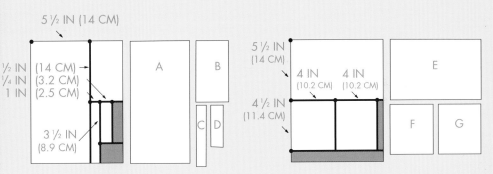

STEP 1 Measure and cut the various pieces from two sheets of bond paper.

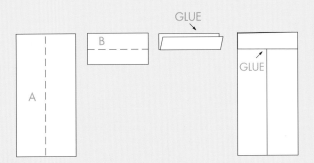

STEP 2 Use piece A to make the fuselage. Fold in half vertically using a valley fold. Unfold. Then valley fold piece B in half horizontally to make nose ballast. Glue halves together. Glue B to A, aligning top edges, as shown.

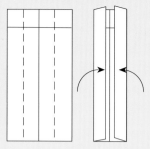

STEP 3 Valley fold so that outer edges meet center crease.

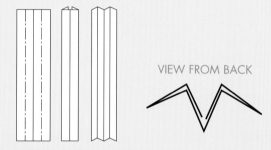

VIEW FROM BACK

STEP 4 Fold each side again using a mountain fold, so that outer edges meet center crease at back. Then adjust folds so that paper looks like an upside-down W, as shown.

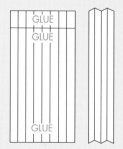

GLUE
GLUE

GLUE

STEP 5 Unfold fuselage completely. Refold, applying glue to contacting surfaces, as shown. Make sure fuselage is straight.

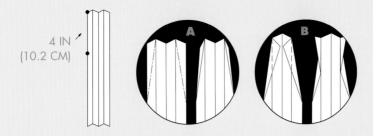

4 IN
(10.2 CM)

STEP 6 On each side, measure from top (front of fuselage), mark, and mountain fold along broken lines, as shown in enlarged view A. Then flip over fuselage. On each side, valley fold the triangle along the broken lines, matching fold line to existing crease, as shown in enlarged view B.

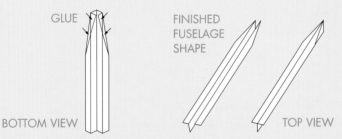

GLUE

FINISHED
FUSELAGE
SHAPE

BOTTOM VIEW

TOP VIEW

STEP 7 Glue triangles. Hold in place until glue sets. It is important that the fuselage stay straight. Do not glue nose yet.

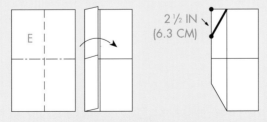

E

2 ½ IN
(6.3 CM)

STEP 8 Lay piece E in a vertical direction to make wings. Valley fold in half vertically. Unfold. Mountain fold in half horizontally. Valley fold so that one outer edge meets center crease, as shown. On each side of horizontal center crease, measure and cut diagonally, as shown by heavy line.

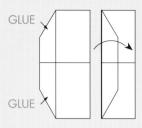

GLUE

GLUE

STEP 9 Apply glue to each diagonal side on top layer only, no more than 1 in (2.5 cm) from the diagonal edge. Refold along the original vertical center crease. The folded-over part is the bottom of the leading edge (front) of wings.

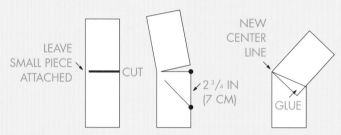

LEAVE
SMALL PIECE
ATTACHED

CUT

2 ³/₄ IN
(7 CM)

NEW
CENTER
LINE

GLUE

STEP 10 To taper wings, cut along center line from the trailing edge (back), leaving a small piece attached at the leading edge. Then measure and draw diagonal line, as shown. Align halves to the diagonal line. Glue. Draw new center line.

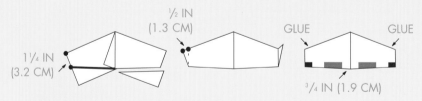

½ IN
(1.3 CM)

GLUE   GLUE

1 ¼ IN
(3.2 CM)

³/₄ IN (1.9 CM)

STEP 11 On each side, measure and cut trailing edge, as shown by heavy line. Then on each side, measure and mountain fold wingtips. Glue. Make ailerons and flaps in locations shown.

AILERONS ¹/₂ in x ¹/₄ in (1.3 cm x .6 cm)
FLAPS 1 ¹/₄ in x ¹/₄ in (3.2 cm x .6 cm)

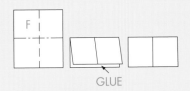

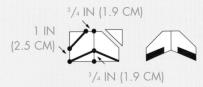

STEP 12 Lay piece F flat in a vertical direction to make the horizontal tail. Valley fold in half vertically. Unfold. Mountain fold in half horizontally. Glue halves together.

STEP 13 On each side, measure and cut, as shown by heavy lines.

ELEVATORS 1 ¼ in x ³/₈ in (3.2 cm x 1 cm)

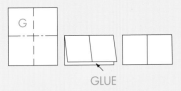

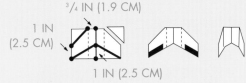

STEP 14 Lay piece G flat in a vertical direction to make the twin vertical tails. Valley fold in half vertically. Unfold. Mountain fold in half horizontally. Glue halves together.

STEP 15 On each side, measure and cut, as shown by heavy lines. Make a rudder on each vertical tail. On each side, valley fold, as shown.

RUDDERS 1 ¼ in x ¼ in (3.2 cm x .6 cm)

STEP 16 Use piece D to make the canopy (see page 11).

CANOPY (TYPE 2) 1 ¼ in x 3 ½ in (3.2 cm x 8.9 cm)
Top point 2 ½ in (6.4 cm)

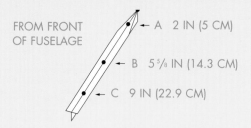

A 2 IN (5 CM)

B 5 5/8 IN (14.3 CM)

C 9 IN (22.9 CM)

STEP 17 Measure from front of fuselage, as shown. Make mark A for positioning the front of the canopy, mark B for positioning leading edge of the wings, and mark C for positioning leading edge of the horizontal tail.

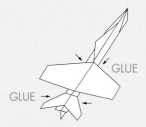

GLUE

GLUE

STEP 18 Apply glue to the inside of the nose and the small triangles on the bottom of the canopy. Position canopy on the fuselage at mark A. Hold until glue sets. Glue wings and horizontal tail in place, making sure they are centered and at right angles to the fuselage.

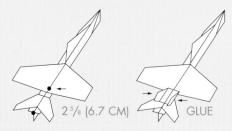

2 5/8 (6.7 CM)

GLUE

STEP 19 Measure from back of fuselage, as shown, and make a mark for positioning the twin vertical tails. Glue vertical tails in place, making sure they are centered and parallel to the fuselage.

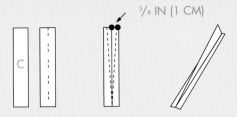

³/₈ IN (1 CM)

STEP 20 Lay piece C in a vertical direction to make the fuselage top. Mountain fold in half vertically. Unfold. On each side, measure and valley fold. Adjust shape, as shown.

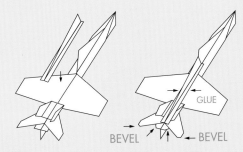

GLUE

BEVEL   BEVEL

STEP 21 Glue piece C onto the fuselage, making sure it fits snugly against the canopy. Bevel the trailing edges of the elevators.

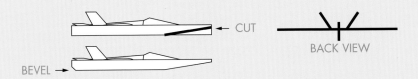

← CUT

BACK VIEW

BEVEL →

STEP 22 Measure and cut nose diagonally, as shown by heavy line. Bevel all corners of the back of the fuselage. Wings and horizontal tail are level. Adjust angles of the canted (tilted) vertical tails, as shown.

747 Jumbo

BACKGROUND INFORMATION

The first jet-powered airliner was the deHavilland Comet built in the 1950s. As more and more people realized the comfort of jet travel, bigger airplanes were needed to carry them. The Boeing 747 was first built in 1968. It is one of the largest passenger airplanes in the world. It is longer than the distance flown by the Wright brothers (120 ft or 36 m) in their first powered flight. The "Jumbo Jet" is used to carry passengers and cargo across the continents and the oceans of the world. This paper airplane is modeled on the 747.

TECHNICAL INFORMATION

The Boeing 747 is a big airplane. From nose to tail it measures 230 ft (70 m). The distance from wingtip to wingtip is 195 ft (58.5 m). Its tail is 64 ft (19.5 m) high, higher than a five-story building. When it is fully loaded with fuel, passengers, and cargo, it weighs 800,000 lb (360,000 kg), and carries 500 passengers or 270,000 lb (122,500 kg) of cargo. Once it reaches high altitude, it cruises at 600 mph (960 km/h). This makes it ideal for use on long-distance passenger routes. Its service ceiling is 40,000 ft (12,200 m) above the ground. Its maximum range is 6,000 miles (9,600 km), allowing it to fly one fourth of the distance around the earth without refueling. The plane is propelled by four 50,000 lb (22,500 kg) thrust turbofan jet engines.

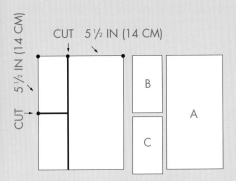

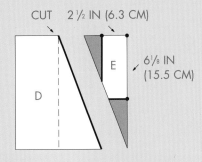

STEP 1 Measure and cut three pieces from a sheet of bond paper, as shown.

STEP 2 Valley fold a second sheet of bond paper in half vertically. Then measure and cut two pieces, as shown.

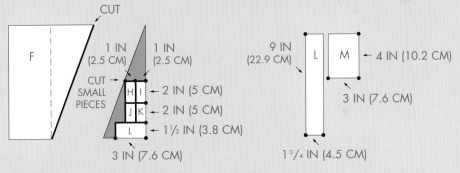

STEP 3 Valley fold a third sheet of bond paper in half vertically. Then measure and cut six pieces, as shown.

STEP 4 Measure and cut two additional pieces, as shown.

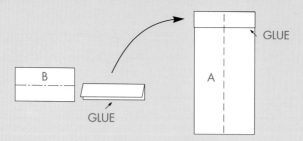

STEP 5 Use piece B to make the nose ballast. Fold in half horizontally using a mountain fold. Glue halves together.

STEP 6 Use piece A to make the fuselage. Glue ballast to the top of fuselage, as shown. Fold in half vertically using a valley fold. Unfold.

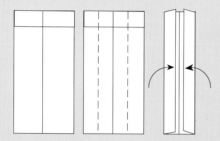

STEP 7 Valley fold each side so that outer edges meet center crease, as shown.

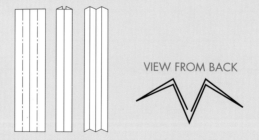

VIEW FROM BACK

STEP 8 Fold each side again using a mountain fold, so that outer edges meet center crease at back. Then adjust folds so that paper looks like an upside-down W, as shown.

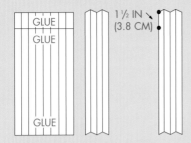

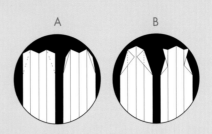

A   **B**

STEP 9 Unfold fuselage completely. Refold, applying glue to contacting surfaces, as shown. Make sure fuselage is straight.

STEP 10 On each side, measure from top (front of fuselage), mark, and mountain fold along broken lines, as shown in enlarged view A. Then flip over fuselage. On each side, valley fold triangle along broken lines, matching fold line to existing crease, as shown in enlarged view B.

GLUE

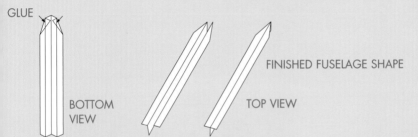

FINISHED FUSELAGE SHAPE

BOTTOM VIEW

TOP VIEW

STEP 11 Glue triangles. Hold in place until glue sets. It is important that the fuselage stay straight. Do not glue nose yet.

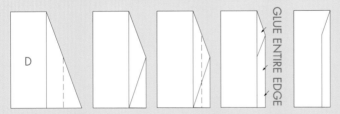

D

GLUE ENTIRE EDGE

STEP 12 Lay piece D vertically to make the right wing. Valley fold vertically so that bottom outer edge meets center crease. Valley fold vertically again so that outer edge meets center crease. Apply glue. Then fold over again along original vertical center crease.

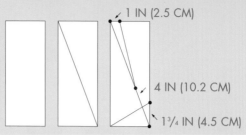

1 IN (2.5 CM)

4 IN (10.2 CM)

1³/₄ IN (4.5 CM)

STEP 13 Flip over, with folded-over edge to the LEFT. Draw diagonal line from upper left to lower right corners. Measure along line from bottom and make a mark. Measure along top edge from left and mark. Join the two marks. Then measure along right edge from bottom and mark. Join this point with the bottom left corner.

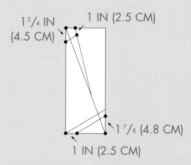

1³/₄ IN (4.5 CM)

1 IN (2.5 CM)

1⁷/₈ (4.8 CM)

1 IN (2.5 CM)

STEP 14 Measure along left edge from top and make a mark. Measure along line from top, as shown, and make a mark. Join the two marks. Then measure along bottom edge from left and make mark. Measure along right edge from bottom and make a mark. Join marks.

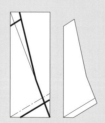

STEP 15 Cut along lines, as shown. Then valley fold along line, as shown.

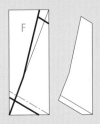

STEP 16 To make the left wing, repeat steps 12–15 using piece F, keeping the folded edge on the RIGHT and reversing the directions of the lines from left to right, as shown.

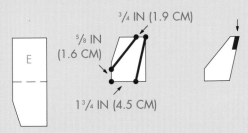

STEP 17 Lay piece E vertically to make the vertical tail. Valley fold in half horizontally and glue halves together. Then cut along heavy lines, as shown. Make rudder on trailing edge.

RUDDER 1 in x ¹/₄ in (2.5 cm x .6 cm)

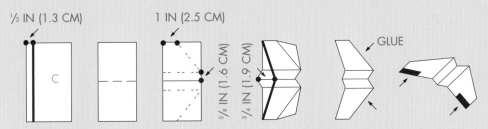

STEP 18 Lay piece C vertically to make the horizontal tail. Measure and cut to size. Valley fold in half horizontally. Unfold. On each side, measure from center crease, as shown, and mountain fold. On each side, measure and mountain fold leading edge along broken lines. Glue. Cut trailing edges and make elevators.

ELEVATORS 1 ¹/₄ in x ¹/₄ in (3.2 cm x .6 cm)

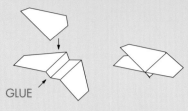

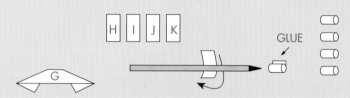

STEP 19 Apply glue to inside of horizontal tail and insert vertical tail, aligning leading (front) edges.

STEP 20 Use piece G to make the canopy (see page 11). Use pieces H, I, J, and K to make the engines. Wrap each piece around a pencil vertically and glue.

CANOPY (MODIFIED TYPE 2) 1 in x 3 in (2.5 cm x 7.6 cm) with top points 1 ¹/₄ in (3.2 cm) from front and back tips

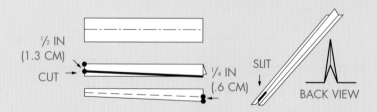

½ IN (1.3 CM)

CUT →

¼ IN (.6 CM)

SLIT

BACK VIEW

STEP 21 Use piece L to make the top of the fuselage. Mountain fold in half horizontally. Measure and cut as shown. Then, on each side, measure and valley fold to form piece, as shown. Cut a 1 in (2.5 cm) slit along center crease at narrow end.

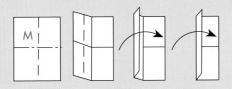

STEP 22 Use piece M to make a spar (support) for the wings. Valley fold in half vertically. Unfold. Mountain fold in half horizontally. Unfold. Then valley fold vertically so that outer edge meets center crease. Fold over again along original vertical center crease.

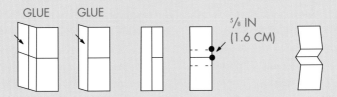

STEP 23 Unfold spar completely. Refold, applying glue to contacting surfaces. Flip over. On each side of center crease, measure and mountain fold, as shown. Folded-over edge is the front.

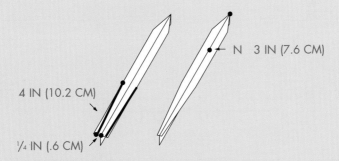

STEP 24 Measure back of fuselage and cut, as shown. Then measure from front and make mark for positioning leading edge of wings at N.

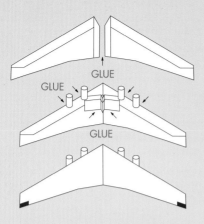

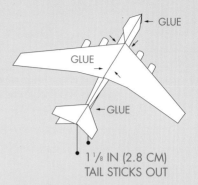

1 ⅛ IN (2.8 CM)
TAIL STICKS OUT

STEP 25 With wings upside down, glue halves together. Glue spar to wings. Glue engines to wings in approximate positions shown (they stick out ½ in (1.3 cm)). Flip over. On trailing edges, make ailerons.

Ailerons ¾ in x ¼ in (1.9 cm x .6 cm)

STEP 26 Apply glue to inside of fuselage, the small triangles on the bottom of canopy, and the center bottom of wings. Slide canopy tabs into fuselage aligning with front tip. Immediately slide wings in place. Then apply glue and slide tail into back of fuselage. Hold until glue sets.

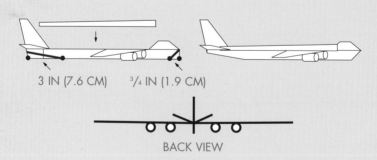

3 IN (7.6 CM)   ¾ IN (1.9 CM)

BACK VIEW

STEP 27 Measure and cut nose and tail ends diagonally along heavy lines, as shown. Glue L onto top of fuselage, as shown, fitting snugly against back of canopy, with vertical tail through the slit. Adjust dihedral (upward slanting of wings and tail), as shown.

TAV Concept

BACKGROUND INFORMATION

We are living on the threshold of a new era in air travel. Already the space shuttle is blasting into space attached to a rocket and returning as an airplane for another mission. The next generation of space planes will take off under their own power from ordinary airport runways, fly into space, and return back to earth. They are called transatmospheric vehicles (TAVs). Sometimes they are called hypersonic transports (HSTs). They will combine jet and rocket engines for propulsion and have stable delta wings (triangle shaped) integrated into the fuselage for lift in the lower atmosphere. They will look something like the ordinary "paper plane." One example is NASA's experimental X30. This paper airplane is modeled on such future space planes.

Transatmospheric vehicles will need powerful and complicated engines and fuel supplies if they are to fly from the ground up into space. It takes a great deal of energy to propel an airplane beyond the limits of the earth's atmosphere and go into space orbit at 22 times the speed of sound. For example, the space shuttle we have now uses over 1,000,000 lbs (450,000 kg) of liquid oxygen and 300,000 lb (135,000 kg) of liquid hydrogen, which it burns in less than ten minutes of flight. The fuel is carried in large external tanks, which are thrown away during each flight. Future TAVs will carry everything onboard, like a regular airplane. In addition to engines for very high altitudes, they will also have engines that can burn fuel using oxygen from the atmosphere at lower altitudes. Only at very high altitudes, where there is not enough oxygen in the air to use, will they switch to an onboard supply of oxygen. Space planes of the future will use less fuel and carry much less oxygen. Such planes will be able to fly completely around the world in just a few hours.

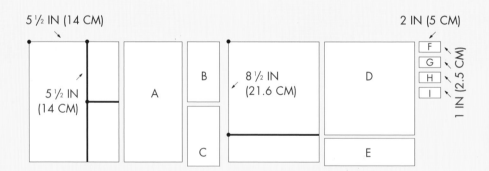

STEP 1 Measure and cut the various pieces from two sheets of bond paper. Four additional small pieces are needed, as shown.

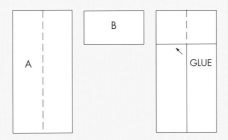

STEP 2 Lay piece A flat in a vertical direction. To make the fuselage, fold in half vertically using a valley fold. Unfold. To make nose ballast, glue piece B in place, aligning the top edges, as shown. Refold center crease. Unfold again.

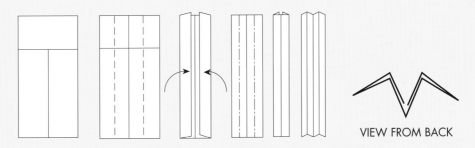

VIEW FROM BACK

STEP 3 Refold in half vertically using a valley fold. Unfold. Valley fold each side so that outer edges meet center crease, as shown. Fold each side again using a mountain fold, so that outer edges meet center crease at back. Then adjust folds so that paper looks like an upside-down W, as shown.

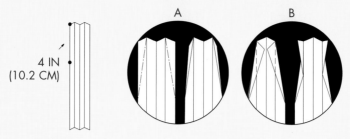

STEP 4 On each side, measure from top (front of fuselage), mark, and mountain fold along broken lines, as shown in enlarged view A. Then flip over fuselage. On each side, valley fold the triangle along the broken lines, matching fold line to existing crease, as shown in enlarged view B.

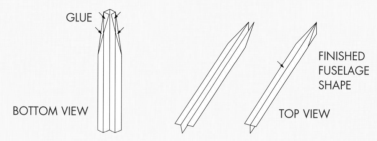

STEP 5 Glue triangles. Hold in place until glue sets. It is important that the fuselage stay straight. Glue fuselage in the middle only, leaving the nose and tail ends unglued.

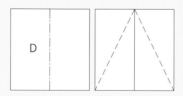

STEP 6 Use piece D to make the wings. Mountain fold in half vertically. Unfold. Then on each side valley fold diagonally along a line running from the top center to the bottom corners. Unfold.

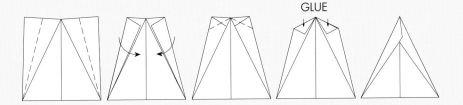

GLUE

STEP 7 On each side, valley fold diagonally so that outer edges meet diagonal crease, as shown. Then fold so that upper edges meet diagonal crease, as shown. Apply glue to the small upper triangles only and refold original diagonal creases.

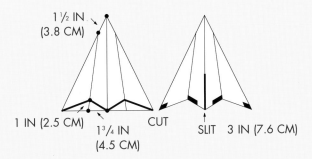

1½ IN (3.8 CM)

1 IN (2.5 CM)

1¾ IN (4.5 CM)

CUT

SLIT   3 IN (7.6 CM)

STEP 8 Lay wings flat, right side up. On each side, measure from front tip and back center and draw lines, as shown. Then cut wings, as shown by heavy lines. Make elevators and ailerons in locations shown. At the trailing (back) edge, cut a slit along center crease, as shown.

AILERONS ¾ in x ¼ in (1.9 cm x .6 cm)
ELEVATORS 1 in x ¼ in (2.5 cm x .6 cm)

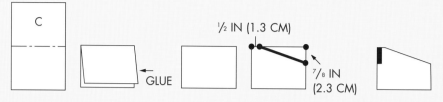

½ IN (1.3 CM)

GLUE

⁷/₈ IN
(2.3 CM)

STEP 9 Mountain fold piece C in half horizontally to make the vertical tail. Glue halves together. Measure and cut, as shown by heavy line. Make rudder, as shown.

RUDDER 1 in x ¹/₄ in (2.5 cm x .6 cm)

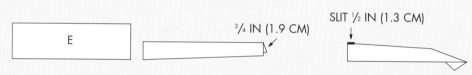

³/₄ IN (1.9 CM)

SLIT ½ IN (1.3 CM)

STEP 10 Use piece E to make the type 1 canopy (see page 11). Note that this canopy is lower at the front than at the back. Cut paper to size first.

CANOPY (TYPE 1) 3 in x 8 ¹/₂ in (7.6 cm x 21.6 cm)
Top point 3 in (7.6 cm), Front ³/₄ in (1.9 cm)

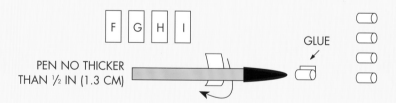

GLUE

PEN NO THICKER
THAN ½ IN (1.3 CM)

STEP 11 Use pieces F, G, H, and I to make the engines. Wrap paper around a felt-tipped pen vertically and glue.

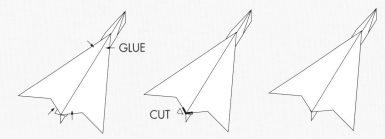

STEP 12 Glue wings to the fuselage, aligning trailing (back) edges. Make sure wings are centered and at right angles to the fuselage. Then trim back of fuselage to match wing trailing edges.

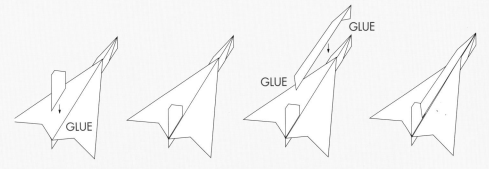

STEP 13 Apply glue and slide vertical tail into fuselage (and the slit in the wings). Align at trailing (back) edges. Apply glue to the lower front tab of the canopy and the inside back. Position canopy by inserting tab into nose end of the fuselage and slipping the back over the vertical tail.

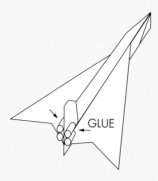

STEP 14 Attach the engines by gluing them to the vertical tail, two on each side, one on top the other, as shown. Align to the trailing edge of the vertical tail.

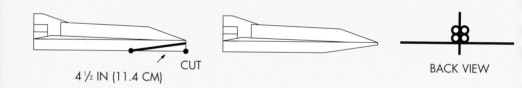

4 ½ IN (11.4 CM)   CUT

BACK VIEW

STEP 15 Measure and cut nose diagonally, as shown by heavy line. This plane has no dihedral.

Decoration

The following pages contain a plan (top) view and sometimes also an elevation (side) view of most paper airplanes contained in this book. They have window outlines, outlines of control surfaces, and other lines that help define each plane's shape, all of which add to an airplane's realism. Decorative patterns add interest.

The patterns can be copied, modified, or you can invent your own. A pattern such as a checkerboard or a camouflage that is shown on one plane can easily be applied to another airplane design. Use your imagination. What you see here are suggestions. Or you can build paper airplanes and leave them undecorated. You may wish to build undecorated trial planes first so you can master their construction and flight before you spend a lot of time on decoration.

It is easier to add decoration to the airplanes before they are completely assembled. Some advance planning is needed. Once you have decided on the pattern or design you want for the plane, decorate the pieces as you cut and fold them. Try each piece for fit and mark it carefully as you go along. Armament can be added to military planes using toothpicks. Draw the decoration lines using a very fine black felt-tipped pen. Narrow colored markers are ideal for filling in. Avoid water-based markers because they wrinkle the paper too much. Stencils can be used to add numbers and letters.

See the photographed airplanes for ideas on color schemes. Some of the patterns may be different from those shown here.

Egret *See page 12 for color suggestions.*

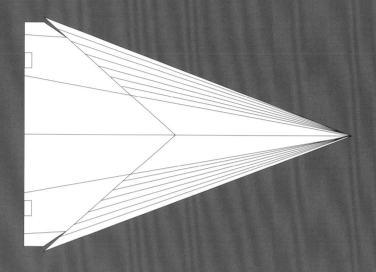

Pipit *See page 16 for color suggestions.*

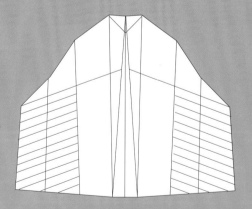

Swallow See page 20 for color suggestions.

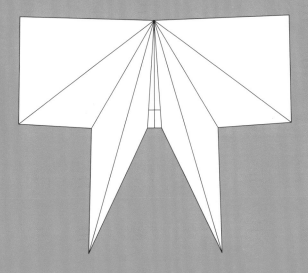

Biplane See page 28 for color suggestions.

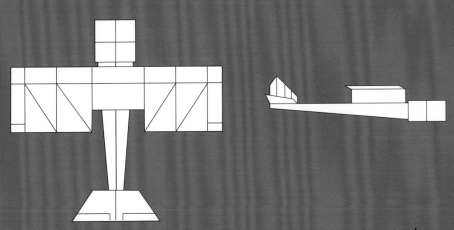

X1 Experimental

See page 34 for color suggestions.

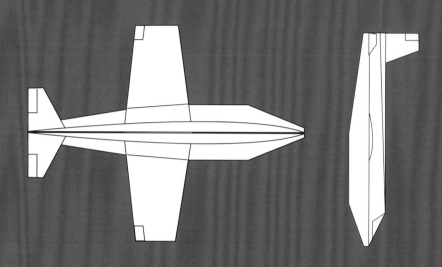

Nighthawk

The Nighthawk has no decoration. It is all black. To add detailing, draw lines (in pencil on black paper) to indicate the engine covers. Add windows to the canopy (see page 45). Also refer to the photograph on page 41.

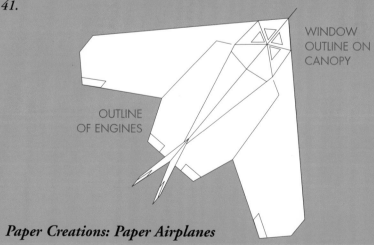

WINDOW
OUTLINE ON
CANOPY

OUTLINE
OF ENGINES

F18 Hornet *See page 48 for color suggestions.*

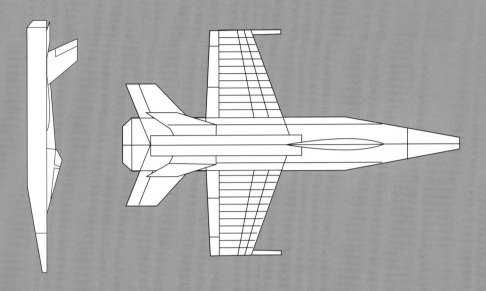

747 Jumbo *See page 56 for color suggestions.*

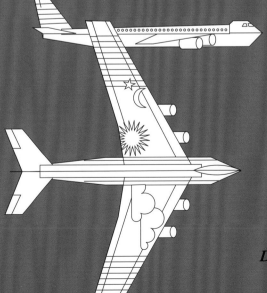

TAV Concept

See page 65 for color suggestions.

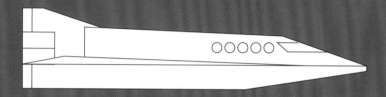

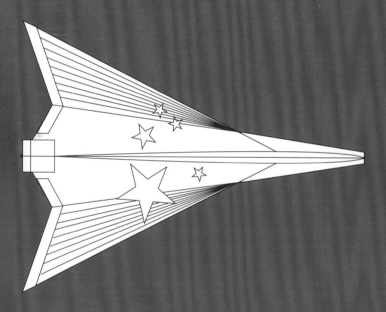

Glossary

ANGLE OF ATTACK The downward slant, from front to back, of a wing.

ANGLE OF BANK The raising of the outside wing and lowering of the inside wing during a turn.

ASPECT RATIO The length of a wing in relation to its width. The longer a wing, the higher its aspect ratio.

ATTITUDE The direction an airplane is pointing in relation to the horizon (banking, yawing, or pitching).

BALLAST Extra weight needed in the nose of an airplane to make the center of gravity coincide with the wings, which provide the lift.

CONTROL SURFACES Small surfaces that can be bent to alter the airflow and change an airplane's attitude—ailerons for bank, elevators for pitch, and rudders for yaw.

DIHEDRAL ANGLE Upward slanting of wings away from the fuselage. (Downward slanting is called anhedral.)

DRAG The resistance of air on moving objects, slowing them down.

FUSELAGE The body of an airplane.

LEADING EDGES The front edges of wings, tails, or other parts.

LIFT The force of air pressure beneath the wings buoying up an airplane.

MANEUVER Skillfully making an airplane fly in a desired direction—turn, climb, dive, stall, spin, or loop.

PITCH Nose-up or nose-down attitude.

ROLL Rotation along the length of an airplane.

SPAR The main internal frame that supports the wing.

STRAKES Wedge-shaped extensions of the wing's leading (front) edges near the fuselage.

TRAILING EDGES The back edges of wings, tails, or other parts.

TRIM Making small adjustments to the control surfaces to affect the attitude of an airplane.

TRIM DRAG The drag (resistance) produced from bending control surfaces into the airflow.

VENTRAL FIN A small stabilizer on each side of the fuselage underneath the tail.

WING LOADING The amount of weight a given area of wing is required to lift.

YAW Nose-left or nose-right attitude.

Index